A Sampler From Marcy's

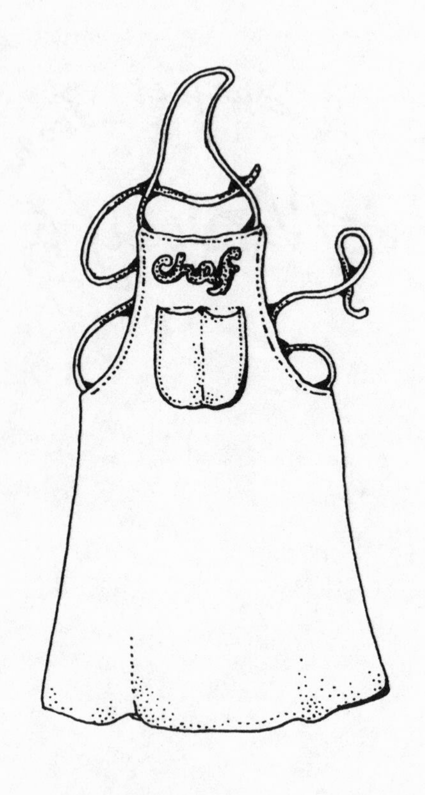
chef

Spanish - English

International Cuisine

Compiled by

Marcella Maize de Widdoes

Translated into Spanish by

Guillermina Garza del Toro

EAKIN PRESS ★ Austin, Texas

FIRST EDITION

Published in the United States of America
By Eakin Press
An Imprint of Sunbelt Media, Inc.
P.O. Drawer 90159 ★ Austin, TX 78709-0159

ISBN 0-89015-875-4

1 2 3 4 5 6 7 8 9

Table of Contents

Acknowledgments

My sincerest thanks to all those friends who had useful suggestions for the preparation of this book, and, most of all, my thanks to the Instituto Mexicano Norteamericano de Relaciones Culturales de Saltillo, which is responsible for all the translations into Spanish presented here. Without the good help of my friends, Gayle Yondorf de Chavez, the director of the Institute, and Guillermina Garza del Toro, our librarian, who did the actual translations, this book would never have been possible. Guillermina studied at a Cordon Bleu School while on leave in Oxford, England.

I wish to thank, also, the two artists who contributed to the book, Patricia Perry Sinex and Reese Kennedy.

Reese Kennedy is responsible for the sketches contained throughout the interior of the book. Mr. Kennedy has been a professor of art at Stephen F. Austin University for many years, and for the past eleven years has conducted a water color workshop in Saltillo during the summers. Mr. Kennedy is widely known. Now retired, he divides his time between Nacogdoches, Texas, and Arteaga, near Saltillo, Mexico, where he paints and conducts classes in his studio.

Patricia Perry Sinex did the cover of the book. She is an American artist presently residing in Saltillo. Mrs. Sinex is well known, primarily for her black art paintings which are shown in galleries in Texas and Oklahoma.

Introduction

Back in 1963, when I first began to practice law in St. Louis, Missouri, some good friends, fellow lawyers, and I had an opportunity to buy a bankrupt restaurant near the county courthouse. We had great plans for an elegant little after-theater bistro with drinks, entertainment and a limited but elegant cuisine. We never followed through on our plan, but it left a yearning in my heart which refused to be satisfied.

Years later, while visiting in Mexico City, I became acquainted with the owners of the beautiful Hacienda de los Morales, where we dined whenever possible, and on one special occasion I was taken to dine at the San Angel Inn. I loved both places, the elegance and antiquity of both impressing me very much. The service and cuisine were elegant, in an ambience of relaxed antiquity.

Still later, my husband and I spent some time in Saltillo, considering making some agricultural investments in the area, and on a Sunday, with nothing to do, I went with a friend to visit an old house in the center of the old city, which had newly come on the market for sale. I entered the house with my friend, and the first thought that came to my mind as we roamed the old Mexican style rooms was what a perfect miniature San Angel Inn this old house would be. I couldn't rest until the house was mine, and then began several years of hard work and planning to open the doors of "Marcy's." For personal reasons I maintained the restaurant for less than two years, but during that time the young women who worked with me and I presented to northern Mexico an ambience of elegant peace and a worldwide cuisine of authentic dishes prepared with loving care. It was, for me, a wonderful and enriching experience, and in response to repeated complaints that "Marcy's" is no longer open, I decided to share some of the recipes we developed during those days.

To all those who love good food, food with style, and to those who love to cook, but without complication and difficulty, elegant and delicious dishes, I dedicate this book. Bon Apetit!

All the recipes presented in this sampler are made with ingredients readily available in Mexico, or have included in them substitutes which are just as good, all of which are available. None of the recipes are complicated nor necessitate large quantities of time in preparation. All have been selected specifically for their ease of preparation.

Appetizers

BAKED STUFFED CLAMS ITALIAN

For this recipe you will have to obtain either some artificial clam shells, or buy a dozen of the big hard shell clams available in the market, and, after having used them once, scrub them well and retain them in a dry place. This first course recipe is well worth it. We served it on opening night at "Marcy's" and it was a very great hit.

1 230 gram can clams, drained and minced (reserve juice) or equivalent amount fresh clams (8 to 10 oz.)
2 cups fresh bread crumbs made from ordinary type white bread with crusts removed
1 cup freshly grated Parmesan cheese (about 4 ounces)
2 tbsps. parsley sprigs, minced
1 tsp. minced garlic
1 tsp. dried oregano, crumbled
1/2 tsp. dried thyme, crumbled
1/2 tsp. dried basil, crumbled
1/2 cup dry white wine
1/2 cup vegetable oil
Freshly ground pepper

Combine all ingredients, reserving 2 tbsps. oil and the wine.

Mix very well

Preheat oven to 450°F. Fill shells with clam mixture, being sure not to overfill, since the filling will puff some baking. Spoon a drop or two of the reserved oil over each filled shell. Arrange in baking dish and pour wine around the bottom of the dish, being careful not to spill into the filling of the shells. Bake in upper part of oven until well browned and crusty on top, about 10–15 min. Add more wine if necessary. Just before serving spoon any remaining pan juices over.

Serve very hot.

BEIGNETS (HORS D'OEUVRE FRITTERS) / (FRANCE)

Makes about 36

BASIC RECIPE

1/2 cup flour
1/8 tsp. salt
1 egg yolk, beaten
1/2 cup beer
1 tbsp. melted butter
1 egg white, stiffly beaten
Oil for deep frying

Mix salt with flour in medium bowl. Stir in egg yolk and beer and blend only until smooth. Add melted butter and blend. Let stand 1 hour. Fold in egg white. Fold selected ingredient (fish, meat, etc.) into batter, coating well.

Heat oil to 375°F. and drop mixture by teaspoonful and fry until browned on all sides. Drain and serve hot.

BEIGNETS DE CREVETTES (SHRIMP)

Fold in 1 cup diced, cooked shrimp.

BEIGNETS DE FROMAGE (CHEESE)

Fold in 1/2 cup diced Gruyere or Manchego cheese.

BEIGNETS DE JAMBON (HAM)

Fold in 3/4 cup chopped ham, 1 tbsp. minced parsley and 2 tbsps. grated onion. Sprinkle with freshly ground black pepper, and fold in.

BRANDIED LIVER PATE

Serves 6–8

1 tbsp. mayonnaise
2 tbsps. vegetable oil
2 medium onions, chopped finely
1 pound beef or calf's liver, cut into 1-inch strips
2 hard boiled eggs, chopped
1 tbsp. brandy
1 tbsp. chopped fresh parsley (optional)
1/4 tsp. ground sage
1/4 tsp. ground marjoram
1/4 tsp. ground nutmeg
1/2 tsp. ground thyme
Salt and fresh ground pepper to taste

Heat oil in medium skillet over medium heat. Add onions and sauté until translucent, about 5 minutes. Add liver and sauté until browned, 6–8 minutes. Transfer to processor and chop finely. Add eggs, brandy, mayonnaise, chopped parsley (if using) and spices and blend until smooth. Season with salt and pepper. Spoon into bowl or mold, spreading evenly. Refrigerate at least 2 hours before serving with French bread or crackers.

CEVICHE

2 lbs. saltwater fish, or 2 lbs. shellfish, cut in pieces and marinated in glass bowl overnight in lime juice (2/3 cup)

Pour off lime juice after marinating and rinse the fish in cold water, then add the following:

2 medium tomatoes, blanched, peeled and chopped
1 medium onion chopped coarsely and blanched about 2 min.
2 large cloves garlic, mashed
1–2 tbsp. olive oil (or to taste)
2 tbsp. minced Chinese parsley (cilantro), if desired
Salt and pepper to taste

Toss well and chill for at least 1 hour before serving.

CREAM PUFFS / (FRANCE)

Use recipe in Dessert Section. Drop puffs from a spoon, about 1 rounded tablespoon each. Recipe makes about 36 small hors d'oeuvre puffs. Bake at 450°F. for 15 min., then reduce heat to 400°F. and bake 15 min. longer, or until golden and tops are firm.

Fill puffs with any of the following:

PINEAPPLE-NUT FILLING

Combine equal parts of:

Chopped celery
Shredded fresh pineapple
A few chopped pecans (or almonds if available)
Mayonnaise

TUNA SALAD FILLING

Mix together:

1 can tuna, drained
1 tbsp. minced pimiento
2 tbsp. minced onion
1/2 cup minced celery
1 tbsp. sweet pickle relish (or sweet pickle minced, if relish unavailable)
1/2 tsp. prepared mustard
1/2 cup mayonnaise (or more if desired)

CHICKEN SALAD FILLING

Mix together:

2 cups chopped cooked chicken
1/2 cup minced celery
1 tbsp. minced onion
1/2 tsp. garlic powder
1/2 tsp. salt
2 tbsp. wine vinegar
1/4 tsp. prepared mustard
1/4 tsp. sugar
1 cup mayonnaise
Fresh ground pepper to taste

If desired, both the tuna salad filling and the chicken salad filling may be given a curry flavor by adding 1 tsp. curry powder to the mix.

CRAB FILLING

Mix together:

2 cups canned crabmeat, drained, or cooked crabmeat or cooked lobster meat, shredded
2 tbsp. minced green pepper
2 tbsp. minced green onion
1 tbsp. catsup
1 tsp. Worcestershire Sauce (Lea & Perrins only)
1 tsp. lemon juice
2/3 cup (or more, if desired) mayonnaise
Salt and pepper to taste

CURRIED TUNA MOLD

2 envelopes (2 tbsps.) unflavored gelatin
1/2 cup cold water
1 cup boiling water
2 packages (8-oz. each) cream cheese, softened
2 tbsps. curry powder
2 tbsps. lemon juice
1/2 tsp. salt
1/2 tsp. garlic powder
1/3 cup finely chopped green onions
2 oz. pimientos chopped
2 cans (7 oz. each) tuna, drained and flaked
1/2 cup chopped nuts (optional)

In large bowl, sprinkle unflavored gelatin over cold water and let stand for 1 minute. Add boiling water and stir until gelatin is completely dissolved. With rotary beater, blend in cream cheese until smooth. Stir in lemon juice, curry powder, salt and garlic powder. Fold in green onions, pimiento, tuna and chopped nuts (if using). Turn into a 5½ cup mold, and chill until firm. Unmold and serve with crackers or small breads. Makes about 5½ cups.

DEEP-FRIED CHINESE SHRIMP TOAST

Makes 16 hors d'oeuvre

½ lb. fresh shrimp in their shells
4 slices plain type square sliced white bread, crusts removed
2 tbsps. fresh pork fat
4 water chestnuts, sliced and chopped, or equivalent amount of raw jicama (about 2 tbsps.)
1 tsp. salt
1 egg, lightly beaten
2 tbsps. cornstarch
1 tbsp. dry white wine
Oil for deep frying

Shell, devein and finely mince shrimp until they are reduced to a fine pulp-like mass.

Cut bread slices diagonally into 4 triangles each slice. Chop pork fat and water chestnuts or jicama together as fine as possible, and, in a small bowl, combine them with shrimp. Add salt, lightly beaten egg, cornstarch and wine, and mix very well (with fingers if necessary). Spread in equal amounts on bread slices, mounding them slightly in the centers, and being sure filling covers entire piece of bread.

Heat the oil to 375°F. Gently drop in the bread triangles, shrimp side down (the filling will not fall off), and fry for about 1 minute. Then gently turn them over in the hot fat with a large slotted spoon and fry for 1 minute longer, until the bread and shrimp topping are golden brown. Then turn them over again and fry for another minute. Drain on paper towels in a baking pan and keep warm in oven until served.

They may be served with hot mustard sauce and/or sweet and sour or plum sauce in small dishes on the side of the plate (see recipe in "Sauces").

HAM, TOMATO, BROCCOLI, CHEESE QUICHE

Makes 8 large servings

Preheat oven to 400°F.

2 slices boiled ham cut in 1″ wide julienne strips and laid across bottom of buttered 10″ pie plate sprinkled lightly with garlic powder
1 medium onion chopped and spread over ham
1 1/2 cup shredded cheese (Gruyere or Manchego or mixed) spread over onion
2 large tomatoes sliced and spread over cheese
4 eggs
1 1/2 cups milk
1 heaping cup baking mix (see recipe in section on "Breads")
1/4 to 1/2 tsp. thyme
1 tsp. salt, pinch pepper, all beaten until smooth

Pour batter over tomatoes and sprinkle generously with grated Parmesan cheese.

(If available, spread 1 cup broccoli flowerettes, which have been previously steamed until tender and allowed to cool, over tomatoes before adding batter.)

Bake at 400°F. 35 or 40 minutes, until brown on top and firm in center.

LIGHT BATTER VEGETABLE FRITTERS "TEMPURA"—JAPAN

3/4 cup cornstarch
1/4 cup flour
1 tsp. baking powder
1/2 tsp. salt
1/2 cup water
1 egg, slightly beaten
1 quart oil for deep frying

In a bowl stir together starch, flour, baking powder and salt. Add water and egg, and stir until smooth. Heat oil to 375°F. Test temperature with a bread cube about 1″ square. If bread turns brown within 50 seconds, oil is ready. If working in high altitudes (5,000 feet or more, increase heat to 390°F.) Dip a few pieces at a time into batter and fry only a few at a time in oil. Fry about 2 minutes, turning once.

Use onion rings, mushrooms, green pepper rings, tomato rings, sliced zucchini, sliced carrots, string beans, strips of eggplant. Skinless chicken breast, uncooked and cut into 1″ cubes, may also be used, or large shrimp, sliced in half lengthwise.

These fritters may be served with or without Japanese style tempura dipping sauces.

MARINATED PORK CUBES (NORTH AFRICA)

Makes about 40

1/3 cup olive oil (vegetable oil may be substituted)
1 tbsp. minced fresh parsley
1/4 to 1/2 tsp. red pepper
2 garlic cloves, crushed
1 tsp. ground cumin
1/2 tsp. dried thyme, crumbled
1/2 tsp. paprika
1 bay leaf, crumbled
3/4 lb. boneless lean pork, cut into 3/4–1-inch cubes
Salt and pepper to taste

Combine olive oil, parsley, red pepper, garlic, cumin, thyme, paprika and bay leaf in medium bowl. Season with salt and pepper. Add meat and stir to coat well; cover and refrigerate several hours or overnight, stirring occasionally.

Remove meat from marinade using slotted spoon. Heat 1 tbsp. marinade in large skillet over medium high heat. Add meat in batches and cook, draining off excess oil, until meat is well browned, about 15 min. Transfer to heated platter. Serve with sherry dip.

SHERRY DIP

1 tbsp. marinade (reserved from pork)
3 oz. coarsely chopped almonds (pecans may be substituted if almonds not available)
1 tsp. flour
1/2 cup sweet sherry
1/4 cup water
1/2 tsp. lemon juice
Salt to taste

Heat marinade in small skillet over low heat. Stir in almonds and cook until lightly colored. Sprinkle with the flour and cook, stirring constantly,

1 to 2 min. Add sherry, water, salt and lemon juice and simmer 1 minute longer.

Use the same amount of dip to serve double this recipe, for a party.

QUICHE LORRAINE
(FRANCE)

Serves 6 to 8

Line a glass 9″ pie pan with the plain pastry: (see plain pastry in "Glossary of Pastries").

PASTRY

1/2 cup plus 3 tbsp. lard or vegetable shortening or butter
2 cups flour
1/2 tsp. salt

Roll out and press into the 9″ pie pan and crimp top edges. (It is important to crimp the edges above the pan with the fingers to handle the amount of filling, as it will rise.)

FILLING

Fry until very crisp, then drain on paper towel and crumble coarsely 6 slices of bacon. Sprinkle bacon over bottom of pan after putting pastry in place.

Blend in blender or mixer or beat with egg beater.

4 eggs
1 tbsp. flour
1/2 tsp. salt
1 cup heavy cream mixed with 1 cup of milk
Dash of nutmeg
1/2 tsp. Worcestershire Sauce (Lea & Perrins preferred)
1 tbsp. brandy

Cover bacon in pastry shell with 1 1/2 cups shredded Gruyere cheese.

Sprinkle chopped green onion (about 1 tbsp.) on top.

Pour filling over all, very gently, so as not to disturb ingredients any more than is unavoidable, and bake in preheated 350°F. oven until custard sets, about 50 minutes. If at altitude above 5,000 feet, bake at 360°F. for about 50 to 60 minutes, or until knife inserted in center comes out clean.

Allow to cool to room temperature before serving. Keeps well in refrigerator, covered with foil, for a day or two.

SHRIMP, LOBSTER OR CRAB QUICHE

Omit bacon and brandy in recipe above and substitute 2/3 cup diced, cooked shrimp, or lobster meat or crabmeat, and 1 tbsp. madeira wine. Be sure shrimp, lobster or crab is well drained.

VEGETABLE QUICHE

Using the Quiche Lorraine recipe above, omit the bacon and brandy, and spread a layer of al dente steamed broccoli or chopped spinach (about 1 cup) over the bottom prior to adding the cheese, and mix 1/2 tsp. dry mustard and 1 tbsp. dry, sweet or cooking sherry into the custard mixture before pouring over the top.

SHRIMP LOUISIENNE

2 lb. raw large to jumbo shrimp, shelled, deveined and tails removed
1 pint vegetable oil
1 tbsp. salt
5 tbsps. catsup
1/2 tsp. basil, crumbled
1/2 tsp. marjoram
2 garlic cloves, mashed

Mix oil, salt, catsup, garlic and spices together thoroughly. Add shrimp and mix. Marinate for at least 2 hours. Remove shrimp from marinade and spread in shallow pan, spreading small part of marinade over. Broil on each side about 3 min. If possible, adjust broiler flame to medium-high.

Serve on cocktail picks with parsley garnish.

Soups

CHINESE HOT AND SOUR SOUP

Serves 4 to 6

4 cups chicken stock or broth
6 oz. lean pork cut in julienne strips
1/2 cup tofu (bean curd) cut in julienne strips (if unavailable this may be omitted, or dried soybean sheets may be substituted)
1/2 cup bamboo shoots, cut in julienne strips (peeled broccoli stems may be substituted if unavailable)
6 dried Chinese mushrooms, soaked in 1/2 cup of water 15 min., stems discarded sliced (fresh mushrooms may be substituted, or canned, if Chinese dried mushrooms unavailable, but the flavor will be less)
1 tbsp. soy sauce
1/4 tsp. sugar
3/4 tsp. salt
3 tbsps. cornstarch mixed with 3 tbsps. water
1 egg, beaten until slightly foamy
3–4 tbsps. red wine vinegar
1/2 tsp. ground white pepper
2 green onions including tops, thinly sliced

Bring chicken stock to boil in uncovered pot. Add pork, tofu, bamboo shoots, and mushrooms. Cook 3 to 5 minutes. Add soy sauce, sugar, salt and cornstarch mixture, mixed together, to soup. Cook only to barely boil. Slowly swirl in egg and turn off heat. Put vinegar and pepper into large bowl. Add soup and green onions. Serve immediately.

NEW ENGLAND STYLE CLAM CHOWDER

Serves 8

4 tbsps. butter
5 tbsps. flour
4 cups milk
1 13-oz. can evaporated milk (reserve can and add 1 can of water)
1 oz. saltpork, rind removed and cut into small cubes
1 small onion, chopped fine
2 small potatoes (peeled and coarsely chopped, and boiled in small amount water until tender)
1 tsp. garlic powder
2 tsps. onion powder
1/4 tsp. basil
1/4 tsp. marjoram
1 1/2 pints minced clams with their juice
Salt and pepper to taste

Melt butter in sauce pan and add flour. Blend in the milk, evaporated milk and water, and cook until thickened.

Fry the pork cubes until crisp, but not brown. Add the onion and cook until soft.

Mix all ingredients together, add the seasonings and salt and pepper to taste and the clams with their juice. Heat over (not in) hot water to serving temperature only. Do not allow to get very hot or boil after clams have been added as soup may tend to curdle if it gets too hot.

Garnish with a little paprika.

COLD CUCUMBER AND SPINACH SOUP

Serves 6–8

2 tbsps. butter
1 onion, coarsely chopped
1 large potato, peeled and coarsely chopped
1 leek with 2 inches of green, split, washed thoroughly and coarsely chopped
3 cups chicken broth or 3 tsp. bouillon or 3 cubes in 3 cups hot water
Salt and pepper to taste
3 sprigs fresh parsley (not cilantro)
2 cucumbers, peeled, seeded and coarsely chopped
1/2 bunch (about 5-oz.) spinach, blanched and chopped
1/2 cup yogurt, or sour cream (if available)
1 tbsp. mayonnaise
1 avocado (for garnish)
Juice of 2 lemons

Melt butter in large pan over medium heat and add onion, potato and leek. Cover and cook over low heat about 5 minutes, or until ingredients are slightly soft. Add chicken stock, parsley, salt and pepper to taste and bring to boil. Reduce heat and simmer 20 minutes. Allow to cool, then puree in blender until smooth. Chill thoroughly. When cold, add remaining ingredients except avocado and blend until pureed and smooth. Chill. Taste and adjust seasoning.

Just before serving, peel, seed and dice avocado and stir into soup.

"AVGOLEMONO" GREEK EGG AND LEMON SOUP

Serves 6–8

8 cups clear chicken broth, canned or homemade
4 eggs
1 cup sliced mushrooms
1½ tbsps. brandy
Juice of 2 lemons (or 3 small limes)

Heat broth in large saucepan, but do not boil.

Beat eggs until light and foamy. Add lemon juice and beat some more. Or put eggs and lemon juice in blender and blend 1 minute. Add 2 cups of the hot broth to the egg-lemon mixture, gradually, stirring thoroughly. Then add the egg-lemon-broth mixture to the rest of the broth.

Sauté the mushrooms lightly in a little butter or oil (not more than 1 tbsp.) and add to soup. Serve immediately.

TOMATO SOUP ALA TORINESE

Serves 6

1 quart tomato juice
2 cloves garlic, mashed
½ tsp. basil
1 tbsp. fresh lemon juice
1 tbsp. sugar
1 tsp. salt
¼ tsp. white pepper
2 tbsps. butter
2 tbsps. flour
1 6-oz. can tomato puree
4 cups chicken broth, or 4 tsp. or 4 cubes bouillon in 4 cups hot water

Sauté the garlic in a little oil in large pot until golden. Add all other ingredients except puree, flour and butter. Cover pot and bring to boil. Reduce heat and simmer 30 minutes. Meantime, in a small saucepan, melt butter, add flour and tomato puree, and blend until smooth. When soup has simmered 30 minutes, add a little at a time to the flour, butter, tomato puree mixture, up to about 1 cup. Then add the mixture and the soup to the pot and bring back up to boil, then reduce to simmer and simmer 5 minutes, until the soup has slightly thickened.

This soup may be served either hot or thoroughly chilled, and with or without croutons on top.

ZUCCHINI SOUP ITALIAN STYLE

Serves 4–6

3 lbs. zucchini, cut in pieces
1 large onion, chopped
2 cups chicken broth or stock
2 cups water
2½ tsps. salt
1 tsp. dried basil
4 slices raw bacon cut up
White pepper to taste
Garlic powder to taste

Bring all ingredients to boil in large pot and simmer 30 minutes. Puree in blender.

Serve hot with freshly grated Parmesan cheese on top and garlic croutons.

CREAM OF ONION SOUP ENGLISH STYLE

Serves 6–8

1 large onion, sliced
¼ cup butter
6 cups chicken stock or broth
¼ tsp. white pepper
1¼ cups heavy cream

Sauté the onion in the butter over medium heat, stirring, for 10 minutes or until the onion is golden.

Add the stock and pepper and simmer, covered, for 30 minutes. Puree in blender, then return to pot. Stir in cream by adding a small amount of soup to the cream in another pan until the cream has been thinned out and heated. Then add all to the original pot and heat over low heat until heated through.

Serve hot, with or without croutons.

VICHYSSOISE

Serves 6–8

4 leeks, white part and 1″ of green only, sliced
1 medium onion, sliced
4 tbsps. butter
5 medium potatoes, peeled and sliced thin
1 quart chicken broth, or water
1 tbsp. salt
3 cups milk
2 cups heavy cream
Finely chopped green onion or chives

Brown the leeks and onion in the butter, then add the potatoes, chicken broth (or water) and salt; boil for 35 or 40 minutes. Puree in blender. Chill well, add the milk and heavy cream and blend. Season to taste. Sprinkle with chopped chives or green onion, and serve cold.

CABBAGE, CAULIFLOWER, AND ROQUEFORT SOUP

Serves 8–10

1 stick butter or margarine, or 1/2 cup
1 large head cabbage, chopped
1 medium cauliflower, coarsely chopped
7 cups chicken stock or broth, or chicken flavored bouillon
1 cup heavy cream
1/4 cup roquefort cheese
Salt and pepper to taste
Croutons

Sauté cabbage in melted fat in large saucepan, 4 quarts or more, slowly, uncovered, until soft, stirring occasionally with wooden spoon. Add cauliflower and broth. Bring to boil over high heat. Reduce heat, cover and simmer 30–45 minutes, until vegetables are tender.

Mix cream and cheese in blender or food processor until smooth. Set aside. Pour soup into blender, in batches if necessary, and puree. Return pureed soup to pot and stir in the blended cream and cheese. Serve hot, garnished with croutons.

BLENDER GASPACHO

Serves 6–8

(This soup is excellent for dieting.)

1 spine of celery (with leaves) cut in pieces
1 carrot cut in pieces
1 medium onion, cut in pieces
1/2 green pepper cut in pieces (other raw vegetables may be substituted or added as desired. Lettuce, zucchini, cucumber seeded and peeled, etc.)
1 large clove garlic, pressed
1 tbsp. Worcestershire Sauce (Lea & Perrins)
1 tbsp. olive oil (optional — if dieting, omit)
1/2 tsp. basil
4–5 cups tomato juice
Salt and pepper to taste

Put all ingredients together in blender (if tomato juice will not all fit, add remainder in a large vessel after blending), and blend at medium speed only until vegetables are coarsely ground, not pureed. Chill for at least 1 hour before serving. Serve with garlic croutons if desired.

DIET MINESTRONE

Serves 6–8

4 garlic cloves, mashed
1 large onion, chopped
5 tsps. or cubes beef bouillon in 5 cups hot water
1 quart tomato juice
1 cup water
1/2 tsp. each of thyme and basil
2 medium zucchini, chopped
1/4 head of small cabbage, chopped
2 carrots chopped
1/2 cup macaroni
1 or 2 stalks or ribs of celery, with leaves, chopped
Salt and pepper to taste
Dash of liquid, or 1/8 tsp. powdered sweetener

Cook all ingredients together in pressure cooker at 15-lb. pressure 8 min. Cool immediately. Serve hot with a little Parmesan cheese sprinkled on top if desired.

SWEDISH MUSHROOM SOUP

Serves 8

3 tbsps. butter
1 lb. fresh mushrooms, with stems, thinly sliced
1/2 tsp. salt
1/4 ground white pepper
1/3 cup flour
2 quarts beef or chicken broth (or bouillon)
1 cup heavy cream
1 tsp. lemon juice
1/4 cup dry white wine
Salt and ground white pepper to taste

Melt butter in 3–4 quart heavy saucepan over low heat. Add mushrooms and sauté over low heat until mushroom juices begin to flow. Pour juices into a 2 cup measure and set aside. Stir 1/2 tsp. salt, 1/4 tsp. white pepper and flour into drained mushrooms. Add broth to mushroom juice to make 2 cups. Stir into mushroom mixture. Stir in 6 cups of remaining broth. Over high heat, cook and stir until soup thickens, almost 5 minutes. Stir in cream and lemon juice. Add salt and white pepper to taste. Stir in white wine. Serve hot.

AVOCADO SOUP WITH GARLIC (SPANISH)

Serves 6

2 tbsps. butter
1 medium onion, chopped
4 cups rich chicken stock
6 large garlic cloves (this seems like a lot, but after simmering with other ingredients in the broth the flavor is lovely) chopped
1 large avocado, ripe, peeled, seeded and chopped
Juice of 1 lime
1 1/2 to 2 cups yogurt
Salt and freshly ground pepper to taste

Sauté onion in the butter over medium heat until soft, in large saucepan. Add stock and garlic and bring to simmer. Cover and cook 30 minutes. When slightly cooled, puree in batches in blender, and transfer to large bowl. Puree avocado and add to the transferred stock. Blend in yogurt and season with salt and pepper to taste.

Serve hot or cold garnished with minced green onion tops.

This soup can be kept for several days in refrigerator, but may not be frozen for future use.

Salads

CAESAR SALAD

Serves 6

There are numerous recipes with many variations of this marvelous salad invented in Mexico, but this is Marcy's favorite:

16 anchovy fillets
$^1/_4$ tsp. dry mustard
3 tbsps. Lea & Perrins
2 tbsps. olive oil
2 tbsps. wine vinegar
Juice of 1 lime
1 coddled egg (it is very important that the egg be coddled, not soft boiled or raw)
3 heads of Romaine lettuce chopped into 1" squares
1 large clove garlic, mashed
2 tbsps. Parmesan cheese
$1^1/_2$ cups garlic fried croutons

Mix all the first 6 ingredients in a small bowl, mashing the anchovies with a fork.

To coddle the egg, place egg in a small pan covered with cold water, and bring slowly to boil. As soon as the water boils, turn off heat. Allow to steep 30 seconds in the hot water, and then quickly drain off hot water, and cool egg in cold water. When cool, continue as follows:

Mix the coddled egg with the Romaine in large bowl before adding other ingredients.

Add the ingredients which have been mixed in the small bowl. Grind on enough fresh pepper to taste.

Using a garlic press, add the clove of garlic and mix well into the greens. Add the Parmesan cheese and mix again.

Mix the garlic fried croutons into the salad just before serving. After the finished salad is served to individual plates, dust top with more Parmesan cheese.

SPINACH SALAD

Serves 8, or 4–6 as a main course

6 tbsps. red wine vinegar
3 tbsps. catsup
3 garlic cloves, mashed
1 tbsp. Lea & Perrins
2 tsps. sugar
1/4 tsp. paprika
1/2 tsp. dry mustard
2/3 tsp. salt
1/4 tsp. freshly ground pepper
1/2 cup vegetable oil
4 bunches spinach, stems removed, thoroughly washed and dried
1/3 cup freshly grated Parmesan cheese or crumbled Roquefort cheese
3 hard-cooked eggs, minced
1/4 pound bacon, cooked until crisp and crumbled

Combine first 10 ingredients and mix thoroughly. Add oil slowly, beating constantly (this is all best done in a blender). Place 1/2 cup of dressing in bottom of large shallow bowl. Tear spinach leaves in pieces and place over dressing mix. Distribute cheese and egg evenly over the top. Sprinkle with bacon bits and toss.

Serve on chilled plates.

JICAMA, ORANGE AND RED ONION SALAD

Serves 12

1 head of Romaine lettuce
1 1/2 pounds of jicama, peeled and sliced paper thin
6 oranges, peeled, seeded and thinly sliced
2 red onions thinly sliced and separated into rings
1/2 cup olive or vegetable oil
1/3 cup fresh lime juice
3 tbsps. red wine vinegar
3 tbsps. orange marmalade
1 tsp. salt
Fresh ground pepper

Line shallow bowl with lettuce. Alternate circles of jicama, orange and onion over top. Cover and refrigerate. (Can be prepared 3 hours ahead.)

Combine remaining ingredients in jar and shake well. Pour over salad and toss to blend. Serve immediately.

NOTE: If mild red onions are unavailable, sliced green onions with part of their green stems may be substituted.

NOTE: This dressing is an excellent tart-sweet dressing for any fresh fruit salad.

BEET AND PINEAPPLE MOLD

Serves 8–10

1 lb. diced, cooked peeled beets (reserve the cooking water)
1 8-oz. can crushed pineapple, drained (juice reserved)
1 6-oz. pkg. lemon flavored gelatin
2 cups boiling water
1/2 cup chopped celery
3 tbsps. lemon juice
Dash salt

Dissolve gelatin in boiling water and add 1 1/2 cups liquid from beets and pineapple, lemon juice, and salt. Chill until partially set. Fold in beets, pineapple, and celery. Pour into 6 1/2 cup ring mold. Chill until firm.

Unmold onto lettuce lined platter and set a small bowl in center with sauce made of mayonnaise mixed with a little pineapple juice and lemon juice.

COBB SALAD

Serves 6 as a main course or 8–10 as a salad

1 medium head iceberg lettuce, finely chopped
2 poached chicken breasts, skinned, boned, and finely chopped
6 hard cooked eggs, finely chopped
6 slices bacon, crisply cooked and finely crumbled
6 oz. Roquefort cheese, finely crumbled
3 medium tomatoes, finely chopped
15 sliced black seedless olives (opt.)
Vinaigrette dressing (see recipe in "Dressings")

Divide lettuce among number of plates to be served. Arrange chicken, eggs, bacon, cheese, and tomatoes in layers atop. If including olives, sprinkle over all.

Chill well before serving.

SUMMER PICNIC CHICKEN SALAD NORTH-AMERICAN STYLE

Serves 10–12

1 whole large boiling chicken, cooked, bones removed and diced
1 whole bunch celery, chopped (discard leaves)
1 large white onion, coarsely chopped
1 medium size jar sweet pickles, coarsely chopped
4 cups mayonnaise (or to taste) mixed with 1–2 tsp. lemon juice.
Salt and pepper to taste

Boil chicken and all giblets in water to cover. Before setting to boil, add to the water the following:

3 large cloves garlic, chopped or mashed
1 large bay leaf (or 3 or 4 small ones)
1 spine of celery, with leaves, cut in 4 pieces
1 carrot, cut into 5 or 6 pieces
1 onion, quartered
1/4 tsp. each thyme, rosemary crumbled
1–2 tbsps. salt
Few sprigs of fresh parsley (not cilantro)

When chicken and giblets are tender, remove from broth and cool (reserve broth for chicken stock for soups or other use). When cold, remove skin and discard; remove meat from bones and dice the meat. Fold in the mayonnaise, thinned with 3 tbsps. juice from the pickles, and all other ingredients. Chill thoroughly before serving.

Dressings to Toss with Your Favorite Greens

ROQUEFORT VINAIGRETTE

Makes almost 2 cups

1/4 to 1/2 tsp. salt
1/2 tsp. white pepper
1/4 tsp. cayenne pepper
1/2 tsp. celery seed or salt
1/4 tsp. dry mustard
2 tbsps. wine vinegar
4 tbsps. tomato juice
1 clove garlic, mashed
1/2 cup oil
1/2 tsp. sugar
2/3 cup roquefort cheese, crumbled

Combine all ingredients in bottle. Cover and shake vigorously. Store in refrigerator.

LEBANESE MINT DRESSING

Makes about 1 cup

Juice of 3 or 4 limes
1/2 tsp. sugar
1/2 to 2/3 cup oil
3 or 4 sprigs of fresh peppermint, chopped
Salt and pepper to taste

Shake all together vigorously in jar. Store in refrigerator.

GREEN GODDESS DRESSING

Makes 3–4 cups

(Use only crisp lettuce with dressing.)

2 garlic cloves, mashed
1 can anchovies
3 tbsps. green onion, chopped
1/2 avocado, mashed
1 tbsp. lemon juice
3 tbsp. wine vinegar
1 cup mayonnaise
1/3 cup chopped parsley (not cilantro)
1 cup sour cream (or yogurt may be used if not available)
Salt and pepper to taste

Mix all above in blender until smooth.

CUCUMBER DRESSING, BAVARIAN

1/2 medium onion
2 cucumbers, peeled
1/2 cup thick sour cream
1 tbsp. red wine vinegar
1 tsp. parsley
1 tsp. dill (fresh if possible)
1 clove garlic, mashed
1 1/2 tsps. salt
1 tsp. sugar
1/2 tsp. fresh ground black pepper

Grind the onion, cucumbers, parsley, dill and garlic in the red wine vinegar in a blender until fine, but not pureed. Add other ingredients and blend only until mixed. Refrigerate for at least 4–5 hours before serving. (Yogurt may be substituted for the sour cream. If using yogurt, do not add it in the blender, but fold gently into the dressing after all other ingredients have been blended).

ORIENTAL SALAD DRESSING

2/3 cup olive or vegetable oil
1/4 cup wine vinegar
4 tbsps. white wine (very dry)
1 large clove garlic, mashed
1/2 tsp. fresh ginger, minced or 1/2 tsp. powdered ginger if fresh is unavailable
1 tbsp. soy sauce
1/2 tsp. sugar

Shake all ingredients well in a bottle and refrigerate for at least 2 hours before using.

MARCY'S VINAIGRETTE

(If dieting, omit the oil and use artificial sweetener in place of sugar and you have a virtually non-caloric dressing.)

2/3 cup oil (do not use olive unless it is very fresh and fine)
1/3 cup wine vinegar
1/4 cup dry white wine
Juice of 1 lime
1 tsp. dry mustard
1 tsp. garlic powder (or 1 garlic clove mashed)
1/4 tsp. sugar (taste and adjust after adding the salt if you like slightly sweeter dressing)
1 tsp. Lea & Perrin's
Salt and pepper (fresh ground) to taste

Shake all ingredients together in a bottle and refrigerate for several hours before using. (If using sweetener, add it after all other ingredients are mixed drop to drop and taste for sweetness until the flavor pleases.)

CREAMY MUSTARD — FRANCE

2 hard boiled eggs
1 1/2 tsp. salt
1 1/2 tsp. sugar
1 tsp. coarsely ground fresh black pepper
1 tbsp. parsley
1 tbsp. mustard (Dijon style if available)
1 large clove garlic, mashed
1/2 cup olive oil (substitute vegetable oil if very fine, light, fresh olive not available)
5 tbsps. heavy cream
1/4 cup wine vinegar

Mix all in blender until very smooth.

Dressings for Your Favorite Fresh Fruits

CUCUMBER YOGURT DRESSING FOR SALADS OR COLD SEAFOOD

Yield — 2 cups

1 cup yogurt
1 tsp. lemon juice
1 clove garlic, mashed
1 tbsp. minced fresh parsley
1 tbsp. minced green onion
1 tsp. mustard (dijon type preferred)
1 cup cucumber, peeled, seeded, and shredded (or if using on cold seafood, sliced)
1/4 tsp. sugar
Salt and pepper to taste

Put all ingredients in a bowl and blend well, but carefully with a whisk or a fork, and store in screw-top container in refrigerator. Keeps well.

TART-SWEET MARMALADE DRESSING

(See Jicama, Orange and Red Onion Salad, in this section.)

1/2 cup olive or vegetable oil (use vegetable if very fresh, light, fine olive not available)
1/3 cup fresh lime juice
3 tbsps. red wine vinegar
3 tbsps. orange marmalade
1 tsp. salt
Freshly ground pepper to taste

Combine all ingredients in bottle or jar and shake well.

CARDAMOM SAUCE FOR FRESH FRUIT

1/2 cup water
1 cup honey (orange blossom if available)
1/4 tsp. cardamom seed, powdered (powder may be used if unavailable)
2 large mint leaves (do not used dried mint) chopped
1/4 tsp. salt
1/2 cup port wine
1/8 cup benedictine liqueur, if available

Simmer the water, honey, salt, cardamom, and mint over low heat for 2 minutes to blend the flavors. Cool to room temperature, and add the port and the benedictine, stirring well. Refrigerate for 1 hour before pouring over any combination of the following fruits:

Melon all kinds
Avocado
Apple
Oranges
Mango
Papaya

GRENADINE DRESSING

1 pint sour cream
2/3 cup powdered sugar
2 tbsps. Grenadine
2 oz. Philadelphia cream cheese
1/4 cup mayonnaise

Mix in blender until smooth. Refrigerate.

POLYNESIAN CHICKEN SALAD

Serves 8

3 cups diced cooked white meat of chicken
$^3/_4$ cup mayonnaise
1 cup finely diced celery
Salt and white pepper to taste

Mix chicken with 1/4 cup of the mayonnaise. Chill for an hour or more. Toss chicken with remaining mayonnaise and celery. Season with the salt and pepper. Place a scoop of salad in center of lettuce lined serving plates. Garnish the plates with asparagus tips, carrot sticks, fresh pineapple slices, halved hard-cooked eggs, ripe olives, tomato wedges, as desired, and top with rum dressing (see below) just before serving.

POLYNESIAN RUM DRESSING

Makes 1 cup

$^1/_4$ cup pineapple juice
$^3/_4$ cup mayonnaise
1 tbsp. rum
1 tsp. rum extract (if available)

Mix well and chill thoroughly before using.

After the dressing has been poured over the salad, garnish the chicken salad scoops with chopped macadamia nuts or, if unavailable, toasted chopped almonds, pistachios or pecans, or even peanuts may be used (if using peanuts, use sparingly).

Entrees

BEEF BOURGUIGNON

Serves 6

2½ cups brown sauce
1½ cups red wine, preferably burgundy
1 bay leaf
½ tsp. thyme
1 slice lemon
1 small piece orange rind
1½ sticks unsalted butter
18 small white onions, peeled
2 tsps. sugar
¼ cup beef broth (see "Stock and Broths"), or canned 18 mushroom caps
4 pieces salt pork, cut into small pieces
2½ lbs. beef fillet, cut into 1¼" cubes
Salt and pepper to taste

Bring wine, bay leaf, thyme, 1 tsp. salt, 1 tsp. pepper, lemon slice and orange rind to a boil, then reduce heat and simmer until reduced to 1 cup. Strain this liquid into the brown sauce, bring to a boil and simmer gently for 25–30 minutes. Cover with plastic wrap and set aside.

Heat 4 tbsp. butter in a skillet. Add onions and sauté over medium heat, sprinkling with the sugar to glaze and brown the onions. Add the beef broth, cover, and steam until just crisp tender. In another skillet, melt 3 tbsp. butter, add the mushrooms and sauté over medium high heat until lightly browned. Remove mushrooms, add 2 tbsp. butter to the skillet, and sauté the salt pork until crisply browned. Remove, drain, combine with onions and mushrooms and set aside, covered with foil.

Just before you are ready to serve, heat 5 tbsp. butter in a heavy skillet and add the beef cubes, a few at time, and sauté over high heat until well seared and browned on all sides. Add the brown sauce, let it just barely come to boil, add the onions, mushrooms and salt pork. Simmer until just heated through. Do not allow the beef to overcook but just heat quickly through.

Serve over boiled noodles or alongside.

CHICKEN CACCIATORE

Serves 6–8

1 2 1/2 or 3 lb. fryer chicken cut into serving pieces or 3 whole large chicken breasts, halved with bone left in
2 medium green peppers, cut into 1″ pieces
2 medium onions, cut into 1″ pieces
16 fresh mushrooms, sliced in thick slices (optional)
3/4 lb. mild Italian sausage, crumbled
3 cups or more, as desired, meatless spaghetti sauce (see recipe in "Sauces")
1/2 cup dry red wine, or more to taste
1/4 cup vegetable oil
1/2 stick sweet butter (salt butter may be used, but sweet is better)
Salt and pepper to taste

Sauté chicken pieces and sausage in butter and oil until browned on both sides and sausage is cooked through. Add green pepper, onion, fresh mushrooms and salt and pepper to taste. Cover all with the spaghetti sauce. Simmer, uncovered, adding the red wine as needed, until chicken is tender and vegetables cooked, about 15–20 minutes.

Serve with plain boiled spaghetti cooked just to al dente, passing Parmesan cheese to sprinkle over all.

The sauce for this and other Italian recipes can be made in large batches and stored indefinitely in the freezer in tightly lidded plastic containers.

CHICKEN OR TURKEY TETRAZZINI

Serves 6 to 8

2 1/2 cups thinly sliced fresh mushrooms
4–5 cups leftover chicken or turkey cut into bite size pieces, using either both brown and white meat or only white meat
1/4 lb. boiled ham slices, cut into julienne strips
1/2 stick sweet butter
1 cup heavy cream
2 tbsp. flour
2 cups chicken broth, from stock of stewed chicken, or canned
Salt and pepper to taste
Pinch of nutmeg, or to taste
1/4 cup sweet sherry
1/3 to 1/2 cup fresh Parmesan cheese
1/2 to 3/4 lb. spaghetti, cooked only until al dente

Melt the butter in a large saucepan and blend in 2 tbsp. flour. Stir in gradually the 2 cups chicken broth and continue to simmer, stirring, until smooth and thickened. Stir in 1 cup heavy cream and the 1/4 cup sherry, salt and pepper and nutmeg. Simmer 10 minutes. Sauté the sliced mushrooms in a little butter and set aside. Cook the spaghetti in rapidly boiling, salted water until just tender. Drain and keep warm.

Add half of the cooked sauce to the mushrooms and mix in the cooked spaghetti. Pour the spaghetti mixture into a generously buttered baking dish large enough to accommodate the entire dish. Add the other half of the sauce to the julienned ham and the chicken and heat until warm. Make a well in the center of the spaghetti mixture and pour the chicken, ham and sauce into the center. Sprinkle the Parmesan cheese over the top and bake in a moderate oven (350°F.) for about 10 minutes, or until the top is lightly browned. Serve at once.

EGGPLANT PARMESAN

Serves 4

1½ lbs. eggplant, peeled and cut in 1/2″ slices lengthwise
Salt
Flour
½ cup olive oil
2 cups meatless spaghetti sauce (see "Sauces")
8 oz. Mozzarella cheese (if not available Asadero, Manchego or Monterrey Jack or any other mild, white, melting cheese will give similar results)
½ cup fresh Parmesan cheese

Preheat oven to 400°F. Oil bottom and sides of a shallow 1½–2 quart baking dish.

Sprinkle both sides of eggplant slices with salt and spread them out in one layer on paper towels for about 20 minutes (the salt will draw out the excess moisture). Dry with paper towels. Dip each slice in flour and shake off excess. In a heavy skillet, heat a little of the oil until hot and brown the eggplant slices on each side a few at a time, adding oil as necessary, and working quickly. Transfer browned slices to paper towels to drain.

Pour about 1/4″ of spaghetti sauce into the baking dish and spread one half of the eggplant slices over the sauce in a single layer. Top them with a layer of Mozzarella or other cheese, and sprinkle half of the grated Parmesan on the top. Repeat with one more layer, first sauce, then the remaining eggplant, then Mozzarella and Parmesan. Top this second layer with sauce, and a little more Mozzarella and Parmesan.

Cover the dish snugly with aluminum foil and bake in the middle of the oven for 20 minutes. Remove foil and bake uncovered for 15 minutes longer.

To turn this dish into a low calorie main dish, steam the eggplant slices until limp instead of frying them, omit the flour and olive oil, and substitute regular or low fat cottage cheese into which has been stirred 1 well beaten egg for Mozzarella.

RED SNAPPER IN THE STYLE OF VERACRUZ

Serves 6

2 lbs. snapper fillets
1/4 cup very fine, fresh olive oil (if not available use vegetable)
2 large onions chopped coarsely
2 large cloves of garlic, mashed
4 very large tomatoes, peeled and coarsely chopped
1 tbsp. minced fresh parsley (not cilantro)
2 tbsps. red wine vinegar
1/2 cup beer
1/2 cup green olives, sliced
1/2 cup capers
1/2 cup chopped jalapeño chiles in escabeche or vinegar (or green peppers if preferred)
1 large or 2 small bay leaves
1/2 tsp. thyme
1/2 tsp. marjoram
Salt and pepper to taste

Sauté the fillets in the oil until lightly browned on both sides. Remove and set aside, keeping hot on a platter. Sauté the garlic and onion until golden. Add the tomatoes, chiles or peppers, bay leaf, parsley, thyme, marjoram and salt and pepper to taste, and the beer and vinegar. Simmer the sauce about 10 minutes until tomatoes, chiles (or peppers) and onions are cooked. Add the green olives and capers and cook 1 minute longer, very slowly.

Pour this sauce over the snapper fillets and serve.

COQ AU VIN

Serves 6

2 frying size chickens, cut in pieces, flour seasoned with salt and pepper and 1/2 tsp. powdered ginger
1 tsp. fresh ginger, mashed, or 2 tsps. powdered
1/2 cup butter
12 tiny white onions
2 cloves garlic, mashed
1 large bay leaf, or 2 small
1 large stick of celery, leaves included
1 cup fresh mushrooms, halved or quartered
2 tbsps. chopped parsley (not cilantro)
1/2 tsp. rosemary
1/2 tsp. marjoram
3 cups dry red wine

Clean chicken, cut into pieces as for frying, and shake in a bag which contains the seasoned flour. Be sure the pieces are well coated. Melt the butter in a large skillet or electric frypan. Shake the pieces of chicken of excess flour and brown on all sides in the butter. Add onions, garlic, bay leaf broken, parsley, celery, mushrooms, ginger, rosemary and marjoram. Simmer about 10 minutes.

Remove the entire mixture to a large casserole, pour over the red wine, cover tightly and cook on top of the stove very slowly 1 to 1 1/2 hours. Add more wine as needed.

CHICKEN POT PIE SUPREME

Serves 8

3 cups chicken breasts (2 whole large breasts) poached and cubed
1/4 lb. cubed boiled ham
2 cups chicken stock (do not use broth or bouillon because it is not rich enough)
1/4 tsp. marjoram
1/4 tsp. thyme
2 medium carrots, cubed and cooked
2/3 to 3/4 cup cooked fresh or frozen peas
1 cup sliced fresh mushrooms
1/2 onion, chopped, or 4 green onions chopped
1 medium potato, cubed and cooked
1 1/2 cups cream
3 tbsps. flour
1/4 cup sherry (medium or sweet)
1/2 stick butter
1/2 cup Parmesan cheese
Salt and pepper to taste

Sauté onion and mushrooms in the butter until tender. Add the chicken and turn off heat. Add a little stock to the flour and mix until blended and smooth. Add the remaining stock a little at a time until all has been used. Heat the mixture in a medium saucepan. If mixture seems too thick, add a little water, but only if necessary. Add cream, seasonings, Parmesan cheese and sherry. When sauce is thickened and smooth add all other ingredients.

Pour into deep baking dish, or individual souffle type dishes, and cover with rich pastry crust (see recipe in the section on "Breads"). Bake at 425°F. for 25–30 minutes, until pastry top is browned. Cool to warm before serving. (If using individual dishes, the baking time will be about 5 minutes less.)

ROULADES OF BEEF

Serves 6

6 long pieces of thin boneless sirloin
Salt and freshly ground pepper to taste
6 tsps. prepared mustard
1 lb. pork sausage (Mexican style mild chorizo sausage covering removed and crumbled may be used, or ground veal or beef may also be used)
1 large garlic clove, mashed
1 large onion, chopped finely
1/2 tsp. thyme
1 large or 2 small bay leaves
1/4 cup cognac (inexpensive brandy may be substituted)
2 tomatoes, peeled and chopped
1/2 cup beef bouillon
2/3 cup dry red wine
1 egg, beaten
3–4 slices bread, crumbled
1/2 cup milk

Spread the meat slices out on a flat surface, and sprinkle lightly with salt and pepper. Spread each slice with a little mustard.

Sauté the garlic and onion in a little oil until golden. Remove from heat and add the thyme, crumbled sausage, cognac, egg, milk, and crumbled bread. Salt and pepper slightly (but do not taste if using raw sausage). Mix together thoroughly. Spread the mixture, divided evenly, over

3/4 of the length of each slice of meat, beginning at the broad end. Roll up and fasten with toothpicks, dredge in a little flour which has been seasoned with a little salt and pepper. Brown the rolls in a little oil in the skillet, reduce the heat, add the bouillon, tomatoes, red wine and bay leaf, cover and simmer until fork tender, about 1 to 1½ hours. Use remaining juices in pan when finished as sauce to pour over. If the pan dries out, the heat is too high. Reduce heat and add more red wine as needed.

BAKED STUFFED SHRIMP

Serves 8–12

24 giant or colossal shrimp
4½ cups chopped onion (red preferred if available)
4½ cups chopped green pepper
1½ lbs. fillet of any very mild, white fish (trout preferred) cut in 1″ pieces
4½ cups croutons (or toasted bread cut into pieces)
1 cup + 2 tbsps. white wine
3 cups chopped celery
⅓ cup mayonnaise
6 cloves garlic mashed
2 sticks butter, softened
Salt and white pepper to taste (about 1 tsp. salt and ½ tsp. pepper)

Preheat the oven to 400°F.

Shell the shrimp, leaving the tail piece intact. Remove the vein and butterfly the shrimp along the outside curve; set aside.

Steam the green pepper, onion, fish and celery in a heatproof container (preferably a small steamer rack if available) over simmering water for about 10 minutes (if using a bowl, cover with foil or plastic wrap).

In a bowl sprinkle croutons with wine and toss. Allow to soften at least 10 minutes.

Combine the steamed vegetables and fish and the crouton mixture together with the mayonnaise and salt in a food processor fitted with steel blade. Blend only until moderately ground, not pureed.

In a small bowl combine the softened butter, the garlic and the white pepper and salt to taste.

Stuff each shrimp with a heaping teaspoon of the vegetable mixture, curling the shrimp tail over it. Arrange shrimp in one layer in a baking dish, dot them with the garlic butter, and bake them in the middle of the oven for 15 minutes (20 minutes or more at altitudes over 5,000 feet) until they are springy to touch.

SEAFOOD CREOLE

Serves 4–6

1/2 lb. fresh (very fresh) mild white fish fillets, raw, cut in 1″ pieces
1/2 lb. shrimp, any size, raw, shelled and deveined
1/4 cup flour
1 cup hot water
1 can (8-oz.) tomato puree
2/3 cup chopped green onions and part of tops
1/4 cup chopped parsley (not cilantro)
2/3 cup chopped green pepper
4 cloves garlic, mashed
1 tbsp. vegetable oil
2 large bay leaves, or 4 small
1/2 tsp. thyme, crumbled
Dash of cayenne pepper
1 lemon slice

Sauté garlic in oil until golden, but not brown. Add water, thyme, bay leaves, lemon slice, cayenne and vegetables. Simmer until tender (about 10 minutes). Make a paste of the flour and tomato puree. When the vegetables are ready, add the hot water, one spoonful at a time, to the tomato mixture until thin enough to pour. Then add the tomato mixture to the vegetable mixture and thicken, stirring constantly. Add the fish and shrimp, and continue simmering only until the shrimp is pink and the fish is white (do not overcook). Remove the bay leaves and serve hot over hot rice.

BREAST OF CHICKEN JACQUELINE

Serves 6

6 small whole chicken breasts or 6 large halves, boned, skinned and flattened slightly
8 tbsps. butter
1/4 cup sliced almonds (omit if unavailable)
Flour
Salt and pepper
3/4 cup chicken stock or bouillon or broth
3/4 cup port wine
1 1/2 cups thick cream
3 tart apples, peeled, cored and cut into eighths

Melt 2 tbsps. butter in heavy skillet over medium heat. Add almonds and stir until golden brown, about 4 minutes. Set aside (this step may be eliminated if the almonds are unavailable.)

Sprinkle salt and pepper into flour and mix well. Lightly dredge chicken in flour, shaking off excess. Melt 4 tbsps. butter in heavy skillet over medium high heat. Add chicken and cook until just springy to touch and lightly browned, about 4 minutes on each side. Transfer to hot platter and place in a warm place.

Add stock or broth to port and pour into same skillet and boil until reduced by half, scraping up any browned bits. Add cream and boil until reduced to saucelike consistency, stirring occasionally.

Meanwhile, melt remaining 2 tbsps. butter in heavy skillet over medium heat. Add apples and cook until just tender, stirring frequently, about 5 or 6 minutes. Arrange 1 chicken breast and 4 apple slices on each plate. Taste sauce and adjust seasoning. Pour sauce over chicken, sprinkle with almonds, if using, and serve.

CHICKEN ROLLATINES

Serves 6

3 whole chicken breasts, halved, skinned, boned and pounded thin
6 thin slices prosciutto ham (boiled ham may be substituted)
6 thin slices Mozzarella type cheese (Manchego or Asadero may be used) or Gruyere cheese
Garlic powder
6 tbsps. fine bread crumbs
1 tsp. herb seasoning
Salt and pepper to taste
6 tbsps. dry white wine
6 tbsps. butter

Preheat oven to 350°F. Lightly grease a shallow baking dish just big enough to accommodate the 6 rollatines.

Sprinkle each chicken piece with garlic powder. Place 1 slice ham and 1 slice cheese on each piece. Add the herb seasoning, salt and pepper to the bread crumbs. Sprinkle bread crumbs in equal portions over the cheese slices on top of the ham and chicken pieces. Roll up, starting at broader end of the chicken piece, and secure with toothpicks. Place in baking dish.

Combine white wine and butter and heat briefly, until butter is melted. Pour over chicken and sprinkle with a little salt. Bake approximately 30–35 minutes at 5,000 ft. or more altitude, 20–25 minutes at lower altitudes.

NORTH AMERICAN "AT HOME" BEEF STROGANOFF

Serves 6–8

2 lbs. beef, tenderloin or sirloin, sliced in very thin strips on the diagonal, about 4" long by 1/2–1" wide
1 large onion sliced and separated into rings
1 lb. fresh mushrooms, sliced
1/2 cup butter
Salt and pepper to taste
2 cans mushroom soup, mixed with 1/2 can water only
1 1/2 tsps. oregano
1 1/2 tbsps. Lea & Perrins
1 cup sour cream (or more to taste if desired) or 1 cup cottage cheese and 2/3 to 1 cup yogurt

Sauté the mushrooms and the onions in butter until limp. Set aside. Sauté the beef strips in very hot pan only until brown (do not overcook as meat will cook more in sauce). Turn heat down to simmer, add mushroom soup and water, oregano, Lea & Perrins, and the sautéed mushrooms and onions. Simmer a minute or two, then add either the sour cream or the cottage cheese and yogurt, and salt and pepper to taste. Turn off heat and cover to warm the last ingredients. If necessary to heat a little, be very careful only to heat to warm — do not allow to simmer or boil.

Serve over boiled noodles, or, if unavailable, over rice or mashed potatoes, although the noodles are much superior.

If desired, this dish can be made with first quality ground beef, fat free, in place of the beef strips.

If a slightly different flavor is desired, a little tomato paste or puree may be added (not more than 1 or 2 tbsps.) for a slight flavor and a rosy color.

CHICKEN COUNTRY CAPTAIN

Serves 8

2 frying chickens, about 2 1/2-lbs. each, cut up
Salt and pepper
2 to 3 tbsps. butter
1 large onion, finely chopped
1 1/2 cups long grain rice
2 green peppers, seeded and chopped coarsely
2 large cloves garlic, minced
1/2 cup raisins
3 tsps. curry powder
2 large tomatoes, peeled and chopped
1 cup tomato puree
1 1/4 cups chicken broth, homemade or canned
3/4 tsp. dried thyme, crumbled
4 tbsps. chutney (or, if unavailable, use same amount of peach preserves or orange marmalade)
1/2 cup slivered, blanched almonds

Cut chickens into serving pieces, excluding the back bones, necks and giblets. Sprinkle with salt and pepper, but only lightly. In a large frying pan brown chicken pieces on all sides in the heated butter, a few at a time. Remove chicken pieces and set aside. Stir the onion and rice in the same pan and cook at medium heat until the onion is soft and lightly browned. Mix in the green peppers, garlic, raisins, chutney and curry powder. Continue to cook, stirring constantly, for about 3–4 minutes. Add tomatoes and puree, broth and thyme, stirring to mix in brown bits from pan. Transfer to a broad, 4 quart casserole and arrange the chicken pieces over the rice, in a single layer if possible, pouring on any accumulated juices.

Cover the casserole and bake in a 375°F. oven for 50 minutes or until the chicken is tender. Remove chicken pieces and stir the rice well. Replace the chicken pieces to top of the rice and sprinkle with the almonds. Continue baking, uncovered, about 15 minutes longer, until chicken and almonds are golden.

This dish keeps well to be rewarmed if there are leftovers.

CARBONNADES FLAMANDE

Serves 8

$1/2$ lb. lean bacon or salt pork, cubed
1 tbsp. salt and 4 twists of the pepper mill of pepper
4 tbsps. butter
5 to 6 large onions, thinly sliced
3 pounds lean boneless beef chuck or rump, cut in 2″ chunks
1 bay leaf
1 tsp. minced garlic
1 tbsp. vinegar
$1\,1/2$ tsps. sugar
1 tsp. dried thyme, crumbled
2 tbsps. finely chopped fresh parsley
3 tbsps. flour
2 bottles dark beer (12-oz. each)
1 tbsp. prepared mustard, spread on one side of 2 slices bread

Heat the oven to 325°F. Grease a large casserole, flameproof with lid.

Cook the bacon in a heavy skillet until most of the fat has been extracted. Transfer the pieces to the casserole. Pour off all but 3 or 4 tbsps. of the fat. Add the butter and heat until hot, but not smoking. Brown the onions, lift them out and set aside. Dredge the meat cubes in the flour which has been seasoned with the salt and pepper, shake off excess, and brown them in the skillet. Add the thyme, garlic, sugar, bay leaf broken into pieces, parsley and vinegar, and stir until well mixed. Transfer the beef to the casserole. Cover with the sautéed onions and bacon. Spread the slices of bread, mustard side down, over the onions. Pour the beer over bread. Bring the casserole to a boil on top of the stove, then transfer to heated oven and cover and bake for 45 minutes. Stir the bread into the beef and onions and continue cooking for $1\,1/2$ hours, or until the beef is tender. After one hour test from time to time.

Serve with boiled potatoes or noodles.

FISH WITH CRABMEAT STUFFING

Serves 6

Choose any 4–5 lb. flat fish with few bones, such as snapper or flounder, increase the size of the stomach slit after the fish has been cleaned and gutted to accommodate the stuffing which follows. This stuffing can also be used on top of boned fillets of any kind of white, mild fish. It is also excellent atop fillets of chicken breast, or slices of turkey breast.

Preheat the oven to 375°F. Choose a flat baking dish sufficiently large to accommodate the single or several fish, or the fillets in a single layer, and butter the dish.

Dry the fish or fishes thoroughly inside and out with paper towels.

1/2 to 3/4 lb. crab meat (or imitation crabmeat may be substituted)
1/2 cup dry white wine
1/3 cup butter
2 tbsps. finely chopped celery
2 tbsps. finely chopped green peppers
2 tbsps. finely chopped onions
1 tbsp. chopped chives, or, if unavailable, tiny green onion
1 large or 2 small cloves garlic, minced
1 tbsp. Lea & Perrins
1 tbsp. prepared mustard
1/2 tsp. salt
Several grindings of black pepper
1 well beaten egg
1 1/2 cups fine bread crumbs
1 tsp. chopped parsley (optional)
1 cup bechamel sauce (see "Sauces")

Sauté the celery, green pepper, onion and garlic in the melted butter until golden brown. Add the bechamel sauce. Mix the crabmeat with the Lea & Perrins, mustard, salt and pepper, beaten egg and breadcrumbs. Add the crab mixture to the sauce and vegetables, mixing thoroughly. Spoon into the prepared fish, or, if using fillets, mound the stuffing on top of each fillet. Place in the prepared dish. Top the fish, or each fish or fillet, with a small pat of butter; pour the wine carefully about the bottom of the baking dish without getting any on the fish. Bake uncovered for about 20–30 minutes for a 4 lb. fish, or 15–20 minutes for small, individually stuffed fish, or for 15 minutes for stuffing-topped fillets. Use the wine as a basting sauce, spooning from bottom of dish over the fish from time to time, as needed. Use more wine if necessary. Test fish before removing from oven. If done, fish should flake easily with fork.

Garnish with lemon slices and sprigs of parsley if desired.

LAMB CURRY

Serves 6

(This recipe seems complicated because of the long list of ingredients, but it is really very simple to make and it makes a superb curry sauce.)

- 1/2 stick butter
- 3 medium onions, minced
- 2 garlic cloves, mashed
- 2 carrots, minced
- 1 celery stalk, minced
- 1/2 green pepper, seeded and minced
- 2 tbsps. minced parsley
- 2 tbsps. flour
- 1 1/2 cups chicken broth or bouillon
- 1/2 cup dry red or white wine
- 1/2 cup fresh tomato, peeled and chopped
- 1/2 cup coconut milk (regular milk may be substituted)
- 1/4 cup lime juice
- 3 tbsps. chutney (or orange marmalade or apricot or peach preserves)
- 2 1/2 tbsps. brown sugar
- 2 tbsps. golden raisins (or brown raisins may be substituted)
- Bouquet garni (2 whole cloves and 1 small bay leaf, tied in cheesecloth)
- 3 tsps. curry powder moistened with a little cold water to mix
- 2 tsps. grated fresh ginger (or 4 tsp. powdered ginger if unavailable)
- 1/2 tsp. cinnamon
- 2 tsps. turmeric
- 2 tsps. coriander
- 4 cardamon seeds, crushed
- 1/8 tsp. nutmeg
- 1/4 tsp. cayenne pepper (or 1/2 tsp. white pepper if unavailable)
- 4 cups cubed cooked lamb (cubes no larger than 1″) trimmed of all fat
- 2 tart large apples, peeled cored and cubed
- 1/2 cup plain yogurt

Melt butter in 5 quart heavy saucepan over medium heat. Add onion, garlic, carrot, celery, green pepper and parsley and sauté until onion is golden.

Combine flour with a little broth in a small bowl, stirring until flour dissolves, and mixture is smooth. Add the sautéed vegtables and the tomato, blending thoroughly. Stir in remaining stock, wine and all spices and simmer very slowly, covered, for 45 minutes, stirring occasionally. Add coconut milk or regular milk, lime juice and chutney or marmalade or preserves and simmer 10 minutes more. Add lamb and cook 15 minutes more. Gently stir in apple and yogurt. Turn off heat. Serve in center of a rice ring or over rice.

If using the sauce to serve over chicken or shrimp, do not add the cubed lamb, apple and yogurt, but serve any or all the following small side dishes either around the platter with the chicken or shrimp covered with the sauce in the center, or in tiny bowls at the top of the place setting of each individual serving of chicken or shrimp and sauce:

"SAMBALS"

Chopped peanuts
Shredded, toasted coconut
Chopped or cubed pineapple (fresh preferred)
Plain yogurt
Chopped green onion
Chopped apple
Chopped, unpeeled, cucumber
Chutney

This sauce is wonderful served over poached chicken breasts, or over freshly boiled shrimp, either medium or large, and may be prepared 2 or 3 days in advance or frozen. If freezing, it is best to double or triple the recipe, because it keeps beautifully in the freezer for 1 or 2 months.

FISH FILLET TURBANS A LA NEWBURG

Serves 6

2 lbs. raw fish fillets (any kind of mild, white fish)
1 tsp. salt
1/4 tsp. pepper
1/4 cup melted butter
3 cups cooked rice
Newburg Sauce

Sprinkle fillets with salt and pepper. Roll each fillet up beginning at broad end and ending with pointed end. Place fish rolls in buttered baking dish in single layer, brush with melted butter and bake at 350°F. 15–20 minutes, or until fish flakes when tested with a fork. Place the rolls on their sides, turban style, on a bed of the cooked rice and pour the following sauce over the top:

1/2 cup butter
1/4 cup flour
1/2 tsp. salt
Dash of cayenne
1 1/2 cups heavy cream
1 1/2 cups milk, scalded
6 egg yolks
1/3 cup Madeira wine (if Madeira is not available, use medium sherry, or white wine)

Melt the butter. Stir in the flour, salt and cayenne. Remove from heat and add the scalded milk a little at a time, blending until smooth. Add the cream. Cook until thickened, stirring constantly. Stir a little of the hot sauce into the 6 egg yolks which have been beaten with the wine. Add the mixture to the saucepan with the remainder of the sauce and heat slowly until thickened. Pour over the fish and serve at once.

PORK TENDERLOIN WITH MANGO SAUCE

Serves 6

2 to 3 lbs. pork tenderloin sliced 1" thick and pounded to about 1/2"
4 slices fresh ginger (or 2 tsps. powdered if not available)
5 strips lemon rind
2/3 cup dry white wine
1/2 cup brown sugar
Juice of 2 small limes or 1 lemon
1/2 cup (about) sweet cream
1/2 cup currant jelly (if not available, orange marmalade may be substituted)
4 small or 2 large fresh mangoes, peeled, seeded, and sliced
4 tbsps. butter
Flour, seasoned with salt and pepper
3 cloves garlic, mashed
1 sliced onion

Dredge each slice of pork lightly with seasoned flour and brown in the hot butter on each side. Remove and set aside. Sauté the garlic and onion until golden in the pan with the remaining butter (add more butter if the pan has become too dry). Return the pork slices to the pan, scraping the pan to loosen any garlic or onion or flour from bottom. Add the wine and heat to boiling. Add the ginger and lemon rind. Cover and simmer until the pork is cooked through and tender (about 25 minutes at low altitudes, 40 minutes above 5,000 feet). Remove meat and set aside on heated platter. Add brown sugar and juice to liquid. Add the cream and the jelly or marmalade, a little at a time, tasting to avoid overcreaming or oversweetening. Cook down a little, gently simmering, to thicken the cream. Fold in the slices of mango and heat through. Pour over the pork and serve.

BEEF TENDERLOIN IN CARAWAY WITH MUSHROOMS

Serves 8

1 4-lb. whole beef tenderloin
2 cups dry white wine
2 sticks sweet butter
1 cup caraway seed
1 lb. fresh mushrooms, sliced

Marinate the beef tenderloin in 1 cup of the dry white wine for at least 2 hours, at room temperature, turning often to insure complete coverage.

Heat oven to 300°F.

Remove meat from wine (reserving the wine to use for basting). Paint generously with 1 stick of the butter, softened, but not melted. Cover all over with the caraway seed, even the bottom, patting gently to make the seeds adhere. The seed should be almost like a crust — do not be afraid to use the amount listed. Roast at 300°F. in roaster or heavy bottom pan, or, preferably in an iron skillet, uncovered, about 30 minutes for rare, 40–45 for medium. (It is important not to overcook this roast.) Baste with reserved wine.

Meanwhile, lightly sauté the mushrooms in the remaining stick of butter. Add 1 cup white wine and gently simmer until reduced by half.

After the meat is roasted, remove to hot platter and pour the juices and remaining wine into mushroom pan. Simmer the sauce for another 10 minutes, keeping the tenderloin hot.

Slice the meat on the diagonal thinly and serve on a platter with the sauce on the side.

This dish is excellent served with plain buttered noodles with a little parsley chopped and sprinkled on top.

SWEET AND SOUR ORIENTAL PORK ROAST

Serves 8–10

4–6 lb. pork roast
2 cups sugar
1 cup vinegar (white preferred)
1 whole small green pepper, seeded and chopped
1 tsp. salt
1 cup water
4 tsps. cornstarch (stirred into 2 tbsps. water)
4 tbsps. soy sauce
1 tbsp. mashed fresh ginger (or 3–4 tsps. powdered)
2 large cloves garlic, mashed and sautéed until golden in oil
2 tbsps. fresh parsley (not cilantro) minced

Sauté the garlic (and the ginger if using fresh) in a little oil in a small frying pan. Set aside. Brown the roast on all sides in a little oil in a frying pan sufficiently large to accommodate it. Transfer to a dutch oven or a deep casserole.

Mix sugar, vinegar, green pepper, salt, soy sauce, cornstarch mixture, water, garlic and ginger. Simmer until the mixture thickens. Add parsley.

Pour the sauce over the roast in the deep casserole or dutch oven. Do not cover. Bake at 300°F. for 2½ hours, or until pork is tender. Baste occasionally.

Remove the roast from the sauce and serve with the sauce on the side.

This recipe may be used for whole roast chicken as well, only adjusting the baking time and temperature. Bake the chicken at 350°F. for about 1 to 1½ hours, until fork tender.

BAKED FISH FLORENTINE

Serves 6

1 4–5 lb. red snapper (or 2 or more smaller snapper or 6, ¾ to 1 lb. trout, or 12 fillets of sole, or trout or other white, mild, firm fleshed fish)

If using a large snapper, removal of the backbone is advised since it makes cutting for serving easier. However, it is a difficult process and not absolutely necessary. If backbone is not removed, cut servings horizontally and scoop out stuffing per serving at table.

Irrespective of the size of the fish, if using whole fish, scale and clean, remove fins, but leave the head and the tail intact. Enlarge stomach slit to accommodate stuffing.

If using fillets, spread stuffing (about 1 tbsp.) on large end of each fillet, roll up and skewer with a toothpick.

4 tbsps. butter
2 large cloves garlic, mashed
3 finely chopped green onions (white part only)
¾ cup finely chopped, cooked spinach
2 cups fine bread crumbs
3–4 tbsps. heavy cream
½ tsp. salt
Freshly ground pepper
¼ tsp. lemon juice

FOR THE FISH

5 tbsps. melted butter
1 cup dry white wine

Preheat oven to 400°F.

Wash any whole fish inside and out under running water and dry thoroughly.

In a heavy skillet melt the 4 tbsps. butter over moderate heat; sauté the onion and garlic until soft, but not brown. Squeeze all possible moisture from the spinach and add to the skillet. Cook over high heat, stirring constantly until most of the moisture has dried out. Transfer to a large mixing bowl; add bread crumbs, cream, salt, pepper and lemon juice, and mix thoroughly.

Brush 1 tbsp. of the melted butter on bottom of shallow baking dish large enough to hold all the fish (if using fillets, or small fish, in a single layer without overlapping). Fill the fish with the stuffing, and close with skewers if necessary. Put fish in prepared dish, brush top with 2 tbsps. of melted butter and season with salt and pepper. Combine remaining 2 tbsps. melted butter with the wine and pour it around, but not on, the fish.

Bake, uncovered, in center of the oven, basting frequently, for 30–40 minutes if using 1 whole fish, or about 20 minutes for small fish or fillets. Do not overcook, but bake only until the fish is just firm when pressed lightly with the finger. If the dish dries out, add a little more wine.

Pour the juices off and serve on the side to pour over the servings of fish.

NOTE: This stuffing is very versatile and can be used to stuff chicken breast fillets or thinly pounded veal scallops, using the same techniques for preparation and, approximately, same cooking time. It is also excellent as a stuffing for tomatoes or mushrooms. (See "Vegetables" section.)

SHRIMP SCAMPI

Serves 6

2 lbs. large (about 36) raw shrimp, shelled, deveined, tails intact
1 1/2 sticks butter
3 tbsps. dry white wine
1 tbsp. mashed garlic
1/4 cup green onions, finely chopped, using a little of the green part
1 tbsp. lemon juice
Salt and pepper to taste

Sauté the garlic and green onion in the butter. Add the shrimp and sauté quickly, turning constantly, only until the shrimp are pink (do not overcook). Remove shrimp from pan and reserve on hot dish, retaining as much of the butter sauce in the pan as possible. Add the lemon juice and the wine to the butter sauce in the pan and cook about 1 minute. Return the shrimp to the pan and turn off heat. Season to taste and serve immediately, pouring the sauce over. Serve with plain rice or buttered pasta, or, for super elegance, fettuccine alfredo (see recipe in "Breads" section).

Although, traditionally, this shrimp dish is made by broiling the shrimp and pouring the sauce over after cooking, Marcy's prefers this method both for ease of preparation and because the shrimp is impermeated with the flavors of the garlic sauce.

VEAL CORDON BLEU

Serves 6

12 3 oz. to 4 oz. veal scallops (preferably cut from the leg)
Salt and freshly ground pepper
6 round, thin slices prosciutto ham (or boiled ham if unavailable)
6 thin round slices Gruyere cheese
2 eggs, lightly beaten
1 tsp. water
1½ cups fresh bread crumbs
½ cup butter
Flour

Season the flour with salt and pepper. Place each scallop between 2 pieces of wax paper and pound with a flat mallet or the bottom of small, heavy skillet until thin. Place 1 slice of ham in the center of six of the scallops and top with a slice of cheese. Beat the eggs and water together. Brush the underside of the veal which has been topped with the ham and cheese with the egg mixture. Place the other slices of veal on top and brush each top with the egg mixture. Carefully dredge the filled meat on both sides with seasoned flour. Dip the pieces in the beaten egg and then in the crumbs until well coated. Pat the pieces lightly with the side of a heavy kitchen knife to help the crumbs adhere.

Transfer the meat to a wire rack and refrigerate for 1 or 2 hours. (This helps the crumbs adhere to the cutlets when they are being cooked.)

Heat the butter in a large skillet and, when it is hot, but not brown or smoking, sauté the cutlets in it until golden on both sides and the cheese melted.

The scallops may be served with a sauce, if desired. At Marcy's the preference is:

½ stick salted butter, sliced
Juice of 2 lemons
1 cup dry white wine
2 tsps. cornstarch

Mix all ingredients together in saucepan and cook until thickened.

Also at Marcy's we add 1 tsp. crumbled Roquefort or blue cheese to the top of each cheese slice before adding top slice of veal for a uniquely different flavor. Delicious!

Vegetables

VEGETABLE TIMBALES

Serves 8

BASIC CUSTARD FOR TIMBALES:

4 eggs, beaten well
1/2 tsp. dry mustard
1/2 cup heavy cream
1 tbsp. light vegetable oil
3 tbsps. Parmesan cheese, grated (optional)
1/2 tsp. salt

Combine all ingredients in top of double boiler and stir over simmering water until mixture begins to thicken. Remove from heat before mixture starts to set, and fold in any combination of vegetables, such as the following:

1. 3 cups mixed diced carrots, turnips, green beans, and peas, all cooked.
2. 3 cups broccoli, chopped small, cooked, and dried between paper towels; add 1/4 tsp basil, crumbled.
3. 3 cups zucchini, diced, cooked, and dried between paper towels; add 1/4 tsp thyme, crumbled.
4. 3 cups cauliflower, chopped small, cooked, and dried between paper towels; add 1 tsp chopped pimiento.
5. 1 1/2 lbs. spinach, washed well, finely chopped, cooked, and pressed dry.
6. 3 cups mushrooms, coarsely chopped or thinly sliced, sautéed lightly in butter and drained well.
7. 2 cups diced cooked potato, 1/2 cup lightly sautéed chopped onion, pinch of thyme.

Bake at 350°F. in a single, buttered 1 1/2 quart baking dish or 8 individual buttered custard cups, in a large pan filled halfway to the top of the dish or cups with hot water, baking 25 to 30 minutes for the 1 1/2 quart dish, or 20 minutes for the individual cups. Serve hot.

If desired, a sauce may be added, but should be served separately for guests to pour as desired. Sauce suggestions are a light tomato sauce, or hollandaise or mushroom.

STUFFED SWISS CHARD OR LETTUCE LEAVES

Makes 6

If using Swiss Chard, cut away the thick part of the stem, being sure to select large, perfect leaves. If using lettuce, select large, perfect leaves of outer part of a large head of iceberg lettuce. Soak the leaves briefly in boiling water. Dry thoroughly and spread on chopping board or flat surface. Stuff with any of the following combinations:

A.

3 eggs, scrambled
1 clove garlic, minced, sautéed in a little butter
6 fresh mushrooms, chopped and sautéed in the butter with the garlic
1/2 medium onion, chopped fine and sautéed with the garlic, and the mushrooms
6–8 spinach leaves, chopped and steamed, then dried in paper towels
1/2 cup shredded Gruyere
Salt and pepper to taste

Mix all the above together thoroughly and place a mound in the center of the stem edge of each leaf. Turn forward once, then fold each side over the center and roll up. Skewer with a toothpick if necessary. Place in one layer in a buttered baking dish, cover with foil, and bake 30 minutes at 350°F.

B.

1/2 medium onion, sautéed in a little butter
1 clove garlic, minced and sautéed with the onion
2/3 cup fine fresh bread crumbs
1 tomato, peeled and chopped
1 small zucchini, chopped fine
6 fresh mushrooms, chopped fine
3 tbsp. Parmesan cheese grated

Mix all the above together thoroughly and follow the same instructions as in A above.

C.

Use 10 leaves — makes 10

2 garlic cloves, minced and sautéed in a little butter
1 medium onion, chopped and sautéed with the above
1 cup finely grated cabbage, sautéed until golden in a little more butter
2 small tomatoes, peeled and chopped fine
1 green pepper, chopped and sautéed until golden
1/2 cup fresh bread crumbs
2 tsps. prepared mustard
1 cup whole kernel corn
1/4 tsp. each of marjoram, basil, chervil, and thyme crumbled and mixed together
3 tbsp. parmesan cheese
Salt and pepper to taste

Mix all the above together thoroughly and follow the same instructions as for A and B above.

VEGETABLE CLAFOUTI

Serves 6 to 8

BASIC BATTER FOR CLAFOUTI:

2 tbsps. dry whole wheat bread crumbs
6 tbsps. fresh, grated Parmesan cheese
3 eggs
1/3 cup whole wheat pastry flour
2 cups milk or light cream
1/2 tsp. salt
Pinch of cayenne pepper

Butter a shallow 10–12″ baking dish, pie dish or tart shell. Dust with mixture of bread crumbs and 2 tbsps. of the Parmesan cheese. Beat eggs until fluffy. Add flour and mix well. Add milk or cream, remaining cheese, salt and pepper, and beat well for 3 minutes. Add one of the following fillings (or invent your own) and bake at 375°F. for 45 minutes, or until the top is slightly browned and puffy, and a toothpick inserted in the center comes out clean. Cut into 6 or 8 wedges and serve hot.

VEGETABLE FILLINGS FOR CLAFOUTI BATTER:

1. Chop coarsely 1/4 cup onion, 1/4 lb. zucchini, 1/4 cup red bell pepper. Add 1 tsp. mashed fresh garlic and 1/4 tsp. dried thyme.

2. Chop 2 large tomatoes coarsely and drain. Add 1 tsp. basil and 1/2 tsp. mashed garlic. Mince 1 tbsp. fresh parsley and add total mixture to the batter.
3. Add 2 tsps. dry mustard and 1/2 tsp. freshly grated nutmeg to basic batter. Place 2 cups cooked (but still slightly crisp) broccoli florets, or 1 cup cauliflower and 1 cup broccoli, in bottom of the baking dish. Pour the batter over and sprinkle 1/4 cup fresh grated Parmesan cheese on top.
4. Add 1 tsp. (or 2 tsps. if definite curry flavor desired) curry powder to basic batter. Spread 1½ to 2 cups fresh or frozen corn niblets in prepared baking dish. Sprinkle with 1/4 cup finely chopped green onion. Add batter.

POTATOES AU GRATIN

Serves 6 to 8

1½ pounds unpeeled potatoes
2 tbsps. butter
2 tbsps. flour
1½ cups hot milk
½ cup shredded sharp cheese (preferably cheddar, Manchego may be substituted but only if necessary)
1 tbsp. fresh, grated Parmesan cheese
2 garlic cloves, mashed (optional)
Salt and fresh ground pepper to taste
Shredded sharp cheese (preferably cheddar), grated Parmesan and paprika for topping

Boil potatoes in lightly salted water until tender. Cool, peel, and cut into 1/4″ slices. Layer slices in buttered casserole.

Melt butter in medium saucepan, sauté the garlic (if using), but do not brown, and stir in flour until the mixture is smooth. Gradually add hot milk, stirring constantly. Stir in sharp cheese and Parmesan and continue cooking until just melted. Season to taste with salt and pepper. Pour over the potatoes and sprinkle the top with sharp cheese, Parmesan and paprika which have been mixed together. Bake 20–30 minutes in a 350°F. oven, then run under the broiler just until brown and bubbly. Serve immediately.

MUSHROOMS OR TOMATOES WITH FLORENTINE STUFFING

Serves 6 to 8

If stuffing tomatoes, select 6 to 8 medium, ripe tomatoes, scoop out all but about 1/4" of the insides, salt the inside of the shells lightly and turn over to drain on paper towels. Cook down the removed part in a saucepan until thick and almost dry. Mix with the prepared stuffing and stuff the tomato shells. Bake uncovered in a preheated 400°F. oven in a well buttered dish for about 35 minutes. About 15 minutes before the tomatoes are cooked, place a small pat of butter on top of each tomato. When shells are soft and top is brown, tomatoes are ready to serve. Serve hot as an accompaniment.

If stuffing mushrooms, select 3 large or 4 medium mushrooms per person. Clean thoroughly, remove stems and chop stems well. Mix chopped stems with prepared stuffing and stuff the shells, rounding the stuffing on the top. Place the mushrooms in a buttered baking dish or aluminum pan sufficient for one layer. Do not crowd. Melt 1/2 cup butter in a saucepan and add 1/2 cup dry white wine. When mixture is blended and hot, pour carefully around the base of the mushrooms, then spoon over the tops of the mushrooms just a little liquid. Bake, uncovered, in a 400°F. oven about 20 minutes or until browned, basting as needed with the liquid in the pan. Serve hot as an accompaniment.

FLORENTINE STUFFING

4 tbsps. butter
3 cloves garlic, mashed
3/4 cup finely chopped, cooked, fresh spinach, or frozen, juices pressed out as much as possible
2 1/2 cups fresh whole wheat bread crumbs
4 tbsps. heavy cream
1/2 tsp. salt
1/2 tsp. lemon juice
Freshly ground pepper

Melt butter over moderate heat and sauté the garlic just a moment to capture the flavor, then add the spinach, juices from which have been pressed out as much as possible, and continue cooking until the spinach is reasonably dry. Turn off heat, add all other ingredients, mix thoroughly, and stuff.

BAKED POTATO CHIPS

Serves 6

4 lbs. unpeeled, medium size potatoes, scrubbed clean
6–7 tbsps. butter, melted
Salt and pepper to taste

Preheat oven to 500°F. and lightly grease 2–3 baking sheets. Slice potatoes, with their skins on, into 1/8″ thick slices. Arrange the slices in single layers on the two or three sheets. Brush generously with the melted butter. Bake 7 minutes with the pans on both upper and lower racks of the oven. After 7 minutes switch the pan positions, upper pans to lower rack, and lower pans to upper rack, and continue baking until potatoes are crisp and browned around the edges, about 7–9 minutes. Transfer to heated platter and sprinkle with salt and pepper. Serve immediately.

If preferred, the potatoes may be peeled before slicing, but we like the whole potato flavor achieved by leaving the skins on the potatoes.

POTATO FRITTERS

Serves 6

1 lb. potatoes, baked until fork tender in 400°F. oven
1 large egg, beaten
3 tbsps. light cream
2 tbsps. minced onion
2 tbsps. butter
2 slices bacon, cooked crisp, drained and crumbled
1½ oz. shredded, mild cheese (such as American)
1 large egg, beaten
2–3 tbsps. milk
½ cup flour
1½ cups soft bread crumbs
Oil for deep frying

Cool potatoes slightly and scoop out the pulp and mash well. Season with salt and pepper to taste. Add the 1 beaten egg and enough cream to hold the pulp together without letting the mixture become too moist. Do not overblend.

Sauté onion in butter and stir in with bacon and cheese. Add to the potato mixture, and roll into small balls, about 1 to 1½″ in diameter.

Combine other beaten egg with milk. Coat the balls with flour, then the egg-milk mixture, and then the bread crumbs, a few at a time, and fry in deep fryer or skillet in oil heated to 375°F. until browned, about 3 to 4 minutes. Be careful not to overcrowd the fritters, frying only 6 or 7 at time.

Keep hot on a cookie sheet which has been covered with paper towels until all are cooked. Then remove the paper toweling and bake 5 to 6 minutes in 400°F. oven to crisp up the coating. Serve hot.

YAM AND APPLE CASSEROLE

Serves 6 to 8

7 medium size yams or sweet potatoes peeled and sliced in 1/2" slices, or 2 (1 lb.) cans yams, drained thoroughly
2–3 medium size tart apples, peeled, cored and sliced in 1/2" slices
8 tbsps. butter, melted
1/2 cup dark corn syrup
1/2 cup firmly packed brown sugar
2 tbsps. dry sherry (if unavailable, use white wine)
1 tsp. cinnamon
1/8 tsp. salt

Cook the potatoes, if using fresh, in enough water to cover. When tender, drain and puree along with the butter, corn syrup, brown sugar, wine, cinnamon, and salt. If using canned potatoes, follow the same procedure.

Cook the apples in just enough water to cover until barely tender. Drain and reserve the apple water.

Spread half the potato mixture into the bottom of a buttered 10" round casserole dish or deep pie dish. Spread the apple slices on top, pour 1/2 cup apple water over, and then spread remaining puree over the top, sprinkle 3 tbsp. apple water on top, dot with butter, and sprinkle a little white or brown sugar over all. Bake, uncovered, at 350°F. for about 35 minutes.

GINGERED CARROTS

Serves 4 to 6

12 medium carrots, peeled and sliced 1/2" thick
1/4 cup butter
1/2 cup cream or evaporated milk
1/4 tsp. ginger
2 tbsps. brown sugar
1/4 cup toasted sliced or slivered almonds (optional)
Salt and pepper to taste

Sauté the carrots in the butter until crisp tender. Add all remaining ingredients except almonds. Cover and simmer gently for 10–15 minutes longer, until tender. Uncover and cook another 5 minutes. Sprinkle with the toasted almonds.

GLAZED JULIENNED BEETS

Serves 6 to 8

2 1/2 cups pear nectar
2 1/2 cups water
3 tbsps. butter
1 1/2 lbs. young beets, peeled and cut into julienne
2 tbsps. sugar
1/2 tsp. dry mustard
1/2 tsp. salt
1/4 tsp. ground ginger

Bring pear nectar and water to rapid boil. Melt butter in deep skillet sufficiently large to hold all ingredients, and add all remaining ingredients, blending well. Pour boiling pear and water mixture over beets and return to boil. Cook slowly, uncovered, until beets are tender, stirring frequently (about 40 minutes, adding remaining water as necessary.) Serve hot.

SWEET 'N SOUR ONIONS

Serves 8

2 lbs. unpeeled small white onions (1 1/2" diam)
1 tbsp. olive oil
1 tbsp. butter
1/8 tsp. allspice, powdered
1/2 to 3/4 cup dry white wine
2–4 tbsp. red wine vinegar
2 tsps. sugar
Salt to taste

Boil 3–4 quarts water, and when boiling rapidly, add rinsed onions in their skins and return to boil, cooking for about 3 minutes. Drain, and rinse onions in cold water and slip off skins.

Heat oil and butter in a heavy large non-aluminum skillet to medium-high heat. Add onions and allspice and sauté until onions begin to turn slightly brown, about 4 minutes, stirring occasionally. Sprinkle with 1/2 cup wine, 2 tbsps. vinegar, and 2 tsps. sugar seasoned with the salt.

Bake at 375°F. for about 30 minutes, stirring frequently, until onions are golden and still slightly firm when pierced with a knife. Remove onions from liquid onto platter and add sufficient remaining vinegar to pan to attain sweet-tart balance. Pour sauce over onions and serve at room temperature.

CREAMED MUSHROOMS

Serves 6 to 8

2 lbs. sliced fresh mushrooms
2 tbsps. minced onion
4 tbsps. butter
4 tbsps. dry white wine
1½ cups hot bechamel sauce (see "Sauces")
½ tsp. marjoram
1–2 tsp. minced fresh parsley (optional)

Sauté the mushrooms and onion in the butter until onion is golden and mushrooms are brown, but not long enough to burn or scorch. Add the wine and continue cooking, stirring constantly, about 2 minutes. Add the hot Bechamel Sauce and seasonings and heat all together thoroughly, stirring constantly. Adjust the seasoning with a little salt and white pepper, if necessary. Serve hot.

CUCUMBERS WITH DILL

Serves 6

3 large cucumbers
2–3 tbsps. butter
2–3 tbsps. minced fresh dill, or 1 tsp. dried dill weed, crushed with 1 tbsp. minced fresh parsley
Salt and pepper to taste

Peel the cucumbers and slice them in half lengthwise. Scoop out the seeds, then cut each half in half again lengthwise. Then cut each length into triangles by cutting diagonally, first to the right and then to the left. Melt the butter, add the cucumbers, and stir over moderately high heat, seasoning to taste with the salt and pepper, until the cucumbers are almost cooked through, but still somewhat crunchy. Stir in the dill and parsley and serve at once.

This dish is the perfect accompaniment to fish entrees.

ITALIAN STYLE FRIED ZUCCHINI

Serves 6

9 medium zucchini, sliced thinly
4 tbsps. very fine, fresh, olive oil
1/2 tsp. basil, crumbled
1/2 tsp. thyme, crumbled
Salt and pepper to taste

Sauté all ingredients together in a large skillet over medium high heat until the zucchini slices are browned and tender. Serve immediately.

EGGPLANT CASSEROLE

Serves 6

2 1/2 cups cubed peeled eggplant
18 saltine crackers, crumbled
1/2 cup shredded, sharp cheese, preferably cheddar (Manchego can be substituted)
1/4 cup finely chopped celery
2 tbsps. chopped pimiento
1 tbsps. melted butter
1/2 tsp. salt
1/8 tsp. pepper
1 cup light cream or evaporated milk
1 large clove garlic, mashed
1 medium onion, minced

Cook eggplant in boiling, salted water 10 minutes. Drain. Sauté the garlic and onion in a little oil until soft. Combine eggplant, garlic, onion, and all other ingredients together and turn into 1 quart buttered casserole. Bake in a moderate oven 350°F. 45 minutes. Serve hot.

SPECIAL ORDER HASH BROWN POTATOES

Serves 6

8 slices bacon, finely chopped
2 large onions, minced
1 lb. potatoes, peeled and shredded
Salt and pepper to taste

Pat the shredded potatoes dry between paper towels. Sauté the bacon in large skillet until crisp. Add onion and continue to sauté until the onions are soft and golden. Add the potatoes and fry until golden brown, turning only once or twice with a broad spatula. Maintain the heat in the skillet at medium high and if browning occurs too quickly and before the potatoes are done, cover the pan with a lid part of the time. Season with the salt and pepper to taste and serve at once.

GLAZED CARROTS

Serves 4 to 6

1 lb. fresh carrots, peeled and julienned
1 1/2 cups fresh orange juice
1/2 cup brown sugar
1 1/2 tbsps. butter
1 tbsp. cornstarch mixed into 1/4 cup cold water
Pinch ground ginger

Steam carrots until just tender. Transfer to serving bowl and keep warm. Combine orange juice, sugar and butter, then add the cornstarch in water. Cook over medium heat until clear and thickened. Add ginger. Pour over the carrots and toss to coat. Garnish with fresh mint leaves, if desired.

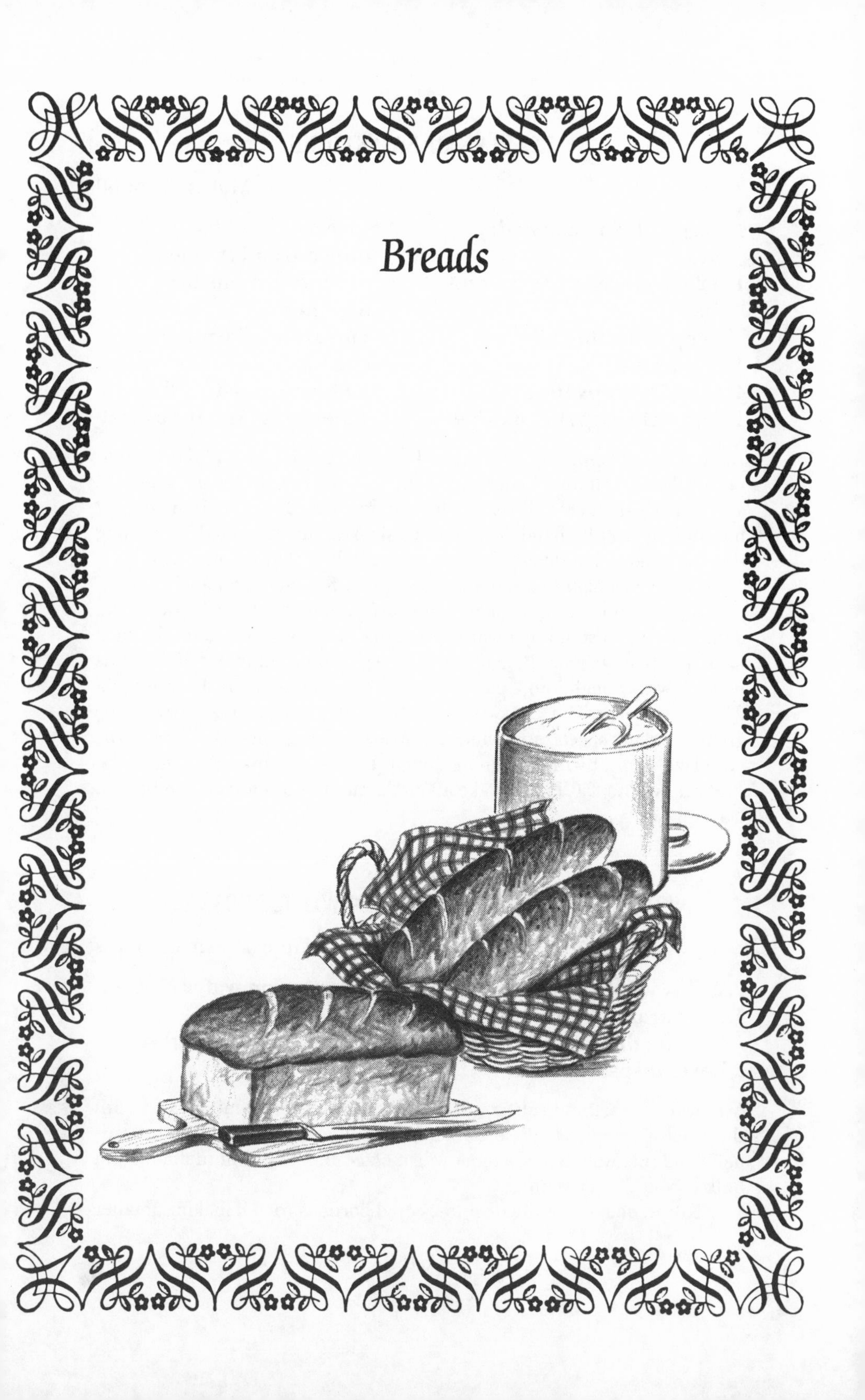

Breads

ITALIAN BREAD STICKS

Makes about 80

1 pkg. (1 tbsp.) active dry yeast
1 12-oz. can beer, warm and flat
3/4 cup vegetable oil
1 1/2 tsps. salt
4 3/4 to 5 1/4 cups flour
1 large clove garlic, mashed
1 tsp. each dried basil, oregano and thyme, ground in a mortar together
1/2 cup grated Parmesan cheese
1 egg blended with 1 tbsp. water for glaze, if desired

In large bowl dissolve yeast in beer. Let stand until foamy, about 10 minutes. Add oil, salt and 3 cups of the flour, together with the garlic, herbs and Parmesan cheese. If using electric mixer, beat at medium speed 2 minutes, or beat by hand 200 vigorous strokes. Stir in enough remaining flour to make a soft dough. Turn out onto lightly floured surface. Grease a bowl large enough to accommodate dough. Knead dough about 8 minutes or until smooth and elastic, and turn into greased bowl; cover with damp towel and stand in a warm place free of drafts to rise until doubled in bulk, about 1 hour. Punch dough down and knead about 30 seconds more. Divide dough into 2 parts. Cover 1 piece and roll out the other to a 22″ x 8″ rectangle. Cut crosswise into about 40 1/2″-wide strips. Arrange on greased baking sheets, stretching the strips to 6–7 inches. Brush with the egg glaze. Repeat with remaining dough. Let rise, uncovered, 30 minutes. Preheat oven to 350°F. and bake about 25 minutes or until golden brown. Cool on racks.

"BLIZBROT" BREAD (GERMAN WHOLE WHEAT)

Makes 2 large or 4 small loaves

2.2 lbs. whole wheat flour
1 1/2 oz. cake of yeast, or 1 1/2 tbsp. dry yeast
2 level tbsps. salt
3/4 quart warm water (110°F., 45°C.)
1 or 2 egg yolks (for glaze)

Mix water, yeast and salt in a large bowl. Let stand 10 minutes or until the yeast is completely dissolved and beginning to foam. Add flour gradually and mix well. Set bowl in a warm place and let rise until doubled in bulk (about 20–30 minutes).

Knead dough and divide into 2 equal portions (or 4 if making smaller loaves). Grease two 8″ x 4 or 5″ loaf pans. Put half of dough into each pan, or, if making 4 small loaves, shape into balls for round loaves and place well apart on greased baking sheet. Brush with egg yolk for glaze.

Place in middle of a cold oven set at 375°F. (190°C.). Place a pan of water on bottom shelf of oven to maintain moisture. Bake 40–50 minutes, or until bread sounds hollow when tapped on bottom.

We like this bread because it has no sweetener in it. Recipe may be cut in half if desired.

ZUCCHINI CHEESE BREAD

Makes 1 loaf

2 eggs
2 cups flour
2 tsps. baking powder
1/2 tsp. baking soda
3/4 tsp. salt
1/8 tsp. paprika
1/4 tsp. dried thyme)
1/4 tsp. dried basil) mashed together in a mortar
1/2 tsp. marjoram)
1 large clove garlic, mashed
2 tbsps. minced onion
1 tbsp. sugar
3/4 cup shredded sharp cheese (Cheddar preferred, but if unavailable, Manchego can be substituted)
1 cup shredded unpeeled zucchini
1/2 cup yogurt
1/4 cup vegetable oil

Beat the eggs until light and fluffy. Add the yogurt and mix well. Combine all dry ingredients in a large bowl, then stir in the cheese and the zucchini, the garlic and the onion. Last, add the egg and yogurt mixture along with the oil. Mix thoroughly until well blended. Pour into a greased 8″ x 4″ loaf pan and bake in a preheated 350°F. oven for about 50 minutes, or until a straw or toothpick inserted in center comes out clean. May be served warm or at room temperature.

MOTHER'S CINNAMON ROLLS

Makes 4 dozen

2 pkgs. dry yeast
1/2 cup warm water
2 cups scalded milk
1/2 cup sugar
6 tbsps. vegetable shortening
2 tsps. salt
2 eggs, beaten
7–8 cups flour
Sugar, cinnamon and raisins

BUTTERSCOTCH TOPPING:

1 cup brown sugar, firmly packed
2 cups light corn syrup
2 sticks butter

Dissolve the yeast in the warm water. Scald (i.e. heat almost to boiling but not quite) the milk with the sugar. Add the shortening to the milk, sugar mixture while hot. Cool about 3 minutes. Then add the salt and the beaten eggs and the yeast mixture. In bowl large enough to accommodate all of the batter, mix in gradually the 7–8 cups flour. Stop adding flour when dough is sticky-stiff. Transfer the dough to a greased bowl, cover with a damp cloth and place in a warm place away from drafts until doubled in bulk.

Divide the dough into 2 equal parts to facilitate rolling out the dough. Roll each half out on well floured board to about 1/2″ thickness in a long rectangle (about 15″ x 11″). Spread with a little melted butter, sprinkle with sugar and cinnamon and cover with raisins. Roll up from one of the long sides to the other, cut into slices about 2″ thick and place on the butterscotch which has been poured into the bottom of an 18″ x 12″ x 2″ baking pan, or two 13″ x 9″ x 2″ pans. Cover with clean cloth and place in warm place out of drafts and allow to rise again until double in bulk. Bake in preheated 400°F. oven 25–30 minutes, until light brown on top. Cool on rack.

For the Butterscotch: Melt the butter in a small saucepan. Add the brown sugar and the corn syrup and mix well but do not heat. Pour into bottom of the baking pan or pans.

FRIED BISCUITS

Makes about 4 dozen

3 1/2 tsps. active dry yeast
2 cups warm milk — not hot
1/4 cup vegetable shortening
3 1/2 to 4 1/2 cups flour
2 tbsps. sugar
2 tsps. salt

Dissolve the yeast in the milk and let stand until foamy (about 10 minutes). Stir in shortening. Mix until shortening is almost melted. Gradually add flour, sugar, and salt and mix until smooth. Cover with damp towel and let stand in a warm place until doubled in bulk, about 2 hours.

Roll out on lightly floured board into a rectangle about 1/2″ thick. Heat oil in deep fryer to 375°F. Cut dough with biscuit cutter and drop a few at a time into the hot oil. When the biscuits are puffed and browned, turn over to brown on other side. Remove with slotted spoon, drain on paper towels and serve at once, or reheat in 200°F. oven for 5 to 10 minutes if not serving at once.

UPSIDE-DOWN PIZZA

Serves 4

1/4 cup chopped onion
1/4 cup chopped green pepper
10 fresh mushrooms, sliced
1/4 lb. any desired meat — beef, sausage or ham — crumbled or sliced, cooked before using if using ground beef or uncooked sausage
1 cup grated Mozzarella type cheese (Manchego is a good substitute for Mozzarella if unavailable)
1 cup marinara sauce (see recipe in "Sauces")
1 3/4 cups baking mix (see recipe this section)
3/4 cup water
1 egg, beaten
2 tbsps. grated Parmesan cheese

Grease a 9″ round cake pan. Sprinkle onion and green pepper over bottom of pan. Layer with sliced mushrooms and arrange whatever meat is being used over them. Spread the grated cheese over this. Last, spread the sauce evenly over the cheese. Mix the water and egg together in a bowl. Add the baking mix and mix only until blended. Do not overmix. Sprinkle the Parmesan cheese over the sauce and then spread the baking mix batter very carefully over the top. Bake in preheated 350°F. oven about 35 minutes, or until top is golden brown. Turn out at once onto heated platter, slice into wedges and serve.

UNFILLED BEIGNETS AS A BREAD

Makes 40

3/4 cup water
1/4 cup unsalted butter
2 tbsps. sugar
1/8 tsp. salt
1 cup flour
4 large eggs
1 tsp. vanilla
1/2 cup sugar
1/4 tsp. cinnamon
Oil for deep frying

Mix butter, water, sugar and salt, and melt over low heat. When mixture is liquid and simmering remove from heat and immediately add the flour all at once, as in making cream puffs, beating with spoon until mixture leaves sides of pan and forms a ball. Return to heat and, over low heat, continue to beat until dough forms a ball. Return to heat and, over low heat, continue to beat until dough films bottom of pan (about 2 minutes). Remove from heat and let stand for 5 minutes. Transfer dough to processor or large bowl of mixer and beat for a few seconds. Add eggs, one at a time, continuing to beat. Add vanilla. If using a processor, stop from time to time to scrape down the sides of bowl.

Heat oil in deep fryer or frying pan to at least 3 inches in depth to 375°F. Using about 2 tsps. batter for each puff, fry in small batches, turning once or twice until puffed and brown on all sides. Be careful not to crowd. Remove puffs and drain on paper towels. If desired, roll beignets in sugar mixed with the cinnamon and keep warm in 200°F. oven until ready to serve. These puffs can, like the fried biscuits in this section, be reheated for later use.

BAKING MIX

Makes 12 cups

9 cups flour
10 tsps. baking powder
2 tsps. salt
10 tbsps. vegetable shortening
6 tbsps. butter, cold, chopped

Mix the flour, baking powder and salt together carefully. When fully mixed, add the shortening and butter. Blend with a pastry blender or in an electric mixer on low speed or with your fingers until the mixture is like coarse meal. Do not knead. Place the mix in an airtight container, or several containers, and store in the refrigerator or freezer. The mix will keep for a month in the refrigerator, or indefinitely in the freezer. Remove and measure according to the recipe being used.

This mix may be used for biscuits, pancakes, shortcakes, etc., as with the commercial "Bisquick."

FRUITED HONEY BUTTER

Makes a scant cup

2/3 cup butter, softened to room temperature
1/3 cup honey
2 tbsps. lemon or orange juice AND
2 tsp. grated lemon or orange peel
OR
1/4 cup marmalade or jam of choice WITH
1 tbsp. lemon juice AND
1 tsp. grated lemon rind

Mix all ingredients in blender, processor or electric mixer until smooth and creamy. Cover and refrigerate until ready to use. Let stand at room temperature 30 minutes before serving.

ORANGE CREAM CHEESE SPREAD

Makes about 1 cup

1 large (8-oz.) pkg. cream cheese, room temperature
1/4 cup orange juice
2 tbsps. confectioners sugar
2 tsps. freshly grated orange peel

In blender or processor or electric mixer blend all ingredients until smooth and fluffy. Cover and refrigerate until ready to use, but return to room temperature (about 30 minutes) before serving as a spread for rolls and sweet breads.

Cakes, Cookies, Frostings, and Fillings

SCANDINAVIAN SPICY APPLE CAKE WITH CARAMEL SAUCE

Serves 8

1 cup butter, softened to room temperature
1 cup sugar
2 eggs, beaten
1 1/2 cups flour
1 tsp. powdered nutmeg (freshly grated if possible)
1 tsp. cinnamon
1 tsp. baking soda
1/2 tsp. salt
3 medium size apples, tart, peeled, cored and finely chopped
3/4 cup chopped pecans
1 tsp. vanilla

Cream butter with sugar in large bowl, and add eggs, beating well. Mix flour, spices, soda and salt and blend into sugar butter mixture. Add apples and nuts, together with the vanilla, and mix thoroughly. Pour into well greased 10″ pie plate and bake in preheated 350°F. oven about 45 minutes. Serve warm with or without ice cream and covered with the following sauce.

CARAMEL RUM SAUCE

1/2 cup sugar
1/2 cup firmly packed brown sugar
1/2 cup heavy cream
1/2 cup butter
1/4 cup rum

Mix sugars and cream in top of double boiler. Cook over gently boiling water for about 1 hour, keeping water replenished as needed in bottom of boiler. Add butter and cook about 30 minutes more. Remove from heat and beat thoroughly. Add rum and blend thoroughly. Serve warm over the cake and, if using, ice cream.

CHOCOLATE HEAVEN CAKE

Serves 10–12

1 18-oz. pkg. devil's food cake mix (or chocolate cake mix)
1 4-oz. pkg. instant chocolate pudding mix (or regular pudding mix)
4 eggs, room temperature
3/4 cup sour cream
1/2 cup vegetable oil
1/2 cup water
1/4 cup mayonnaise
3 tbsps. Kahlua liqueur
1 cup semisweet chocolate morsels
1/2 cup toasted, chopped almonds (pecans may be substituted)
Unsweetened cocoa powder

Grease a 10″ bundt pan and dust with cocoa powder. Combine cake mix, pudding mix, eggs, sour cream, oil, water, mayonnaise and liqueur in large bowl or in large bowl of mixer. Beat until smooth. Stir in chocolate chips and nuts. Pour batter into prepared pan, and bake in preheated 350°F. oven approximately 1 hour, or until toothpick or straw or other tester comes out clean. Cool in pan 10 to 15 minutes. Invert onto wire rack. Cool slightly before removing pan. Dust with powdered sugar. Allow to cool before serving. Garnish with whipped cream if desired.

If using the chocolate cake mix which is more available in place of the devil's food cake mix indicated, add 1 tbsp. cocoa to the batter. If the box of chocolate cake mix is 500 grams, which is about 1/2 ounce short of 18 ounces, also add 1 tbsp. flour to the batter.

RICH CARROT CAKE

Serves 12

2 cups sugar
1 1/2 cups vegetable oil
3 eggs, beaten
2 cups grated carrot
1 cup chopped pecans
1 cup chopped dates (optional)
1 1/2 cups flour
1 cup crushed, canned pineapple, drained
1 tsp. vanilla
1 tsp. soda
1/2 tsp. salt
1 tsp. cinnamon

Blend sugar and oil. Add eggs, beating well. Blend in other ingredients. Grease a 9″ x 13″ x 2″ baking pan. Pour batter in and bake in preheated 350°F. oven 40–45 minutes or until firm in center. Frost with cream cheese frosting if desired.

CREAM CHEESE ICING

1/4 cup softened butter
3 oz. cream cheese
1/2 lb. powdered sugar
1 tsp. vanilla

Mix all ingredients thoroughly and spread over cake.

PINEAPPLE NUT CAKE

Serves 12–15

2 eggs
2 cups sugar
1 tsp. vanilla
2 cups flour
2 tsps. baking soda
1 cup drained crushed canned pineapple
1 cup coarsely chopped pecans

Beat eggs, sugar and vanilla in large bowl. Beat in flour, baking soda and pineapple. Fold in nuts. Pour batter into greased and lightly floured 13″ x 9″ x 2″ baking pan. Bake for approximately 60 minutes in a preheated 350°F. oven. Cool and spread with favorite frosting.

APPLE UPSIDE DOWN SPICE CAKE

Serves 6

1/4 cup vegetable shortening
1/2 tsp. salt
1/2 tsp. cinnamon
1/4 tsp. nutmeg
1/4 tsp. allspice
3/4 cup sugar
1 egg, unbeaten
1 1/4 cups flour
1 1/2 tsps. baking powder
1/2 cup milk
2 medium size tart apples, peeled cored and sliced
4 tbsps. butter
1/2 cup brown sugar, firmly packed
2 tbsps. milk

Cream shortening, salt, spices and sugar until light and fluffy. Add the egg and beat thoroughly. Sift flour and baking powder together and add small amounts to creamed mixture alternately with milk, beating after each addition until smooth. Grease an 8″ x 8″ baking dish or pan and arrange apples over the bottom. Melt butter, brown sugar and milk in saucepan, mixing well. Spread over apples and pour batter over all. Bake in preheated 350°F. oven about 60 minutes. Serve upside down with whipped cream.

YELLOW CAKE

Serves 8 to 10

1/2 cup fresh vegetable shortening
1 tsp. vanilla
1 cup milk
2 1/4 cups flour
1 1/2 cups sugar
3 tsps. baking powder
1/2 tsp. salt
2 eggs

Cream shortening, vanilla and sugar until creamy. Add eggs and continue beating until smooth. Mix together flour, baking powder and salt. Add the dry mixture a little at a time to the creamed mixture alternately with the milk, beating until smooth. Grease and flour two 8″ layer cake pans. Pour batter in equal parts into the two pans and bake in preheated 350°F. oven 25 to 30 minutes, or until cake center springs back when lightly pressed with fingertip. Fill and frost with any desired frosting.

QUICK AND EASY POUND CAKE

Serves 12 or more

1 white box cake
4 whole eggs
2/3 cup oil
2/3 cup water
1 box dry Jell-O (lemon or orange)
1/2 tsp. mace, powdered

Put all ingredients into large bowl of electric mixer and beat at medium high speed for 5 minutes. Or beat with a rotary beater for 7 minutes. Preheat oven to 325°F. Grease a tube pan with butter or vegetable shortening. Pour batter in and bake 45–55 minutes until cake is firm and golden on top.

ITALIAN CASSATA

Serves 12 or more

1 9″ x 5″ loaf shape pound cake (see recipe in this section for pound cake)
2 cups ricotta cheese (the cheese for this cake is very important, so if ricotta is not available, use the mild cheese called "requeson" or cottage cheese. Mix 1 1/4 cups requeson or cottage cheese to 3/4 cup cream cheese. The cream cheese will soften the other to make it more spreadable, but retaining the correct flavor.)
2/3 cup chopped, toasted almonds or pecans (optional)
4 oz. semisweet chocolate chips, chopped
2 oz. orange liqueur or creme de cacao
1 1/4 cups seedless raspberry jam (orange marmalade or apricot jam may be substituted, but the raspberry is better. Or chopped candied fruit may be used, like the real Italian style, but we think the jam or marmalade is better.)
Chocolate frosting or whipped cream, or more cheese piped through a pastry tube or any combination for topping

Chill the cake for 1 to 2 hours. Slice the cake horizontally into 4 layers. Chop the chocolate chips in a blender or food processor with the liqueur. Do not chop too much, or the texture will be lost. Add this mixture to the jam in a bowl and set aside. If using 2 cheeses, mix them together until well blended and spreadable. If using ricotta, blend it to spreading consistency. Spread the bottom layer of the sliced cake with 1/3 of the cheese. Next spread the cheese layer with 1/3 of the jam mixture. Add 1/3 of the chopped nuts, if using, and then repeat this procedure 2 more times, placing the 4th layer of cake on the top. Press the filled cake gently and even up the sides with a spatula. Cover with plastic wrap or foil and chill in the refrigerator overnight or more. Frost with chocolate butter cream frosting and pipe the edges if desired with more cheese through a pastry tube, or frost with sweetened whipped cream. Return to refrigerator for another 30 minutes or more before slicing and serving.

This makes a very rich dessert, so it should go a long way.

POUND CAKE

Serves 6 to 8

This cake is included here because of the versatility of its uses. The flavorings can be changed and adjusted to include almost any flavor, and the texture is such that it makes an excellent base for ice cream cakes, always a favorite with children and for special parties.

1/2 cup vegetable shortening
1/4 cup butter, softened to room temperature
3/4 tsp. salt
1/2 tsp. mace
1/2 tsp. grated fresh lemon rind
1 1/4 cups sugar
3 eggs, unbeaten
2 3/4 cups sifted flour
1 1/2 tsps. baking powder
1/2 cup milk

Cream the shortening, salt, butter, mace and lemon rind with the sugar, until fluffy. Add eggs, one at a time, beating well after each addition. Sift the flour with the baking powder several times until very airy and fluffy. Add to the creamed mixture alternately with the milk, mixing thoroughly after each addition until smooth. Line a 9″ x 5″ x 3″ loaf pan with wax or parchment paper, greased on top side. Pour batter into pan and bake in a preheated 300°F. (slow) oven for 1 hour, then increase heat to 325°F. and bake 45–50 minutes longer, until cake springs back in center when touched with fingertip or until toothpick or straw tester comes out clean. Invert onto wire rack and remove paper while still warm.

If using for ice cream cake, allow cake to cool completely and slice horizontally into 3 or 4 layers, then soften any desired flavor or combination of flavors of ice cream until spreadable, spread between layers and cover with aluminum foil or return to loaf pan and freeze. When frozen the loaf may be spread with sweetened whipped cream before serving if desired. Unmold onto platter, frost with the cream or any kind of frosting, or more ice cream, then slice and serve.

1 tsp. of lemon extract, or any other desired flavor, may be substituted for the 1/2 tsp. mace called for above, to change the flavor of the cake layers, and custard filling of any flavor may be substituted for the ice cream.

RICH AND ELEGANT ORANGE FILLED CAKE

Serves 12–16

Have all ingredients at room temperature for this cake.

3 cups flour
3/4 tsp. salt
3 1/2 tsps. baking powder
Grated rind of 1 orange
1 1/2 cups sugar
3/4 cup butter
3 eggs
1/2 cup orange juice
1/2 cup water
2 tbsps. fresh lemon juice

Cream the sugar and butter together until creamy. Add the eggs one at a time, beating until smooth. Add the sifted dry ingredients alternately with the juices and water which have been mixed together, beating after each addition until smooth. Add orange rind. Grease and flour the bottoms of 3 9″ round baking pans. Pour the batter into the three pans in equal portions and bake in preheated 375°F. oven for about 30–35 minutes, or until layers are tan on top and centers spring back when touched lightly with fingertip. Remove from pans and when cool spread between the layers the following orange cream filling:

ORANGE CREAM FILLING

1 tsp. plain gelatin, soaked in 1 tbsp. water for 5 minutes
2 tbsps. cornstarch
2 tbsps. flour
3/4 cup sugar
3/4 cup water
1 tbsp. butter
2 egg yolks, beaten
Grated rind of 1 orange
3 tbsps. each orange and lemon juice
1/2 cup whipping cream

Mix dry ingredients all together in top of double broiler. Add the water and cook until thickened, stirring constantly (about 12 minutes). Add butter. Beat yolks and add a little of the custard to them until eggs have been warmed. Then add egg mixture to the custard and heat the mixture to almost boiling, stirring constantly. Do not boil. Add the soaked gelatin. Stir until dissolved and remove from heat. Add the orange rind and the juices. Cool the custard. Beat the 1/2 cup cream until stiff and gently fold into custard. Chill one hour and spread between the layers of the cake. Then ice with the following:

FLUFFY SEVEN MINUTE ORANGE ICING

2 unbeaten egg whites
1 1/2 cups sugar
5 tbsps. orange juice
1/4 tsp. cream of tartar
OR
1 1/2 tsps. light corn syrup

Mix all ingredients together in top of double boiler over boiling water. With a rotary beater, beat the mixture over the boiling water continuously until it stands in wet peaks (about 8 minutes). Remove from heat and add

1 tsp. grated orange rind

Continue beating until the icing is the right consistency for spreading on the cake.

Keep cake chilled until ready to serve.

RICH COCOA DEVIL'S FOOD CAKE

Serves 12

2/3 cup vegetable shortening
1 1/4 cups sugar
2 eggs
1 tsp. vanilla
1 1/2 cups flour
1/2 cup cocoa
3/4 tsp. salt
1 1/4 tsps. soda
1 cup sour milk or buttermilk (sour milk may be achieved by adding 1 tsp. vinegar to sweet milk)
1 tsp. cinnamon, powdered
1/2 tsp. allspice, powdered

Beat shortening with sugar until creamy. Add eggs and vanilla. Mix flour, cocoa, salt and spices together. Mix soda with the soured milk. Add the mixed dry ingredients alternately with the milk mixture to the shortening, sugar, egg mixture and beat until smooth. Pour into 2 9″ cake pans which have been greased and lightly floured on the bottom. Bake approximately 35 minutes in a preheated 350°F. oven. Cake is done when it springs back when touched. Cool on wire rack before removing from pans. Frost with Seven Minute Fluffy Frosting (see "Frostings" in this section).

CHOCOLATE FUDGE BROWNIES

Makes about 30

An all-American favorite, brownies seem very easy. They are easy to make, but how they are made is important. To achieve the fudgey, chewey texture most admired in a good brownie, the size of the pan for the amount of batter is very important. This recipe calls for a 13″ x 9″ x 2″ cake pan. If you do not want to make this large a batch, cut the recipe in half and use an 8″ x 8″ square pan.

1/2 cup vegetable shortening or butter
4 oz. unsweetened chocolate
4 eggs, room temperature
1/4 tsp. salt
2 cups sugar
1 tsp. vanilla
1 cup flour
1 cup chopped pecans (optional)

Melt the shortening or butter and the chocolate in top of a double boiler over boiling water. Set aside until cool (do not use until cool because it is important not to melt the sugar with which it will be mixed.) Beat the eggs, together with the salt, until light in color and thick. Gradually add the sugar and vanilla and continue beating until blended. By hand blend the chocolate mixture into the egg and sugar mixture, and then, just as it is almost blended, add 1 cup of flour, and mix the whole batter until well blended. If adding nuts, do so at this point, just before pouring the batter into a well greased and floured pan. Bake in a preheated 350°F. oven about 25 to 30 minutes, until center is firm. Cool completely before cutting into squares. Serve plain or frosted or with a dollop of sweetened whipped cream or ice cream.

Cookies

REFRIGERATOR COOKIES

Makes about 3 1/2 dozen

These cookies are wonderful filled, which see below

1/2 cup butter, room temperature
1 cup sugar
1 beaten egg
1 tsp. vanilla
1/2 tsp. grated lemon rind
1/4 tsp. salt
1 1/2 tsps. baking powder
1 1/4 to 1 1/2 cups flour

Cream the butter, sugar, egg, vanilla and rind together until fluffy. Add salt and baking powder, and then flour, and mix together thoroughly, adding only enough of the flour to make a firm ball. Turn the ball out onto a large piece of waxed paper or aluminum foil and shape into a long roll. Roll the paper or foil up around the roll and chill in refrigerator for several hours or overnight, until firm. Slice about 1/4" thick onto greased cookie sheet and bake in preheated 400°F. oven 8 to 10 minutes, or until golden. Cool on paper or foil on wire rack.

To turn these cookies into filled cookies, place one cookie on the sheet, place about 1/2 tsp. of filling or a piece of dried fruit on top, cover with another cookie and crimp the edges all around with a fork to seal. Marmalade of any kind can be used for filling, chopped dried fruit mixed with a little orange liqueur, or, if you have it, fill with 1/2 tsp. mincemeat.

BUTTERSCOTCH REFRIGERATOR COOKIES

Follow the recipe above, except substitute 1 1/4 cups firmly packed brown sugar for the 1 cup white sugar, and add some chopped pecans to the dough before rolling out.

PECAN PUFFS

Makes about 3 1/2 dozen

1 cup butter, room temperature
2 tbsps. sugar
1 tsp. vanilla
1 cup pecans meats, ground coarsely
1 cup flour
Powdered sugar

Cream the butter, sugar and vanilla together until fluffy. Mix in the flour and stir or knead until thoroughly mixed. Knead in the ground nutmeats. Form dough into small balls and place on a greased cookie sheet. Bake for about 30 minutes in preheated 300°F. oven. While the cookies are hot, roll them in powdered sugar. Cool completely before serving. These cookies may be successfully kept for some time in the freezer in a tightly sealed container.

BROWN RIM COOKIES

Makes about 4 dozen

1 cup vegetable shortening
1 tsp. salt
1 tsp. vanilla
2/3 cup sugar plus 2 tbsps.
2 eggs, well beaten
2 1/2 cups flour

Cream sugar, shortening, salt and vanilla until fluffy. Add eggs and continue beating until smooth. Add flour; mix well. Drop from tip of spoon, or roll into small balls with the hands, onto greased cookie or baking sheet. Dampen a clean smooth cloth very slightly, and place over a wide flat bottom glass. Holding the cloth tightly over the glass press each ball flat. Bake in preheated 375°F. oven about 8–10 minutes until delicately browned. Turn out at once onto wax paper covered flat surface, preferably a wire rack.

The flavoring of these cookies can be changed by using 1/2 tsp. almond extract with 1/2 tsp. vanilla, or by using 1/2 tsp. lemon extract with grated rind of one lemon.

This recipe makes a very crisp, delicate cookie, suitable for afternoon tea or coffee.

SUGAR COOKIES

Makes 3 dozen

2 cups sifted flour
1/2 tsp. baking powder
1/4 tsp. salt
1/2 cup table fat (preferably butter)
1/2 tsp. grated lemon rind
1/2 tsp. nutmeg
3/4 cup sugar plus 2 tbsp.
1 egg
1 tbsp. milk

Knead all ingredients together until smooth ball can be formed. Chill for about 30 minutes before rolling out on floured board about one-fourth batch at a time. Cut into desired shapes. Turn cookies onto greased cookie sheets and bake in preheated 400°F. oven for 12 to 15 minutes, until golden. Frost, if desired, after cookies have cooled.

Frostings and Fillings

SEVEN MINUTE FLUFFY FROSTING

2 egg whites
1 1/2 cups sugar
1 1/2 tsps. light corn syrup, or 1/4 tsp. cream of tartar
1/3 cup cold water
Dash of salt
1 tsp. vanilla extract

Place all ingredients except vanilla in top part of double boiler. Mix thoroughly. Cook, beating constantly with rotary or electric beater over boiling water, until mixture forms peaks, about 7–8 minutes. Remove from heat and add vanilla. Continue beating until thick enough to hold up after spreading.

BUTTERCREAM FROSTING

1/3 cup softened butter
2 1/2 to 3 cups (1 lb.) powdered sugar
1/4 cup cream, evaporated milk or milk
2 egg yolks or 1 whole egg
1 tsp. vanilla extract

Beat the butter and about 1/3 of the powdered sugar in mixing bowl until well blended. Alternately add cream or milk, egg yolks or egg and remaining powdered sugar. Beat until smooth, fluffy and consistency for spreading. Add vanilla extract. If too thin, add a little more powdered sugar. If too thick, add a few drops of milk.

LEMON BUTTERCREAM FROSTING

Using above recipe, add 3 1/2 tbsps. lemon juice instead of vanilla, and mix in grated rind of one lemon. Also use only egg yolks, not a whole egg.

CHOCOLATE FUDGE FROSTING

3 oz. unsweetened chocolate
3 tbsps. butter
1/4 cup cream or evaporated milk
1 tsp. vanilla
2 to 2 1/2 cups powdered sugar

Melt butter and chocolate in saucepan over low heat. Remove from heat, cool about 3 minutes and add cream or milk. Beat into sugar with rotary or electric beater and add vanilla. If too thin, add a little more sugar. If too thick, add a little more milk, until spreading consistency is reached.

BAKE-ON FROSTING

6 tbsps. melted butter
$^2/_3$ cup firmly packed brown sugar
$^1/_4$ cup evaporated milk
1 cup granola, chopped pecans or shredded coconut, as preferred

Blend all ingredients together in bowl. When cake is baked, remove from oven and quickly spread topping over hot cake. Return to oven and cook under broiler as far away from flame as possible for about 5 minutes. The frosting may also be spread on cooled cake and placed under broiler itself until it bubbles.

ALMOND CUSTARD FILLING

$^3/_4$ cup sugar
3 tbsps. cornstarch
$^1/_4$ tsp. salt
2 cups milk
2 eggs, beaten
$^3/_4$ tsp. vanilla extract
$^3/_4$ tsp. almond extract
1 cup whipping cream, whipped (optional)

Mix together sugar, cornstarch, and salt. Add milk and mix until smooth. Bring slowly to boil, stirring constantly. Cook until thick. Stir a little into beaten eggs and then return eggs and mixture to the main pan and continue to cook over very low heat until the custard is hot but not yet boiling, about 2 to 3 minutes. During this time, stir mixture vigorously. Remove from fire and add extracts. Cool and fold in whipped cream if using.

VANILLA CUSTARD FILLING

Use above recipe exactly, except use $1^1/_2$ tsps. vanilla and omit almond extract.

CHOCOLATE CUSTARD FILLING

Use almond custard filling recipe above, but add 2 ounces unsweetened chocolate and 2 tbsps. butter which have been melted together, to the milk before adding to the dry ingredients, and substitute $1^1/_2$ tsp. vanilla extract for the 3/4 tsp. vanilla, and omit the almond extract.

QUICK LEMON FILLING

1/4 cup sugar
1 1/2 tbsps. cornstarch
1/2 cup water
3 tbsps. lemon juice
1/2 tsp. grated lemon rind
1 tbsp. butter
1 egg yolk, beaten with 1 tsp. milk

Mix sugar, cornstarch and salt together in medium saucepan. Stir in water, lemon juice, rind and butter. Cook over medium heat to rolling boil, stirring constantly for about 2 minutes. Remove small amount and add to beaten yolk mixture, then return mixture to remainder of filling in saucepan. Bring just to below the boil again, stirring constantly. Cool. Beat with rotary beater until smooth and thickened.

Pies

TART LEMON CHIFFON PIE

Serves 6 to 8

Pinch of salt
1 cup sugar
1 1/4 cups water
1 tbsp. butter
1/4 cup cornstarch
6 tbsps. lemon juice
1 tsp. grated lemon rind
3 eggs, separated
1 9″ baked pastry shell (see "Plain Pastry" in glossary)
2 tbsps. milk

Combine sugar, salt, butter and cornstarch and mix well in saucepan. Add water and mix well. Cook, stirring constantly, over low heat until thick. Add the 6 tbsps. lemon juice and the grated lemon rind. Beat the egg yolks with the milk until fluffy. Slowly add a little of the cornstarch mixture to the egg yolks and then return all to the saucepan. Bring to almost a boil, but do not boil, and remove from heat when thickened to cool.

Beat egg whites until stiff but not dry. Fold 1/3 of beaten whites into the lemon filling. Spread into the baked pastry shell and prepare fluffy meringue topping as follows:

1/2 cup sugar
1/8 tsp. salt
1/4 cup water
1/8 tsp. cream of tartar

Combine all above ingredients and cook in small saucepan, stirring only occasionally, over low heat, to light thread stage. Gradually pour over beaten egg whites, beating constantly. Continue beating until mixture holds its shape, 3 or 4 minutes. Add 1 tsp. lemon juice or 1/8 tsp. vanilla and spread over top of pie. Chill pie for at least 2 hours before serving.

FRESH PINEAPPLE PIE

Serves 8

1 cup or 1 1/2 cups sugar (depending on how tart or sweet the fresh pineapple is)
3 tbsps. flour
1/2 tsp. nutmeg
1 tsp. cinnamon
1 tbsp. butter
2 beaten eggs
4 cups pineapple cut in 1″ pieces
1 unbaked 9″ pastry shell (see plain pastry in glossary at end of section) plus 1/2 recipe for top

Blend sugar, flour, nutmeg and cinnamon and a small pinch of salt. Cut the butter into the mixture until mixture is like cornmeal. Spread bottom of unbaked pastry shell with the cut up pineapple. Mix the 2 beaten eggs into the sugar, flour, butter mixture and mix well. Pour over the pineapple, evenly, being sure to cover all the pieces. Roll the other one-half recipe for plain pastry in an oblong to about 1/4″ thickness and cut into strips 1/2″ wide. Lay half of the strips across the pie top in one direction and the other half across them at right angles to form a lattice crust. Press the ends into the crimped edges of the pastry shell. Bake in preheated very hot oven (450°F.) for 10 minutes, then lower temperature to 350°F. and continue baking for 30 to 40 minutes, or more if necessary, until custard is set and top is golden. Serve warm or at room temperature.

CARIBBEAN LIME PIE

Serves 8 to 10

1/2 cup fresh lime juice
2 tbsps. or 2 envelopes unflavored gelatin
5 egg yolks
1 cup sugar
1/4 cup rum
1 tbsp. orange liqueur
Grated peel of 2 limes
5 egg whites, beaten with 1/2 cup sugar
3 or 4 drops of green food coloring
1 cup whipping cream, whipped
Lime slices and 1/2 cup whipping cream, whipped with 1 tbsp. confectioners sugar for garnish (optional)
1 coconut pie crust (see below)

Mix gelatin and lime juice in small pan and heat over low heat until gelatin is thoroughly melted. Beat egg yolks with 1/2 cup sugar in top of double boiler until blended. Mix in gelatin mixture and continue beating over simmering water until mixture is thick enough to coat a spoon well (about 10–15 minutes). Remove from heat and cool. Blend in rum, orange liqueur and grated peel.

Beat egg whites with the food coloring in large bowl of electric mixer until stiff but not dry, adding the sugar gradually as soon as the whites become bubbly but before beginning to stiffen. Gently fold the custard into the whites, only until a marbleized effect is obtained. Do not overfold. Gently fold in whipped cream. Spoon filling into crust, and either refrigerate or freeze, if desired.

Just before serving, spread the other cup of whipped cream over the top and sprinkle with reserved toasted coconut and edge with lime slices.

COCONUT CRUST

3 cups shredded fresh coconut
6 tbsps. melted butter

Spread the coconut in a thin layer over the bottom of a cookie sheet or shallow, large pan and toast lightly in a 350°F. preheated oven for 8 minutes.

Reserving 1/2 cup of the toasted coconut for garnish, combine remaining coconut with the melted butter and toss lightly until thoroughly blended. Press firmly into 9" pie shell with deep sides. Be sure sides are covered and firm with coconut mixture. Cover lightly with foil and refrigerate until ready to use.

If you have guests who may not like coconut, a graham cracker crust may be substituted (see recipe for "Simple Cheese Cake" in "Desserts") or a chocolate cookie crust may be substituted, using the same proportions as the graham cracker crust recipe but omitting the cinnamon and chilling the crust instead of baking it.

PECAN PIE MADE WITH KAHLUA

Serves 8

1 9" unbaked pastry (see "Plain Pastry" in glossary)

1/4 cup butter (softened but not melted)
3/4 cup sugar
1 tsp. vanilla
2 tbsps. flour
3 eggs
1/2 cup kahlua
1/2 cup dark corn syrup
3/4 cup evaporated milk
1 cup very coarsely chopped pecans

Cream together butter, sugar, vanilla and flour. Mix well. Beat in whole eggs, one at a time. Stir in kahlua, corn syrup, evaporated milk and pecans. Mix well and pour into pie dish lined with the plain pastry. Bake for 15 minutes in preheated 400°F. oven, then reduce heat to 325°F., leaving the oven door open for 3 or 4 minutes to cool down from 400°F. to 325°F., then closing oven door and beginning to time the baking for about 45 minutes or until the custard is firm. Chill before serving and garnish with whipped cream and pecan halves, if desired.

LEMON ANGEL TORTE

Serves 6 to 8

4 eggs, room temperature, separated
3/4 cup sugar
1/4 tsp. salt
1/4 tsp. cream of tartar
1 cup heavy cream, whipped
1 recipe lemon filling (see below)

Beat egg whites together with sugar, salt and cream of tartar in mixer at high speed until very stiff peaks form. Spread in well greased 9″ pie dish and bake at 225°F. in preheated oven for 1 1/2 to 2 hours, until shell is firm when touched and slightly golden. Cool.

Fill shell with 1/2 of the whipped cream, then spread the lemon filling carefully over and spread the other 1/2 of the whipped cream on top. Chill thoroughly before serving.

LEMON FILLING

Beat the 4 egg yolks until thick and lemon colored. Gradually beat in 1/2 cup sugar, dash of salt, 1 tbsp. grated lemon peel and 3 tbsps. lemon juice. Cook over slow heat until thick (about 6 minutes). Cool before spreading over the whipped cream in the meringue.

The top of the pie may be garnished with a little grated lemon peel.

YOGURT APPLE PIE

Serves 8

1 unbaked 9″ pie shell (see "Plain Pastry" in glossary)

1/4 cup sugar
1/4 cup firmly packed brown sugar
2 tbsps. cornstarch
1/4 tsp. salt
1/2 tsp. cinnamon
4–5 cups thinly sliced, peeled, cored apples, preferably tart
1/2 tsp. lemon juice
1 cup yogurt
1 egg
1/2 tsp. vanilla
1/4 cup toasted crushed almonds)
1/2 cup firmly packed brown sugar)
1 tsp. cinnamon)

Combine sugar, cinnamon, salt and cornstarch. Mix with apples. Sprinkle in lemon juice. Pour apple mixture into unbaked pastry shell, distributing apples evenly. Bake in preheated 400°F. oven 30 minutes.

Beat egg until foamy. Add yogurt and vanilla and mix well. Reduce oven heat to 350°F. Allow oven to cool 2 minutes with door open before replacing pie after pouring the yogurt mixture over the top of the apples, distributing evenly. Continue baking for about 40 minutes longer, until custard is set and apples done.

Cool pie for 10 minutes, and then sprinkle evenly over the top the crushed almonds, remaining 1/2 cup brown sugar and cinnamon which have been mixed together. Serve warm or at room temperature.

DOUBLE DECK FRESH FRUIT PIE

Serves 8

Baked 9″ pie shell (see "Plain Pastry" in glossary)

1/2 cup confectioners sugar
1/2 tsp. vanilla
1/2 tsp. almond extract
1 large pkg. (6 oz.) cream cheese
1/2 cup heavy cream whipped (prewhipped, artificial cream (1 cup) such as Cool Whip may be used if necessary, but if using presweetened prewhipped product, cut down confectioners sugar to 1/4 cup)
1/3 cup sugar
3 tbsps. cornstarch
1/3 cup water
1/3 cup light corn syrup
1 tbsp. lemon juice
2 cups fresh fruit (whole strawberries, sliced peaches, sliced or cubed mango, sliced or cubed pineapple, sliced plums, etc.)
Several drops of food coloring, a color which matches the particular fruit being used

Add confectioners sugar, vanilla and almond extract to cheese and beat until smooth and creamy. Fold in whipped cream. Spread evenly over bottom of baked pie shell. Chill thoroughly several hours.

Combine 1/3 cup sugar and cornstarch in saucepan. Add water slowly, stirring to make a smooth mixture. Add syrup and lemon juice and food coloring. Cook, stirring constantly, until thick and clear. Cool.

Add to the fruit, stir to coat with the glaze. Spread over top of chilled layer. Chill thoroughly before serving. Serve with a dollop of sweetened whipped cream on top of each piece, if desired.

ITALIAN MARMALADE PIE
CROSTATA DE MARMALADA

Serves 8

Use recipe in "Glossary of Pastries" for Italian Crostata.

Roll the larger piece out on a lightly floured surface to fit on a 10″ pie plate. Crimp the top edge of the crust with the fingers and prick the bottom of the crust and the sides as well. Bake at 400°F. in preheated oven for 10 minutes and remove. Set aside. Roll out the smaller piece of pastry in an oblong shape and cut 8 to 10 strips about 3/4″ wide to form the lattice for the top of the pie. Spread marmalade filling over the bottom of the pie shell. Lay half of the strips over the filling in one direction 1″ apart. Weave remaining strips in opposite direction in diamond or square pattern. Sprinkle with sugar and bake for 20–25 minutes, until strips are golden. Let stand 2 to 3 hours before serving at room temperature.

MARMALADE FILLING

1 lb. (about) tart orange marmalade, or any other favorite flavor marmalade or jam or preserves
1/4 cup warm water

Mix the marmalade with the water until spreading consistency (if the marmalade you are using is sufficiently spreadable without thinning, omit the water).

MANGO RUM PIE OR TARTS

Serves 8

1 baked 9″ pie shell or 8 baked 4″ tart shells (see "Plain Pastry" in glossary)

3 large, ripe mangoes, peeled and thinly sliced
1/2 cup sugar
1/4 cup dark rum
2 tbsps. cornstarch
1 tsp. lemon or lime juice
2 egg yolks
1/4 tsp. powdered ginger
Sweetened whipped cream flavored with 2 tsps. rum or 1 tsp. rum flavoring

Slice the mangoes into a saucepan. Add sugar and rum. Cook over low heat for about 10 minutes, stirring constantly. Combine cornstarch with juice and 1 tbsp. water, mixing until smooth. Add beaten egg yolks. Add a little of the hot fruit to egg mixture and then stir egg mixture into saucepan. Continue cooking over low heat, stirring constantly, until thick and smooth. Stir in the ginger. Cool and pour into baked shell or tart shells. Serve with the sweetened, rum-flavored whipped cream.

PUMPKIN CHIFFON PIE

Serves 8

1 9″ baked pastry shell (see "Plain Pastry" recipe in glossary)

3 egg yolks
1/2 cup sugar
1 1/4 cups cooked fresh or canned pumpkin
1/2 cup milk
1/2 tsp. ginger
1/2 tsp. cinnamon
1/2 tsp. nutmeg
1 tbsp. (1 envelope) unflavored gelatin
1/4 cup cold water
1/2 tsp. salt
3 stiffly beaten egg whites
1/2 cup sugar

Beat egg yolks and 1/2 cup sugar until thick. Add pumpkin, milk, salt and spices. Cook over low heat, stirring constantly, until thick. Add gelatin which has been softened in cold water, and stir until gelatin has dissolved. Add egg whites beaten with remaining 1/2 cup sugar. Pour into baked shell and chill. If desired, top with sweetened whipped cream.

COLONIAL INNKEEPER'S PIE

Serves 8 to 10

1 unbaked 9″ pie shell (see glossary for "Plain Pastry")

2 oz. unsweetened chocolate
2/3 cup water
2/3 cup sugar
8 tbsps. butter, softened but not melted
2 tsps. vanilla
1 cup flour
3/4 cup sugar
1 tsp. baking powder
1/2 tsp. salt
1/2 cup milk
1 egg
1/2 cup chopped pecans (optional)
1 cup whipping cream, whipped

Melt chocolate in water over very low fire, stirring constantly. When melted and blended, mix in sugar and 4 tbsps. butter and bring to boil, continuing to stir constantly. Add 1 tsp. vanilla and set finished mixture aside.

Mix flour, 3/4 cup sugar, baking powder and salt together thoroughly. Place in large bowl of electric mixer, or large bowl sufficient for beating by hand. Add milk and remaining 4 tbsps. butter and vanilla. Beat until mixed well. Add egg and beat for 2 or 3 minutes until thoroughly blended. Pour batter into pie shell. Stir chocolate mixture and very carefully pour over the batter. If using, sprinkle with the nuts. Bake in preheated 350°F. oven for about 55 minutes to an a hour, until tester inserted in center comes out clean. (A toothpick, a small knife, or a broomstraw all do nicely as testers).

Serve warm or at room temperature, but not chilled, with the whipped cream on top.

ANGEL CHOCOLATE PIE

Serves 6 to 8

2 eggs whites (have eggs at room temperature)
1/8 tsp. salt
1/8 tsp. cream of tartar
1/2 cup sugar
1/2 cup chopped pecans
1/2 tsp. vanilla
2 tbsps. sugar
1 8-oz. pkg. semisweet chocolate morsels
3 tbsps. milk
4 eggs, separated (room temperature)

Beat the 2 egg whites until foamy, then add the salt and cream of tartar and the sugar. Continue beating until stiff but not dry. Fold in pecans and vanilla. Grease a 9″ pie pan. Spread meringue mixture into the greased pan, building up the sides so that the meringue is 1/2″ above the sides. Bake in preheated 225°F. oven for $1^{1}/_{2}$ to 2 hours, until meringue is slightly golden and firm. Turn off oven, open the door, but do not remove the meringue for at least 10–15 minutes. Cool.

Melt the 2 tbsps. sugar, the chocolate morsels and the 3 tbsps. milk in a saucepan. Beat the 4 egg yolks together with 1 tsp. vanilla, or, if desired, 1 tbsp. rum or kahlua. Beat only until well mixed. Cool the chocolate mixture slightly, and add the egg mixture slowly. Beating thoroughly. Reheat until the chocolate, egg mixture is hot but not boiling. Set aside. Beat the egg whites until stiff but not dry, then fold very, very gently into the chocolate mixture. Fill meringue with the filling and chill thoroughly.

Top with slightly sweetened whipped cream and chocolate curls, or chopped chocolate morsels, or chopped nuts.

Glossary of Pastries

PLAIN AMERICAN-STYLE PASTRY:
(Single Crust 9″ Pie)

$1\frac{1}{4}$ cups flour
$\frac{1}{2}$ tsp. salt
$\frac{1}{3}$ cup vegetable shortening
2–3 tbsps. water, room temperature

With 2 knives, one held in each hand, or with a pastry mixer, cut shortening into the flour and salt mixture until the mix is like a bowl of tiny peas, or very coarse meal. Add water, 1 tbsp. at a time, and blend the dough together with hands only until the dough makes a soft ball. (It is important not to knead the dough at all!) roll out in a circle on a floured board until the circle will fit into a 9″ pan with a slight overlap. Flute the edges with the fingers and fill. Or, if the crust is to be baked partially or wholly before filling, prick the bottom and sides of the crust closely with a fork, and all around the bottom of the crust where it meets the sides to avoid bubbling or swelling of the crust while baking. Bake 10 minutes at 400°F.

DOUBLE CRUST, OR LATTICE TOP CRUSTED 9″ PIE:

$2\frac{1}{2}$ cups flour
1 tsp. salt
$\frac{3}{4}$ cup vegetable shortening
4–6 tbsps. water, room temperature

Use the same technique as above, except separate the dough into 2 balls, one slightly smaller than the other, using the larger one for the bottom crust. If making lattice for topping, roll second ball into an oblong and cut dough into 1/2″ or 3/4″ strips.

In either of the above recipes, if the dough seems too dry and a ball cannot be formed, do not be afraid to add another tbsp. or so of water. Remember, however, not to knead the dough.

This recipe for plain pastry can be multiplied by any number of times, leaving out the water, and divided into portions sufficient for 1 pie, placed in tight-closing plastic containers and stored in the freezer indefinitely, making a handy ready mix when needed.

FRENCH SHORT PASTRY, OR PATE BRISEE:

(Single 9″ Pie Shell or 8–10 2″–3″ Tart Shells)

$1\frac{1}{2}$ cups flour
$\frac{1}{4}$ tsp. salt
6 tbsps. unsalted butter, chilled and cut into $\frac{1}{4}$″ bits
2 tbsps. vegetable shortening, chilled and cut into $\frac{1}{4}$″ bits
3–4 tbsps. water, chilled

In a large chilled bowl, combine flour, salt, 6 tbsps. butter bits and vegetable shortening bits. With fingertips, rub flour and fat together until you have a mixture like coarse meal. Add the water, 1 tbsp. at a time, sprinkling it over the mixture so that it is disbursed well among the meal-like mixture. Gather the dough into a ball, being careful not to knead it. Cover the dough with a damp cloth and rest it in the refrigerator for at least 2 hours. Roll out on a board floured only as much as is necessary to avoid sticking.

Use this dough for meat or other main dish pies.

FRENCH SHORT PASTRY, OR PATE SUCREE:

Use the same recipe as above, adding 4 tsps. sugar to the flour and fat mixture before adding the water.

This recipe is for use as a dessert crust for cream pies and tart or fruit pies.

ITALIAN EGG PASTRY, OR CROSTATA:

(10″ pie shell plus lattice top)

2 cups flour
3/4 cup butter, room temperature
1/2 cup sugar
1/2 tsp. salt
2 whole eggs
2 tsps. vanilla
2 tsps. grated fresh lemon rind

In a bowl, combine flour, butter, sugar, salt, eggs, vanilla and lemon rind. Work mixture with hands until mixed. Shape into smooth ball, cover tightly and refrigerate for at least 30 minutes. Separate part of dough for lattice top and roll remainder into a circle sufficiently large to slightly overlap the 10″ pie tin. Roll smaller piece into an oblong and cut strips 1/2 to 3/4″ wide for lattice top. Fill with desired filling.

If making a crust for use with vegetables or meat fillings, omit sugar, vanilla and lemon rind and proceed as above.

SCANDINAVIAN COTTAGE CHEESE PASTRY:

(9″ double crust pie)

1 cup cold, firm butter
2 cups flour
1 cup cottage cheese, small curd if available
1–2 tbsps. ice water, if needed

In a large bowl, cut butter into flour until mixture is crumbly and pieces about the size of peas. Stir in cottage cheese until mixture forms a crumbly dough. Knead lightly to shape into a ball, adding ice water a few drops at a time and only as much as may be necessary to obtain the ball. Chill for at least 30 minutes before rolling out.

This recipe makes a firm pastry which can be shaped around meats or fish or mixture of vegetables or cheese, but it is also a delicious pastry for any kind of filling, for main dishes, side dishes or desserts.

Desserts

MOUSSE AU CHOCOLAT

Serves 6 to 8

9 squares semisweet chocolate, or 9 ounces chocolate chips
1/4 cup strong coffee, hot
6 eggs
3/4 cup plus 2 tbsps. sugar
1 tbsp. dark rum

Add the chocolate to the hot coffee in a small saucepan and cook over low heat until chocolate melts. Separate the egg yolks from the whites and set the whites aside. Beat the yolks with one half of the sugar until creamy. Add the rum to the yolks and then combine eggs with the hot chocolate mixture. Beat the egg whites until just foamy. Add remaining sugar and beat until the whites form stiff peaks. Fold carefully into the chocolate mixture. Spoon into individual stemmed glasses or custard cups, if desired. Chill until firm. Top with sweetened whipped cream just before serving.

ORANGE BAVARIAN CREAM

Serves 10 to 12

7 egg yolks
2 large oranges
3/4 cup sugar
2 tsps. cornstarch
1 1/2 cups warm milk
2 tbsps. unflavored gelatin
5 egg whites
2 tbsps. sugar
1 cup whipping cream
2–3 tbsps. orange liqueur

Grate peel of oranges and set aside. Squeeze juice and set aside. Beat yolks with electric mixer or rotary beater until fluffy and light. Add cornstarch to sugar and mix well. Gradually add the 3/4 cup sugar mixture to egg yolks, beating constantly until mixture is thick. Add warm milk and blend well. Transfer to heavy saucepan and add orange juice and gelatin which has been softened in part of the orange juice. Heat gently, stirring constantly, until mixture thickens and coats spoon, but do not boil. Remove from heat and let stand to cool slightly.

Beat whites in large bowl until soft peaks form. Gradually add 2 tbsps. sugar and continue beating until stiff peaks form. Stir the custard in a small stream gradually into the egg white mixture, stirring in a folding motion until well blended. Refrigerate, stirring occasionally, until the custard is slightly thickened and mounds lightly on the spoon (about 1 1/2 hours — do not allow it to set firmly). Whip the cream until stiff. Add the orange liqueur, folding gently. Fold the cream into the custard, blending well. Pour into parfait glasses or stemmed glasses or dessert dishes and refrigerate for several hours. Garnish with whipped cream and/or decorate with a little fresh fruit.

This dessert can be frozen and the flavor can be changed to whatever is desired by the addition of the same amount of juice from another fruit, and/or rind of another fruit. And the recipe will make either chocolate or mocha Bavarian by substituting 1/2 cup water for the juice, omitting the rind, and adding 2–3 oz. melted sweet chocolate and/or 3 tsps. instant coffee, plus 1 tsp. vanilla to the milk before adding it to the eggs.

STRAWBERRY MOUSSE

Serves 10

2 egg whites, room temperature
1/4 tsp. cream of tartar
Pinch of salt
2 cups whipping cream
1 1/4 cups powdered sugar, sifted
2 cups strawberries, washed, dried, stems removed and pureed, then chilled before using

Beat the egg whites together with the cream of tartar and salt in a small bowl until stiff and glossy. Whip the cream with the sugar in medium bowl until stiff. Whisk strawberry puree gently into whipped cream. Gently fold in egg whites, blending well. Spoon mousse into stemmed glasses. Refrigerate at least 1 hour before serving. Garnish each glass with additional whipped cream just before serving, and if desired, place a whole strawberry on top.

This recipe can be adapted to use any fresh fruit which lends itself to being pureed, such as peaches, apricots, pineapple.

SIMPLE CHEESE CAKE

Serves 6 to 8

8 oz. cream cheese, softened to room temperature
2 tbsps. butter, softened to room temperature
1/2 cup sugar
1 whole egg
2 tbsps. flour
2/3 cup milk
1/4 cup lemon juice
2 tbsps. grated lemon rind

Cream the cheese and butter together until well blended. Add sugar and egg, then flour and milk and blend well. Stir in juice and rind. When mixture is fully blended, pour into unbaked 9″ graham cracker crumb crust. Bake in preheated 350°F. oven for 35 minutes. Chill well before serving. Fresh sweetened fruit may be served over the top of each serving, if desired.

GRAHAM CRACKER CRUST

1 1/2 cups graham cracker crumbs
1/3 cup sugar
1/2 tsp. cinnamon
1/2 cup melted butter

Thoroughly mix together crumbs, sugar and cinnamon. Add melted butter and mix all together until well blended. Press into a 9″ pie dish and fill with above batter.

CHARLOTTE

Serves 12

Line a charlotte mold or a steep sided bowl with ladyfingers (which can be purchased at most bakeries or found in the cookie section of most supermarkets — making ladyfingers is extra unnecessary work since, in our opinion, homemade ladyfingers taste the same as well made bakery products).

Fill the interior of the mold with any the mousses for which recipes have been provided in this chapter, or any of the Bavarian cream variations which have been provided. After filling chill thoroughly before unmolding onto serving plate.

To vary the charlotte, the ladyfingers may be sprinkled with or soaked lightly in brandy or a liqueur which is compatible with the filling being used, and after unmolding, whipped cream may be piped around the edges with a pastry bag.

LADYFINGERS

Makes about 15

All ingredients should be at room temperature

1/3 cup flour, sifted several times until light
1/3 cup powdered sugar, sifted well
1/8 tsp. salt
1 whole egg
2 egg yolks
1/2 tsp. vanilla
2 egg whites, beaten until stiff, but not dry

Beat the 2 egg yolks and 1 whole egg together with the vanilla until thick and lemon colored. Fold the sugar and salt gradually into the egg whites, which have been beaten until stiff, but not dry, and continue beating until the mixture thickens again. Fold in the egg yolk mixture and then the flour. Shape the dough into strips 3 1/2" long by 1 1/4" wide (a pastry tube is really necessary for this operation, unless you have a ladyfinger pan) on a paper lined cookie sheet or pour into greased ladyfinger molds. Bake in a preheated 375°F. oven 12 to 15 minutes, until golden. When cool, dust with powdered sugar and keep in an air tight container if reserving for later use.

MANGO MOUSSE

Serves 12

5 medium, ripe mangoes, peeled, halved and seeded (about 2 1/2 pounds)
1/3 cup fresh lime juice
3 egg whites, room temperature
Pinch of salt
1/3 cup sugar
1 cup whipping cream

Puree the mangoes with the lime juice. Beat whites with the pinch of salt in large bowl of electric mixer or with rotary beater until soft peaks form. Gradually add sugar and continue beating until stiff but not dry. Whip cream in another large bowl until it forms soft peaks. Gently fold whites into the cream, then fold in the mango puree. Pour into stemmed glasses or glass dessert dishes. Chill at least 6 hours before serving.

This recipe is heavier on the fruit than the recipe for strawberry mousse, which see, and is better for use with a less tart, sweet fruit.

CREAM PUFFS OR ECLAIRS

Makes about 15 medium

1 cup boiling water
1/2 cup vegetable shortening
1/4 tsp. salt
1 cup flour
4 eggs

Before starting, preheat the oven to 450°F. and generously grease a cookie sheet or two.

In a medium saucepan mix boiling water, shortening and salt. When shortening has melted, add flour all at once and stir vigorously, continuing to cook on low heat, until mixture is damply solid and comes cleanly away from the sides of the pan. Remove from heat and cool for about 1 minute. Add the unbeaten eggs, one at the time, beating constantly, until batter is smooth. Drop batter by one heaping tbsp. at a time onto cookie sheet, allowing 2" between each mound. If making eclairs, mound the dough in an elongated mound for each eclair.

Bake at 450°F. for 15 minutes. Reduce the oven temperature to 400°F. and continue to bake for 15 to 20 minutes more. Puffs are done when a puff used to test the batch does not fall when removed from the oven, and when tops are golden in color.

Cool completely. Cut tops off with sharp knife and fill with custard filling, fruit or ice cream, or sweetened whipped cream.

These puffs can be made a little larger simply by increasing the baking time by only 2 minutes or so. The larger puffs are ideal for filling with creamed vegetables or creamed meats, or fish, or for filling with meat or fish salads. Use your imagination. Cream puffs are delicious and very versatile.

Sauces, Dressings, Relishes
Side Dishes, Broths and Stocks

BASIC SPAGHETTI SAUCE WITHOUT MEAT

Makes 1 1/2 quarts

10–15 medium size, very ripe tomatoes, peeled, chopped
1 pint tomato puree
1 very large, or 2 small green bell peppers, chopped
2 large onions, chopped
3–4 cloves garlic, mashed
1 large or 2 small bay leaves
1–2 tsps. each rosemary and thyme, ground in a mortar
3/4 tsp. oregano, ground with the rosemary and thyme in a mortar
Salt to taste
1 tsp. white pepper
2 tsps. sugar (or to taste)
1 cup (or more if needed) dry red wine
2 cups sliced fresh mushrooms (optional)

Sauté the mashed garlic in a little oil (preferably olive, but use olive oil only if very fresh, very fine is available — vegetable oil is better than heavy olive oil) until translucent. Add onions and sauté a minute or two, along with the mushrooms, if using. Add the peppers, bay leaf or leaves, herbs, pepper, sugar, tomatoes, tomato puree and salt to taste (start out with 1 tbsp. and test for taste after 10 minutes or so). Bring to boil, add the 1 cup of red wine and turn heat down to very low simmer. Simmer uncovered, adding wine from time to time if mixture gets too thick, for at least 4, but preferably 5–6 hours, stirring from time to time with a wooden spoon.

If using meat, either ground beef or Italian style mild sausage, sauté the meat until cooked thoroughly and add to the sauce about 1 hour before using to allow the flavors to blend. Use the amount of meat desired, but not less than 1/2 lb. for this size recipe.

This recipe may be doubled, quadrupled, etc. and frozen in 1 quart plastic containers covered tightly for an indefinite period of time, at least 6 months. Since it takes so many hours to do the sauce properly, we recommend that it be made, whenever possible, in large quantities and stored thus until needed.

MARINARA SAUCE

(For meats or pasta)

Makes about 6 cups

1/2 cup fresh, light olive oil
8 cloves garlic, mashed
8 cups peeled, stewed and chopped tomatoes, or 1 1/2 quarts tomato puree plus 2 cups fresh tomatoes, peeled and chopped
1/2 tsp. oregano, pulverized in a mortar
Salt and pepper to taste

Sauté the garlic in the olive oil over high heat until the garlic is lightly browned. Reduce heat to low and add tomatoes, or tomatoes and puree, and the oregano. Cover the pan and cook for 30 minutes or until the sauce thickens. It is important to the sauce that some pieces of tomato be evident in the final sauce, so do not crush all the tomatoes beyond recognition.

CARBONARA SAUCE FOR SPAGHETTI

Serves 4

5 tbsps. butter
8 slices bacon
3/4 cup medium cream
2 whole eggs
1 egg yolk
1 cup freshly grated Parmesan cheese
1 tsp. dried red pepper flakes (optional)
1 lb. spaghetti

Cut the bacon slices crosswise into 1/4″ strips. Cook slowly over moderate heat until crisp. Remove bacon and drain on paper towels, then crumble into a bowl and set aside. Drain off all but 1 tbsp. of fat in pan and blend the cream into that 1 tbsp. Heat gently, but do not allow to boil. Cool for 2 minutes. Meanwhile, beat the eggs and the egg yolk, add the cheese, red peppers, if using, and salt to taste. Then add the cream and return the whole mixture to the skillet and heat gently, but do not boil.

Melt the 5 tbsps. butter and set aside. Cook the spaghetti al dente and drain. Blend the sauce, melted butter and reserved bacon crumbles into the hot spaghetti.

TRATORIA STYLE SAUCE

(Also known as Al Burro, or, in the U.S. Alfredo)

Serves 6

1½ lbs. fettucine, cooked al dente
8 tbsps. butter
2 cups heavy cream
3 egg yolks
2 cups fresh grated Parmesan cheese
Salt and white pepper to taste

After cooking the fettucine, drain it well and put it in a warm serving bowl and gently stir in 2 tbsps. of the butter, melted. Keep warm.

In a saucepan melt remaining butter and stir in the cream. Heat the mixture thoroughly. In a bowl lightly beat the egg yolks and stir into them, a little at a time, the heated butter and cream. Return the mixture to saucepan and reheat it, but do not let it boil. Blend in 1 cup of the cheese and add the salt and pepper. Pour sauce over the pasta and toss, along with the remaining cheese. Serve at once.

BECHAMEL SAUCE OR "WHITE SAUCE"

Makes 3 cups

2 cups milk
1 small bay leaf
3 tbsps. butter
4 tbsps. flour
Pinch white pepper and salt to taste
1 egg yolk, mixed well in 2 tbsps. light cream
1¼ tbsps. sweet sherry

Melt the butter in a small saucepan. Remove from heat and add the flour. Mix well until blended thoroughly. Gradually add the milk, then bay leaf and pinch of white pepper. Cook, stirring constantly, over medium heat until thick. Turn off heat and cover. Cool for at least 3–4 minutes to allow the bay leaf to flavor the sauce. Meantime, beat the egg yolk and the cream together until well blended. Add the sweet sherry. Mix the whole mixture into the sauce and return to heat until almost, but not quite, to the boil, and thickened. Remove bay leaf. Cool if not using at once, cover tightly and refrigerate. Will keep well for a day or two in the refrigerator.

This sauce is called "White Sauce," which it is not. Plain White Sauce should remain unmade. It is nothing like this lovely, flavorful sauce.

NEWBURG SAUCE

Makes 1 cup

1/2 cup butter
1 medium garlic clove, mashed
1/4 cup sweet Madeira wine (if unavailable sweet sherry can be substituted, but the Madeira is very much better)
1 cup cream
3 egg yolks

Melt the butter and sauté the garlic until translucent, but not browned. Remove from heat. Beat the egg yolks until thick and lemony. Add the cream and the wine and mix well. Pour this mixture into the butter and cook over low heat until just below boiling — do not boil or eggs will curdle — and sauce has thickened. Use at once.

Use for crab and lobster.

If the sauce needs to be kept for a little while it is possible to substitute milk and flour for the cream as follows:

Add 2 1/2 tbsps. flour to the melted butter and garlic then pour in 1 1/4 cup milk and blend well

Cook until thick. Whip the egg yolks with the wine and add to the thickened mixture and heat to just below boiling. This recipe can be cooled and kept refrigerated until ready to use, then reheated.

MORNAY SAUCE

Makes about 4 cups

This sauce is very dependent upon the cheese which is used. Basically this sauce requires a very sharp, aged, meltable cheese. If the recipe calls for "Mornay Sauce" no other cheese will do.

2 cups Bechamel sauce (see recipe)
2 cups light cream
2 cups very sharp cheddar cheese, grated
1 tsp. Lea & Perrins
1 tbsp. sweet sherry
Dash of cayenne pepper

Heat the 2 cups Bechamel sauce. Add the cream and cheddar, the Lea & Perrins, the sherry and the dash of cayenne, and heat, stirring constantly, only until the cheese has melted and all ingredients well blended.

This sauce, like Bechamel, will keep well covered in the refrigerator for several days or a week.

WHITE CLAM SAUCE FOR LINGUINE

Serves 4–6

1/3 cup very fresh, very fine olive oil
3 large cloves garlic, mashed
1/2 cup clam juice, bottled, reserved from fresh or canned clams, or both
1/4 tsp. salt
Freshly ground pepper
Large pinch dried oregano, ground in mortar
Large pinch dried thyme, ground in mortar
10 1/2 oz. can minced clams, or equivalent
2 tbsps. chopped fresh parsley
1/2 cup minced carrot
1/2 cup minced celery
1/2 cup minced green pepper
1/2 cup minced onion
1/2 cup dry white wine
2 tbsps. flour
1 lb. linguine

Heat oil in a large, heavy skillet. Sauté the garlic until pale yellow. Add the clam juice, salt, pepper, spices, herbs and minced vegetables. Simmer, covered, for about 10 minutes, until vegetables are soft. Mix the flour carefully with the wine. Stir the clams into the vegetable mixture along with the wine and flour mixture and cook uncovered for about 2 minutes, until the flour has thickened the sauce slightly. Stir in the parsley and turn off heat.

Cook the linguine al dente only, drain and put in heated bowl. Add half the clam sauce and toss well. Serve in heated bowls with remaining sauce spooned over.

RED CLAM SAUCE FOR LINGUINE

Serves 4–6

1/4 cup olive oil
2 medium onions, chopped
2 cloves garlic, mashed
3 cups chopped tomatoes, stewed, or 4 cups tomato puree
3/4 tsp. salt
Freshly ground pepper
1/2 tsp. red pepper flakes
1 tsp. dried oregano
10 1/2 oz. canned minced clams, or 15 fresh shucked clams
3/4 cup clam juice, bottled or reserved from the clams
4 anchovy fillets, chopped
1 lb. linguine

Heat oil in a very large heavy skillet. Sauté the onions and garlic until soft. Add the tomatoes or puree, salt, black and red pepper, oregano and anchovies. Bring to boil and simmer gently uncovered for 10 minutes, stirring once or twice. Add the clams and their juice, stir well and simmer, uncovered, for another 3–4 minutes, stirring frequently. If this sauce seems a little thin, it may be thickened with 2–3 tbsps. flour, mixed with a little red wine.

Cook the linguine al dente only, drain and put in heated bowl. Add half the clam sauce and toss well. Serve in heated bowls and top with remaining sauce.

WHITE WINE SAUCE

Makes 2 cups

3 tbsps. butter
3 tbsps. flour
1 cup fish stock
1/4 cup dry white wine
Salt and white pepper to taste
1/2 cup heavy cream blended with 2 egg yolks

Melt the butter in a saucepan. Stir in the flour. Remove from heat and gradually add the fish stock and the wine, and mix until well blended. Cook, stirring constantly, until thickened and smooth. Season to taste with the salt and pepper. Pour a little of the hot sauce into egg yolk cream mixture and stir. Add this to the sauce in the pan and cook gently, over low heat, until thickened. Do not allow to boil or eggs will curdle.

Serve over or with fish dishes, particularly hot poached fish.

MUSHROOM SAUCE

Serves 8

3 cups onion, sliced thin
5–6 tbsps. butter
1 lb. fresh mushrooms, sliced thin
1 tbsp. beef base such as bovril, or two beef bouillon cubes or 1 tbsp. beef bouillon granules
1/4 tsp. marjoram, crumbled
1/4 tsp. basil, crumbled
Pinch of thyme, crumbled
1/2 cup whole milk
1 cup Bechamel sauce (see recipe)
1 1/2 cups sour cream

Braise the onion in the butter until golden. Add the mushrooms and sauté

2–3 minutes. Stir in the bovril or the bouillon and the herbs, together with the milk. Simmer for 2 or 3 minutes, stirring constantly. Add the Bechamel sauce and heat but do not boil. Add the sour cream and stir in until well blended and hot, but, once again, do not boil.

This sauce can be refrigerated and reheated, but as above, do not boil or the sauce will curdle.

Delicious served as a sauce over medallions of beef fillet, or any roast meat.

CUCUMBER SAUCE

Makes 2 cups

2 large cucumbers
1 tsp. salt
1 cup sour cream
1 cup mayonnaise
1 tbsp. cream style horseradish (may be omitted if unavailable)
1 tsp. grated onion
1 tbsp. tarragon vinegar (add 1 tsp. crushed fresh or dried tarragon to 1 cup red or white wine vinegar and allow to sit for a few hours, then strain, to make tarragon flavored vinegar if unavailable)
1/4 tsp. white pepper

Peel cucumbers and slice very thin. Place in a 2 quart mixing bowl and cover with cold water. Add the 1 tsp. salt and stir well. Allow to sit for 30 minutes and then drain and dry on paper towels. Combine sour cream, mayonnaise, horseradish (if using), grated onion and vinegar in bowl. Add cucumbers, and stir gently. Season with a little more salt, if desired and the white pepper.

This sauce is delicious on hot or cold poached, or hot baked fish, especially salmon or trout.

HOT MUSTARD SAUCE

Makes 1 cup

1/4 cup dry mustard
2 tbsps. vegetable oil
2 tbsps. water
1/4 cup sugar
1 tbsp. cornstarch
1/2 tsp. salt
1/2 cup water
1/4 cup white vinegar

Blend sugar, cornstarch, salt and 1/2 cup water and 1/4 cup vinegar in medium saucepan. Cook over low heat until mixture thickens. Add mustard, oil and 2 tbsps. water which have been mixed together until smooth, and blend thoroughly. Serve at room temperature.

Use for fritters and shrimp toast (see recipes in "Appetizers").

QUICK HOLLANDAISE SAUCE

Makes 1 cup

3 whole eggs, room temperature
5 tsps. lemon juice
3 tbsps. water
7 tbsps. butter
1/2 tsp. salt
Pinch white pepper
1/8 tsp. ground marjoram
1/8 tsp. ground thyme

Melt the butter in a medium saucepan. Add the juice and water to the melted butter and mix well. Beat the eggs in a small bowl or the small bowl of the electric mixer until thick and yellow. Heat the melted butter and the juice and water until on the edge of boiling, and then, while beating, pour steady stream of the liquid into the eggs. Beat until thick, add the marjoram, thyme, salt and pepper, mix thoroughly, and return mixture to the saucepan. Heat very slowly over very low fire, mixing constantly until thick. (If too thick to pour, add a little more water.) When thick, remove from heat and cover until ready to use.

This sauce will hold its shape, unlike traditional Hollandaise, and will keep for a day or two in the refrigerator, and may be reheated to serve later.

CHINESE SWEET AND SOUR SAUCE

Makes 1 1/4 cups

1/2 cup pineapple juice
1/2 cup white wine vinegar
2 tbsps. vegetable oil
2 tbsps. brown sugar, firmly packed
1 tbsp. soy sauce
1/2 tsp. white pepper
2 tbsps. cornstarch mixed with enough water to thin it (about 2 tbsps.)

Mix all ingredients except the cornstarch mixture and bring to boil in a medium saucepan. Stir in cornstarch mixture and cook until sauce is clear and thickened.

Use for shrimp toast or for any type of fritter (see recipes in "Appetizers").

HERB SAUCE

Makes about 1 1/2 cups

1/2 cup dry white wine
1/2 cup chopped fresh parsley (not cilantro)
1/4 cup white vinegar
1 small onion, quartered
2 large cloves garlic, cut in quarters
2 1/2 tsps. dried tarragon leaves, crushed
1/4 tsp. dried chervil leaves, crushed
1/8 tsp. white pepper
1 cup mayonnaise

Blend all ingredients except the mayonnaise in blender on high speed until pureed. Remove to small saucepan and cook over low heat until reduced to about 1/3 cup. Strain and return liquid to saucepan. Stir in the mayonnaise and heat until just warm.

Use with red meats or fish as a bearnaise sauce.

GREEN MAYONNAISE

Makes 2 cups

1 large handful spinach leaves, washed, stems removed
1/2 cup finely chopped fresh parsley, tarragon, chervil and dill leaves, or 1 tsp. each if using dried
1 tsp. minced green onion
2 cups mayonnaise
Salt and freshly ground pepper to taste

Blanch the spinach in boiling water for 1 minute and quickly run cold water over and drain. Then chop very finely. Mix in the herbs and chop everything together. If using dried herbs, be sure the mixture is well blended. Mix in mayonnaise and season with salt and pepper to taste. Allow to chill an hour or two before using in order to blend the flavors.

Use this mayonnaise as an accompaniment to any fish dish, but it is especially good with any cold, poached fish.

RICH HOT FUDGE SAUCE

Makes about 1 1/2 cups

1 14-oz. can sweetened condensed milk
1 tbsp. water
1/8 tsp. salt
2 oz. unsweetened chocolate
1/2 tsp. vanilla extract

Mix milk with salt and water in top of double boiler. Add chocolate. Place over boiling water and cook over high heat, stirring constantly, until sauce is thick and smooth, about 20 minutes. Remove from heat and stir in vanilla.

CITRUS SAUCE

Makes 3/4 cup

1/2 cup sugar
4 tbsps. cornstarch
1 1/2 cup water
3 tbsps. butter
2 tsps. grated lemon or orange rind
6 tbsps. lemon juice or 6 tbsps. orange juice (depending on which flavor you wish to predominate)
1/8 tsp. salt

Combine all ingredients and cook, stirring constantly, in top part of double boiler over boiling water until thickened.

Makes a delicious sauce for puddings, gelatins or ice cream desserts.

JUBILEE SAUCE

About 1 1/2 cups

1 cup preserved cherries (or other preserved fruit may be used, if cherries are not available)
1/4 cup brandy
2 tbsps. kirsch liqueur, or, if not available, orange liqueur may be substituted

Heat the fruit, add the brandy which has been slightly warmed. Ignite and when the flame has died down, add the kirsch or other liqueur. Serve over ice cream while still very warm.

If desired, the fruit may be mixed with the brandy and they may be heated together and not ignited before adding the liqueur. The flaming brandy is more for effect than out of necessity, and is usually done at the table in a chafing dish.

CARAMEL SAUCE

About 2 cups

1 cup sugar
1 1/2 cups milk
1 tbsp. flour
3 egg yolks, beaten
1/2 tsp. vanilla extract

Cook sugar over low heat in a small skillet until golden brown. Blend the flour and milk together, gradually, until well blended. Add to the caramelized sugar. Boil over low heat for 3 to 4 minutes, stirring constantly. Put beaten egg yolks in top of a double boiler. Add the caramel mixture and the extract and cook over boiling water, stirring constantly, until thickened.

BUTTERSCOTCH SAUCE

Makes about 2 1/2 cups

1 1/4 cups brown sugar, firmly packed
2/3 cup light corn syrup
4 tbsps. butter
2/3 cup light cream

Combine sugar, corn syrup and butter in skillet or heavy saucepan. Bring to boil over low heat and simmer, stirring constantly, until a small quantity dropped into cold water forms a soft ball. Gradually add the cream. Remove from heat and stir to blend.

CHICKEN STOCK

Makes 2 quarts

This recipe is the same for stewing chicken as for simply making stock. So, when stewing a chicken, always use enough water to leave some stock. Reserving the liquid left after stewing a whole chicken makes richer stock than when only giblets and bones are used, as in this recipe.

- **2 lbs. chicken gizzards**
- **2 lbs. chicken necks and backs**
- **1 large onion, peeled and chopped**
- **1 leek, washed and trimmed, but with most of green part still on (optional)**
- **4 garlic cloves, peeled and chopped coarsely**
- **1 large or 2 small bay leaves**
- **2–3 sprigs parsley**
- **1 tsp. dried thyme, pounded in mortar**
- **1/2 tsp. dried rosemary, pounded in mortar**
- **6 peppercorns**
- **3 quarts water**
- **Green tops of 3 stalks of celery**
- **1 tbsp. salt**

Put all ingredients into large pot and bring to boil. After a few minutes, skim the scum off surface and reduce heat to simmer. Cover the pot and simmer for 2–2 1/2 hours. Strain the stock through a sieve lined with several thicknesses of cheesecloth into another container. Chill thoroughly in refrigerator, and when stock is cold, remove the fat from the top. If you used chicken gizzards, reserve them for eating. Refrigerate or freeze the stock until needed.

FISH STOCK

Makes 6 cups

- **2 lbs. fish bones and heads, or 2 lbs. bony fish (do not use oily fish)**
- **3 cups water**
- **3 cups dry white wine**
- **1 or 2 slices of lemon with skin on**
- **1 large celery stalk, or 3 tops**
- **1 small onion sliced**
- **1 tsp. fennel seeds**
- **1 small bay leaf**
- **1 medium carrot, sliced**
- **1/2 tsp. thyme**
- **4 sprigs fresh parsley**
- **6 peppercorns, crushed**
- **Salt**

Wash the fish well and remove gills from heads. Combine in a large pan all the other ingredients except the salt. Bring to a boil, reduce heat to simmer and simmer 20–30 minutes. Strain. Salt to taste.

BEEF STOCK

Makes 2½ to 3 quarts

2 to 3 lbs. bones (beef or veal)
Flour
5 lb. piece of leg bone with some meat
1 large onion, peeled
1 carrot, cleaned
1 leek, washed and trimmed
1 white turnip, peeled
4 garlic cloves, peeled but left whole
1 large or 2 small bay leaves
2–3 sprigs fresh parsley
1 tsp. dried thyme
1 tbsp. salt

Dredge the bones and the leg bone with meat lightly in flour. Place on broiling rack and broil with rack at lowest point under broiler (or place in a preheated 500°F. oven on center rack) until beef and bones are nicely browned, turning from time to time. Place the bones and meat, after browning, together with all remaining ingredients in a large pot with water to cover. Bring to boil over high heat for 5–6 minutes, skimming off scum which rises to the surface. Reduce heat until water just simmers. Cover the pot and cook for 3 hours. Remove the pot from the heat, remove the bones with the meat on them for use as boiled beef, then strain the broth into a large bowl through a sieve lined with cheesecloth. Chill overnight, then remove the fat from the top. Return broth to fire and simmer slowly for several hours longer to reduce the stock. Then strain the broth once more and refrigerate or freeze until ready for use.

Miscellaneous

How-tos, Conversion Tables

HIGH ALTITUDE ADJUSTMENTS

BREADS:

At altitudes above 3,500 feet, use slightly more liquid or a little less flour because flour is drier and absorbs more liquid at higher altitudes. On a rainy day, however, more flour needs to be used than on a dry day.

Dough also rises faster at high altitudes, so to obtain the fullest flavor, allow the dough to rise twice before doing the final shaping and rising.

Reduce baking powder or baking soda, or both, in recipes for quick breads by 1/4 tsp. or slightly less.

Decrease sugar in sweet quick breads by 1½ tbsps. per cup of flour to prevent thick crusts.

To stabilize the leavening action and to get it started for better yeast bread, increase the oven temperature for 10 minutes at the beginning of the baking time. An increase of about 20°F. is the usual rule, but this may vary from recipe to recipe. Do a test run the first time you bake a new bread.

CAKES:

Decrease the amount of leavening agent at altitudes of 2,500 feet or more, i.e. the baking powder, baking soda or cream of tartar, by 1/4 tsp. per 1,500 feet.

Decrease the amount of air beaten into egg whites. If the recipe calls for stiff beaten egg whites, do not let them become very stiff and dry, but beat only until the eggs form soft peaks and are satiny.

Increase the amount of liquid used by 2 tbsps. per cup at altitudes of 2,500 feet or more, for each 1,500 feet.

Increase the amount of flour at altitudes of 3,500 feet or more, by 1 tbsp. per 1,500 feet.

Increase the baking temperature by 10°F. above 4,000 feet up to 6,500 feet, then increase by 25°F. above 6,500 feet.

Decrease the amount of sugar used at altitudes above 2,500 feet by 1 tbsp. per 1,500 feet.

BOILING AND DEEP FAT FRYING:

Since the boiling point of liquids is lower at higher altitudes, the cooking process on top of the stove takes a little longer.

You must also increase the temperature of fat for deep frying by 5 to 15°F., depending on the altitude where you are cooking, and also depending on the type of food you are frying. But never let the oil or other fat smoke before introducing the food. Use a thermometer if possible, and test the particular food at your altitude. Test the temperature by tossing in a 1″ cube of bread. If it turns brown in 50 seconds the oil is correct.

HINTS ABOUT FISH:

The technique for knowing fresh fish from that which should be avoided is easy:

1. Eyes should be bright and shiny, with clear, identifiable pupils;
2. Scales should be shiny and tight against the fish;
3. Gills should never be gray in color.

Thaw frozen fish in milk. This eliminates fishy odors and any possible freezer odors.

If freezing fresh fish for future use, clean it thoroughly in cold, running water and either freeze it in a plastic bag or a milk carton or other container which can be sealed well which has been filled with water.

Or, freeze whole, large fish by wrapping carefully in heavy-duty aluminum foil, sealed well, and then placing in a large plastic bag, all air squeezed out and sealed with a tie or elastic.

Before cooking fresh fish, soak it in cold water with about 1/4 cup white vinegar, white wine or lemon added. This gives saltwater fish a sweeter flavor and gives a delicate flavor to all fish. Rinse the fish in cold water briefly and pat dry before cooking.

SHRIMP:

Really fresh shrimp are always firm, never floppy, and do not have a strong scent.

Frozen shrimp may be thawed in cold water with a little vinegar, or may be cooked frozen. If cooking frozen, plunge into rapidly boiling water and bring back up to simmer.

Never allow shrimp to come to a boil because this makes the shrimp tough. Start fresh shrimp in cold water and slowly bring almost to the boil, lower heat and simmer only until the shrimp turns pink. The same rule applies to the cooking of the shrimp while frozen (see above).

Shrimp may be cooked in the shell and peeled and deveined after cooking, or may be shelled and deveined before cooking. Cook in lightly salted water, and drain immediately after cooking, and rinse in a cold bath, then redrain.

Never overcook any fish, including all types of shellfish. Cook fish only until the flesh is no longer opaque in color but has taken on its final coloring, white, pink or red. Test with the prick of a fork (down to the bone if cooking a whole fish). This same rule applies to scallops and oysters. If cooking shrimp or lobster, the fish is done when it turns pink or orange.

Remember, if you overcook fish it loses flavor and becomes tough.

OTHER GENERAL HINTS AND HOW-TO'S

DEALING WITH EGGS IN COOKING:

1. Bring eggs, the whites of which are to be whipped, to room temperature before separating.

2. Whites should never be beaten until dry, but only until stiff and satiny looking.

3. To get more volume and a fluffier end product, the eggs should be separated and the whites beaten separately and added to cakes by folding them in at the end of the mixing process. (However, remember the high altitude rules, and test this hint before preparing a cake for company if you live up high.)

4. Never pour raw eggs or egg yolks, whether beaten or not, directly into a hot mixture. Instead, add a little of the hot mixture to the eggs until they are warm, then pour the warmed eggs back into the hot mixture. This prevents curdling.

5. After adding egg yolks to sauce, never allow the mixture to boil. This causes separation and curdling. Heat according to recipe directions, but do not boil. Also, do not prolong the cooking period. Heating the eggs is sufficient to cook them.

6. If curdling occurs, pour out the curdled mixture at once into a cold bowl and beat vigorously with a rotary beater, and, if necessary, add a little cold cream.

HOW TO STORE COOKED PASTA UNTIL READY TO SERVE:

1. Never cook pasta beyond the al dente stage.

2. As soon as this stage is reached, rinse pasta in hot water, drain and cover with cold water. If storing for the next day, cover and refrigerate until ready to use.

3. When ready to use, bring another pot of water to boiling, drain the refrigerated pasta and cook it for one minute in the boiling water, drain in hot water and serve.

4. Taste for saltiness just before serving, and add salt to the hot water if needed.

5. To cook pasta, bring the water (3 quarts to 8 oz. of pasta) to a rolling boil before adding the pasta, with 3–4 tbsps. salt or to taste and 1/3 cup vinegar (prevents the pasta from sticking together). Return to the boil, lower heat and boil gently, uncovered, until the al dente stage is reached (8 to 10 minutes depending on the altitude).

HOW TO REFRESH LIMP LETTUCE OR CELERY:

Cut a little slice from the stem so that the water can penetrate, then stand in about 1/4″ of cold water in a pan, covered with a plastic bag, loosely, in the refrigerator overnight. Then remove, wrap in paper towels, place in a plastic bag and tie with a twist tie and return to the refrigerator until ready for use. The crispness will be réstored by the night in the cold bath, and will remain as long as the lettuce or celery is stored as indicated.

HOW TO MAKE SMOOTH GRAVIES AND BUTTER SAUCES:

Use 2 tbsps. butter or fat from the meat or chicken for each 1 or 2 tbsps. of flour, and melt the fat before adding the flour. Blend thoroughly, then add the liquid, gradually, whether milk or stock, and seasonings, blending thoroughly, then cook until thick.

HOW TO CHOOSE AND STORE FRESH MUSHROOMS:

1. If picking fresh mushrooms which are displayed in bulk at the market, choose only those which are dry and closed, not open and showing the brown underside and/or slippery to the touch.

2. If purchasing mushrooms which have already been packaged by the market, remove them from the containers immediately because retaining them stored in plastic makes them become moist and spoil rapidly.

3. Lay the mushrooms in single layers, not touching, on a dish or pan (styrofoam tray preferred), completely encased in paper toweling. The paper towels will keep the mushrooms dry, and fully covering the mushrooms helps them retain their interior moisture. It is important not to lay the mushrooms directly on the tray or pan, but on a paper towel covering the bottom of the tray.

Kept this way in the refrigerator, mushrooms can be kept up to 3 weeks before using. If they begin to dry out, they may be treated like dried mushrooms, which are restored for use by soaking in a little water for a few minutes. But, if properly covered, as instructed, and firm and fresh when put away for storage, they will keep for at least 2 and usually 3 weeks.

Do not clean the mushrooms before storing, but only immediately before using.

Entremeses

ALMEJAS RELLENAS HORNEADAS A LA ITALIANA

Para esta receta debe obtener, ya sea, algunas conchas de almejas artificiales, o comprar una docena de conchas de almejas gruesas y grandes, las cuales están disponibles en el mercado y, después de haberlas usado una vez, lávelas muy bien y guárdelas en un lugar seco. Este platillo principal es muy bueno. Nosotros lo servimos la noche de la inauguración del restaurant Marcy y fue un gran éxito.

1 lata de 230 gramos de almejas, drenadas y picadas (reserve el jugo), o el equivalente en almejas frescas (8 a 10 onzas)
2 tazas de pan fresco, desmoronado, hecho de pan blanco ordinario sin cortezas
1 taza de queso parmesano fresco, rallado (cerca de 4 onzas)
2 cucharadas de ramitos de perejil, picadito
1 cucharadita de ajo, picadito
1 cucharadita de orégano seco, desmoronado
1/2 cucharadita de tomillo seco, desmoronado
1/2 cucharadita de albahaca seca, desmoronada
1/2 taza de vino blanco seco
1/2 taza de aceite vegetal
Pimienta recién molida

Combine todos los ingredientes, reservando 2 cucharadas de aceite y el vino. Mezcle muy bien.

Precaliente el horno a 450°F.

Rellene las conchas con la mezcla de almejas, asegurándose de no sobre-llenar, ya que el relleno se esponjará un poco al hornearse. Con una cuchara ponga una o dos gotas de aceite reservado sobre cada concha rellena. Acomódelas en un platón para hornear y vierta vino alrededor en el fondo del platón, teniendo cuidado de no derramar vino en el relleno.

Hornee en la parte superior del horno hasta que las cubiertas estén bien doradas y crujientes, cerca de 10–15 minutos.

Si es necesario agregue más vino. Justo antes de servir, vierta encima, con una cuchara, los jugos restantes del platón. Sirva muy caliente.

BEIGNETS (HORS D'OEUVRE FRITTERS) (FRANCIA)

Rinde 36 aproximadamente

RECETA BASICA

- **1/2 taza de harina**
- **1/8 cucharadita de sal**
- **1 yema de huevo, batida**
- **1/2 taza de cerveza**
- **1 cucharada de mantequilla derretida**
- **1 clara de huevo, batida hasta que esté dura**
- **Aceite para freído profundo**

En un tazón mediano mezcle la harina y la sal. Revuelva con la yema y la cerveza, bata hasta que esté tersa solamente. Añada la mantequilla derretida y bata. Déjela reposar por 1 hora. Mezcle en la clara de huevo. Agregue el ingrediente seleccionado (pescado, carne etc.) en la mezcla, cubriendo bien.

Caliente el aceite a 375°F. y deje caer cucharaditas de la mezcla y fría hasta que estén bien doradas, en todos lados. Escurra el exceso de grasa y sirva caliente.

BEIGNETS DE CREVETTES (CAMARON)

Mezcle con 1 taza de camarón cocido, en cubitos.

BEIGNETS DE FROMAGE (QUESO)

Mezcle con 1/2 taza de queso Manchego o Gruyere, en cubitos.

BEIGNETS DE JAMBON (JAMON)

Mezcle con 3/4 taza de jamón picado, 1 cuchara de perejil, picado y 2 cucharadas de cebolla rallada. Espolvoree con pimienta recién molida, y mezcle de manera envolvente.

PATE DE HÍGADO AL BRANDY

6–8 Porciones

1 cucharada de mayonesa
2 cucharadas de aceite vegetal
2 cebollas medianas, finamente picadas
1 libra de hígado de res o ternera, rebanado en tiras de 1 pulgada
2 huevos duros, picados
1 cucharada de brandy
1 cucharada de perejil fresco, picado (opcional)
1/4 cucharadita de salvia seca
1/2 cucharadita de tomillo seco, molido
1/4 cucharadita de mejorana seca, molida
1/4 cucharadita de nuez moscada, molida
Sal y pimienta recién molida al gusto

Caliente el aceite en una sartén mediana, a fuego moderado. Añada las cebollas y sofríalas hasta que estén transparentes, aproximadamente 5 minutos. Agregue el hígado y fríalo hasta que esté dorado, 6 a 8 minutos. Transfiéralo al procesador y píquelo finamente. Añada los huevos, brandy, mayonesa, perejil picado (si lo usa) y las especies, muela hasta que esté terso. Sazone con sal y pimienta. Vacíelo a cucharadas, en un tazón o molde, esparciéndolo en forma pareja. Refrigere por lo menos 2 horas antes de servirlo, con pan francés o galletitas.

CEVICHE

2 libras de pescado de agua salada, o 2 libras de mariscos, cortados en trozos y marinado en jugo de limón (2/3 taza) durante toda la noche, en un recipiente de vidrio

Escurra el jugo de limón después de marinar y enjuague el pescado en agua fría, después agregue lo siguiente:

2 tomates medianos, sumergidos en agua hirviendo (30 segundos aproximadamente), pelados y picados
1 cebolla mediana, toscamente picada y sumergida en agua hirviendo cerca de 2 minutos
2 dientes de ajo grandes, machacados
1–2 cucharadas de aceite de oliva (o al gusto)
Sal y pimienta al gusto
2 cucharadas de perejil chino, picadito (cilantro), si lo desea

Mezcle bien y refrigere por lo menos 1 hora antes de servir.

CHOUS CREMOSOS / (FRANCIA)

Use la receta en la sección de "Postres." Ponga los chous a cucharadas, cerca de 1 cucharada redonda cada uno. Esta receta hace 36 chous pequeños. Hornee a 450°F. durante 15 minutos, luego reduzca la temperatura a 400°F. y horneé 15 minutos más, o hasta que las puntas estén doradas y firmes.

Rellene los chous con cualquiera de los siguentes rellenos:

RELLENO DE PIÑA Y NUEZ

Combine partes iguales de:

Apio picado
Piña fresca desmenuzada
Unas pocas nueces (o almendras si están disponibles)
Mayonesa

RELLENO DE ENSALADA DE ATÚN

Mezcle junto:

1 lata de atún, drenada
1 cucharada de pimiento morrón rojo, enlatado, picadito
2 cucharadas de cebolla, picadita
1/2 taza de apio, picadito
1 cucharada de salsa de pepinillo (o pepinillo dulce, picadito si no está disponible la salsa de pepinillo)
1/2 cucharadita de moztaza preparada
1/2 taza de mayonesa (o más si desea)

(Si desea un sabor a curry, puede obtenerlo agregando 1 cucharadita de curry en polvo.)

RELLENO DE ENSALADA DE POLLO

Mezcle junto:

2 tazas de pollo cocido, picado
1/2 taza de apio, picadito
1 cucharada de cebolla, picadita
1/2 cucharadita de ajo en polvo
1/2 cucharadita de sal
2 cucharadas de vinagre de vino al gusto
1/4 cucharadita de mostaza preparada
1/4 cucharadita de azúcar
1 taza de mayonesa
Pimienta recién molida al gusto

(Si desea un sabor a curry, puede obtenerlo agregando 1 cucharadita de curry en polvo.)

RELLENO DE JAIBA

Mezcle junto:

2 tazas de jaiba enlatada, drenada, o cocida o langosta cocida, desmenuzada
2 cucharadas de pimiento morrón verde, picadito
2 cucharadas de cebolla cambray, picadita
1 cucharada de catsup
1 cucharadita de salsa inglesa (Lea & Perrins solamente)
1 cucharadita de jugo de limón
Sal y pimienta al gusto
2/3 taza de mayonesa (o más si desea)

MOLDE DE ATÚN AL CURRY

2 sobres de gelatina sin sabor (2 cucharadas)
1/2 taza de agua fría
1 taza de agua hirviendo
2 paquetes (8-onzas cada uno) de queso crema, suavizado
2 cucharadas de jugo de limón
2 cucharadas de curry en polvo
1/2 cucharadita de sal
1/2 cucharadita de ajo en polvo
1/3 taza de cebollita cambray, finamente picada
2 onzas de pimiento morrón rojo, enlatado, picado
2 latas (7 onzas cada una) de atún, drenado y desmenuzado
1/2 taza de nuez picada (opcional)

En un recipiente grande, espolvoree la gelatina sin sabor, sobre el agua fría y déjela reposar un momento. Añada el agua caliente y revuelva hasta que la gelatina esté completamente disuelta. Con un batidor giratorio, mezcle la gelatina con el queso crema hasta que esté terso. Agregue el jugo de limón, el curry en polvo, la cebolla cambray, pimiento morrón, atún y nuez picada (si desea). Vacíe está mezcla en un molde con capácidad de 5 1/2 tazas y refrigere hasta que esté firme. Desmolde y sirva acompañado de galletitas o panecillos. Rinde aproximadamente 5 1/2 tazas.

TOSTADAS DE CAMARÓN FRITAS

Rinde 16

1/2 libra de camarón en su cáscara, fresco
4 rebanadas de pan blanco, sin corteza
2 cucharadas de grasa fresca de puerco
4 castañas de agua, rebanadas y picadas, o la cantidad equivalente de jicama, cruda (cerca de 2 cucharas)
1 cucharadita de sal
1 huevo, ligeramente batido
2 cucharadas de fécula de maíz
1 cucharada de vino blanco seco
Aceite para freído profundo

Pele, desvene y pique finamente el camarón, hasta que se reduzca a una pulpa fina, como masa.

Corte las rebanadas de pan diagonalmente en 4 triángulos cada una.

Pique la grasa de puerco y las castañas de agua o jicama, juntos, tan fino como sea posible y, en un pequeño tazón, combínelos con el camarón. Agregue la sal, el huevo ligeramente batido, fécula de maíz y vino, y mezcle muy bien (con los dedos si es necesario).

Extienda en cantidades iguales en las rebanadas de pan, amontonando ligeramente en el centro de cada triángulo, y asegurándose de que el relleno cubra la pieza entera de pan.

Caliente el aceite a 375°F. con cuidado meta los triángulos de pan, con el lado del camarón hacia abajo (el relleno no se caerá), y fría durante 1 minuto. Luego, con sumo cuidado volteélos en la grasa caliente, con una cuchara ranurada y fría 1 minuto más, hasta que el pan y la cubierta del camarón estén dorado obscuro. Luego volteélos de nuevo y fría otro minuto. Drene en toallas de papel en un molde para hornear y manténgalos calientes en el horno, hasta que los sirva.

Puede servirlos con salsa de mostaza caliente y/o salsa agridulce o salsa de ciruela en pequeños platitos al lado del plato. (Ver recetas en "Salsas.")

QUICHE DE JAMON, TOMATE, BROCOLI, QUESO

8 Porciones Grandes

Precaliente el horno a 400°F.

2 rebanadas de jamón cocido, cortado en tiras de 1 pulgada, estilo juliana, y colocando en el fondo del molde para pay de 10 pulgadas, engrasado con mantequilla y ligeramente espolvoreado con ajo en polvo.
1 cebolla mediana, finamente picada y distribuida encima del jamón
1 1/2 tazas de queso rallado (gruyere, o manchego, o mezclados) extendido encima de la cebolla
2 tomates grandes, rebanados y extendidos sobre el queso
4 huevos
1 1/2 tazas de leche
1 taza copeteada de mezcla para hornear (ver receta en la sección de "Panes y Pastas")
1/4 a 1/2 cucharadita de tomillo
1 cucharadita de sal
1 pizca de pimienta

Bata los huevos, leche, mezcla para hornear, tomillo, sal y pimienta, hasta que esté terso.

Ponga la mezcla encima de los tomates y espolvoree generosamente con queso parmesano rallado.

(Si tiene disponible, extienda 1 taza de florecitas de brocoli, previamente cocidas al vapor hasta que estén suaves, permita que se enfrien, sobre los tomates antes de añadir la mezcla).

Horneé a 400°F. durante 35 ó 40 minutos, hasta que la parte superior esté dorada y firme.

FRITURAS DE VEGETALES CUBIERTAS "TEMPURA"—JAPON

3/4 taza de fécula de maíz
1/4 taza de harina
1 cucharadita de polvo para hornear
1/2 cucharadita de sal
1/2 taza de agua
1 huevo ligeramente batido
1 litro de aceite para freír

En un tazón mezcle la fécula de maíz, harina, polvo para hornear y sal. Agregue agua y el huevo, y mezcle hasta que esté terso. Caliente el aceite a 375°F. y pruebe la temperatura con un cubito de pan de 1 pulgada. Si el pan se dora en 50 segundos, el aceite está listo. Si está preparándolas en altitudes altas (5000 pies o más, aumente la temperatura a 390°F.). Bañe unas cuantas piezas a la vez en la masa fría, agregue unas cuantas a la vez, en el aceite. Fríalas durante 2 minutos, volteando una vez.

Use aros de cebolla, champiñones, aros de pimiento morrón verde, rebanadas de tomate, rebanadas de calabacitas, rebanadas de zanahoria, trozos de ejotes, tiras de berenjenas. También puede usar pechuga de pollo sin piel, cruda y cortada en cubitos de 1 pulgada, o camarones grandes, rebanados a la mitad, a lo largo.

Estas frituras pueden servirse con o sin salsa tempura estilo japonés.

CUBITOS DE CARNE DE PUERCO MARINADOS (AFRICA DEL NORTE)

Rinde 40 aprox.

1/3 taza de aceite de oliva (puede substituirlo con aceite vegetal)
1 cucharada de perejil fresco, picadito
1/4 a 1/2 cucharadita de pimienta roja
2 dientes de ajo, machacados
1 cucharadita de comino molido
1/2 cucharadita de tomillo seco, desmoronado
1/2 cucharadita de paprika
1 hoja de laurel, quebrada
Sal y pimienta al gusto
3/4 libra de carne de puerco sin grasa, deshuesada, cortada en cubitos de 3/4–1 pulgada

En un tazón mediano combine el aceite de oliva, perejil, pimienta roja, ajo, comino, tomillo, paprika y hoja de laurel. Sazone con sal y pimienta. Agregue la carne y mezcle para cubrir bien. Tape y refrigere varias horas o toda la noche, meneando de vez en cuando.

Retire la carne de la marinada utilizando una cuchara ranurada. En un sartén grande caliente 1 cucharada de la marinada, a fuego medio alto. Agregue la carne en tandas y cueza, drenando el exceso de grasa, hasta que la carne esté bien dorada, cerca de 15 minutos. Transfiera a un platón precalentado. Sirva con salsa de jerez.

SALSA DE JEREZ

1 cucharada de marinada (reservada del puerco)
3 onzas de almendras, toscamente picadas (si no están disponibles puede substituirlas con nueces)
1 cucharadita de harina
1/2 taza de jerez dulce
1/4 taza de agua
Sal al gusto
1/2 cucharadita de jugo de limón

En una sartén chica, caliente la marinada a fuego lento. Mezcle en las almendras y cueza hasta que estén un poco coloreadas. Espolvoree con la harina y cueza, meneando constantemente, 1 ó 2 minutos. Agregue el jeréz, agua, sal y jugo de limón y cueza a fuego lento 1 minuto más.

Para una fiesta, use la misma cantidad de salsa para servir con el doble de esta receta.

QUICHE LORRAINE / (FRANCIA)

6–8 Porciones

Forre un molde para pay de 9 pulgadas con Pasta Básica para pay — ver la receta en el Glosario de Pastas. Extiéndala con un rodillo y presiónela en el molde para pay y ondule las orillas. (Es importante ondular con los dedos, las orillas encima del molde, para manejar la cantidad de relleno, ya que podría levantarse).

RELLENO

Fría 6 rebanadas de tocino hasta que estén muy crujientes o doradas, luego drene la grasa en una toalla de papel y desmoronelo toscamente. Distribuya el tocino encima de la pasta que colocó en el molde de pay.

Mezcle en la licuadora o batidora, o bata con un batidor de huevo:

4 huevos
1 cucharada de harina
1/2 cucharadita de sal
1 taza de crema mezclada con 1 taza de leche
1 pizca de nuez moscada
1/2 cucharadita de salsa inglesa (Lea & Perrins de preferencia)
1 cucharada de brandy

Cubra el tocino en la pasta con 1 1/2 tazas de queso Gruyere rallado.

Espolvoree cebolla cambray picada encima — cerca de 1 cuchara.

Ponga el relleno con sumo cuidado, para que los ingredientes no se mezclen más.

Hornee a 350°F. hasta que el relleno esté firme, cerca de 50 minutos. En una altitud mayor de 5000 pies horneé a 360°F. por 50 a 60 minutos aproximadamente, o hasta que al insertar un cuchillo en el centro, salga limpio.

Permita que se enfríe a la temperatura ambiente antes de servir. Puede guardarlo en el refrigerador, cubierto con papel aluminio, durante uno o dos días.

QUICHE DE CAMARON, LANGOSTA O JAIBA

Omita el tocino y el brandy en la receta de arriba y substituyalos con 2/3 taza de camarón, pulpa de langosta o jaiba, cocidos en cubos, y 1 cuchara de vino de madéra o jeréz dulce. Asegúrese de que el camarón, langosta o jaiba estén bien escurridos.

QUICHE DE VEGETALES

Usando la receta de arriba para Quiche Lorraine, omita el tocino y brandy, y extienda una capa de brocoli cocido al vapor, al dente, o espinaca picada (cerca de 1 taza) sobre el fondo y antes de agregar el queso, y mezcle 1/2 cucharadita de mostaza seca y 1 cuchara de jeréz seco, dulce o para cocinar, a la mezcla antes de vertirla encima.

CAMARONES LOUISIENNE

2 libras de camarón crudo grande o gigante, pelado, desvenado y sin colas
1 pinta de aceite vegetal
1 cucharada de sal
5 cucharadas de catsup
1/2 cucharadita de albahaca seca, desmoronada
1/2 cucharadita de mejorana seca, desmoronada
2 dientes de ajo, machacados

Mezcle el aceite, sal, catsup, ajo y las especies. agregue el camarón y mezcle. Marine por lo menos durante 2 horas. Retire el camarón y colóquelo en una sartén poco profunda y extienda encima una pequeña cantidad del aceite en que marinó los camarones. Dore 3 minutos en cada lado. Si es posible ajuste la flama a fuego medio alto.

Sirva en palillos de cocktel adornados con perejil.

Sopas y Cremas

SOPA CHINA—CALIENTE AGRIA

4–6 Porciones

4 tazas de consomé concentrado o caldo de pollo
6 onzas de carne de puerco magra, cortada estilo juliana
1/2 taza de tofú (requesón de soya) cortado estilo juliana (si no se consigue puede omitirlo, o utilizar hojas de frijol de soya secas, cortadas también estilo juliana)
1/2 taza de tiras de bambú, cortadas estilo juliana (si no están disponibles puede substituirlas con tallos pelados de brocoli)
6 champiñones chinos secos, remojados en 1/2 taza de agua durante 15 minutos, sin tallos, rebanados (si no están disponibles, pueden substituirse con champiñones frescos o enlatados, pero se disminuye el sabor)
1 cucharada de salsa soya
1/4 cucharadita de azúcar
3/4 cucharadita de sal
3 cucharadas de fécula de maíz, disuelta en 3 cucharadas de agua
1 huevo, batido hasta que esté ligeramente espumoso
3–4 cucharadas de vinagre de vino tinto
1/2 cucharadita de pimienta blanca molida
2 cebollitas cambray, incluyendo el tallo, finamente rebanadas

Ponga a hervir el consomé en una olla sin tapar. Agregue el puerco, tofú, bambú y champiñones. Cueza de 3–5 minutos. Agregue la salsa soya, azúcar, sal, fécula de maíz disuelta, mezclado junto, a la sopa. Cueza solo hasta que apenas llegue a hervir. Lentamente agregue el huevo y apague el fuego. Ponga el vinagre y la pimienta en un tazón grande. Agregue la sopa y la cebollita de cambray. Sirva inmediatamente.

CREMA DE ALMEJAS ESTILO NUEVA INGLATERRA

8 Porciones

4 cucharadas de mantequilla
5 cucharadas de harina
4 tazas de leche
1 lata (13 onzas) de leche evaporada reserve la lata y agregue una lata de agua
1 onza de tocino, cortado en cuadros chicos
1 cebolla chica, finamente picada
2 papas chicas, (peladas, toscamente picadas y hervidas en un poco de agua hasta que estén tiernas)
1 cucharadita de ajo en polvo
2 cucharaditas de cebolla en polvo
1/4 cucharadita de albahaca
1/4 cucharadita de mejorana
1 1/2 pintas de almejas picaditas en su jugo
Sal y pimienta al gusto

En una sartén derrita la mantequilla y agregue la harina. Mezcle en la leche, leche evaporada y agua, y cueza hasta que espese.

Fría los cubitos de tocino hasta que estén crujientes pero no muy dorados. Agregue la cebolla y cueza hasta que esté suave.

Mezcle todos los ingredientes, agregue las especies y sal y pimienta al gusto y las almejas en su jugo. Caliente a vapor, sobre agua caliente (no en) para servir solo a la temperatura. Es importante que la crema no llegue a hervir o estar muy caliente después de haber agregado las almejas ya que puede cuajarse.

Adorne con un poco de paprika.

SOPA FRIA DE PEPINO Y ESPINACA

6–8 Porciones

2 cucharadas de mantequilla
1 cebolla, toscamente picada
1 papa grande, pelada y toscamente picada
1 poro con 2 pulgadas de la parte verde, cortado a la mitad, bien lavado y toscamente picado
3 tazas de caldo de pollo, ó 3 cucharaditas ó 3 cubitos de caldo de pollo disuelto en 3 tazas de agua caliente
Sal y pimienta al gusto
3 ramitas de perejil fresco (no cilantro)
2 pepinos, pelados, sin semillas y toscamente picados
1/2 manojo (aproximadamente 5 onzas) de espinacas, sumergidas en agua hirviendo 1–2 minutos y picadas
1/2 taza de yogurt, o crema ácida (si está disponible)
1 cucharada de mayonesa
1 aguacate (para adornar)
Jugo de 2 limones

En una sartén grande a fuego moderado derrita la mantequilla y agregue la cebolla, papa y poro. Tape y cueza a fuego lento durante 5 minutos o hasta que los ingredientes estén apenas suaves. Agregue el caldo de pollo, perejil, sal y pimienta y deje que hierva. Reduzca la flama y cueza a fuego lento 20 minutos. Deje que se enfríe y licúela hasta que esté tersa. Enfríe completamente en el refrigerador. Cuando esté fría agregue el resto de los ingredientes, excepto el aguacate, y hágala puré en la licuadora y enfríe de nuevo. Refrigere. Pruebe y ajuste el sazón.

Justo antes de servir, pele, deshuese y corte en cubitos el aguacate y mézclelo en la sopa.

"AVGOLEMONO"
SOPA GRIEGA DE HUEVO Y LIMON

6–8 Porciones

8 tazas de caldo de pollo colado, hecho en casa o enlatado
4 huevos
1 taza de champiñones rebanados
1 1/2 cucharadas de brandy
Jugo de 3 limones

En una sartén grande caliente el caldo, pero sin hervirlo.

Bata los huevos hasta que estén ligeros y espumosos, agregue el jugo de limón y bata un poco más. O ponga los huevos y el jugo de limón en la licuadora y licúelos durante 1 minuto. Agregue, poco a poco, 2 tazas del caldo a la mezcla de huevo y limón, incorporando completamente. Entonces agregue la mezcla de huevo, limón, caldo, al resto del caldo.

Sofría ligeramente los champiñones en un poco de mantequilla o aceite (no más que 1 cucharada).

Agregue los champiñones y el brandy a la sopa y recaliente hasta que esté bien caliente, pero no hirviendo.

Sirva de inmediato, o, si no la va utilizar al momento, no agregue los champiñones ni el brandy, y refrigere la sopa. Cuando esté lista para servirla, si la sopa ha sido refrigerada durante varios días o más, colóquela en la licuadora para volverla a mezclar, ya que la sopa tiende a separarse y asentarse. Luego recaliente y agregue los champiñones sofritos y el brandy justo antes de que esté muy caliente.

SOPA DE TOMATE A LA TORINESE

6 Porciones

1 litro de jugo de tomate
2 dientes de ajo, machacados
1/2 cucharadita de albahaca
1 cucharada de jugo de limón fresco
1 cucharada de azúcar
1 cucharadita de sal
1/4 cucharadita de pimienta blanca
2 cucharadas de mantequilla
2 cucharadas de harina
1 lata (6-onzas) de puré de tomate
4 tazas de caldo de pollo, ó 4 cucharaditas ó 4 cubitos de caldo de pollo disueltos en 4 tazas de agua caliente

En una olla grande sofría el ajo en un poco de aceite hasta que esté dorado. Agregue todos los demás ingredientes excepto el puré, harina y mantequilla. Tape y deje que llegue a hervir, reduzca la flama y cueza a fuego lento durante 30 minutos.

Mientras tanto, aparte en una sartén chica, derrita la mantequilla, agregue la harina y el puré de tomate y mezcle hasta que esté terso. Cuando la sopa se haya cocido a fuego lento durante 30 minutos, agregue un poco a la mezcla de harina, mantequilla y puré de tomate, aproximadamente 1 taza. Luego agregue esta mezcla y la sopa a la olla. Ponga a hervir, luego reduzca la flama y cueza a fuego lento 5 minutos, hasta que la sopa esté ligeramente espesa.

Esta sopa se puede servir caliente o completamente fría, y con o sin cubitos de pan tostado encima.

SOPA DE CALABACITA ESTILO ITALIANO

4–6 Porciones

3 libras de calabacitas, cortadas en trozos
1 cebolla grande, picada
2 tazas de consomé concentrado o caldo de pollo
2 tazas de agua
2 1/2 cucharaditas de sal
1 cucharadita de alabhaca seca
4 rebanadas de tocino crudo en trocitos
Pimienta blanca al gusto
Ajo en polvo al gusto

En una olla grande ponga a hervir todos los ingredientes durante 30 minutos. Hágalos puré en la licuadora.

Sirva caliente con queso parmesano fresco rallado encima y cubitos de pan de ajo tostado.

CREMA DE CEBOLLA ESTILO INGLES

6–8 Porciones

1 cebolla grande, rebanada
1/4 taza de mantequilla
6 tazas de consomé concentrado o caldo de pollo
1/4 cucharadita de pimienta blanca
1 1/4 tazas de crema espesa

Sofría la cebolla en la mantequilla a fuego moderado, meneando, por lo menos durante 10 minutos o hasta que la cebolla esté dorada.

Agregue el consomé y la pimienta y cueza tapado a fuego lento durante 30 minutos. Ponga esta mezcla en la licuadora y hágala puré, luego regresela a la olla. En otro recipiente, mezcle en la crema agregando un poco de sopa a la crema para hacerla más ligera y calentarla. Luego agregue todo a la sopa y caliente a fuego lento hasta que esté completamente caliente.

Sirva caliente, con o sin cubitos de pan tostado.

VICHYSSOISE

6–8 Porciones

4 poros, la parte blanca y 1 pulgada de la parte verde solamente, rebanados
1 cebolla mediana, rebanada
4 cucharadas de mantequilla
5 papas medianas, peladas y finamente rebanadas
1 litro de caldo de pollo, o agua
1 cucharada de sal
3 tazas de leche
2 tazas de crema espesa
Chives o cebollita cambray finamente picada

Dore los poros y la cebolla en la mantequilla, luego agregue las papas, caldo de pollo (o agua) y sal. Hierva durante 35–40 minutos. Hágalo puré en la licuadora. Enfríe bien, agregue la leche y la crema espesa y mezcle. Sazone al gusto. Espolvoreé con la cebollita cambray o chives picaditos, y sirva frío.

SOPA DE REPOLLO, COLIFLOR Y ROQUEFORT

8–10 Porciones

1 barra de mantequilla o margarina, o 1/2 taza
1 repollo grande, picado
1 coliflor mediana, toscamente picada
7 tazas de consomé concentrado o caldo de pollo, o cubitos de pollo
1 taza de crema espesa
1/4 taza de queso roquefort
Sal y pimienta al gusto
Cubitos de pan tostado

En una olla grande (con capacidad de 4 litros o más) sofría a fuego lento el repollo en la mantequilla derretida, sin tapar, hasta que esté suave, meneando ocasionalmente con una cuchara de madera. Agregue la coliflor y el caldo. Ponga a hervir a fuego alto. Reduzca la flama, tape y cueza a fuego lento durante 30–45 minutos, hasta que los vegetales estén suaves.

Mezcle la crema y el queso en la licuadora o procesador de alimentos hasta que estén tersos. Ponga aparte. Vierta la sopa en la licuadora, en partes si es necesario, y hágala puré. Regrese la sopa molida a la olla y mezcle en la crema y queso. Sirva caliente, adornada con cubitos de pan tostado.

GASPACHO EN LA LICUADORA

6–8 Porciones

(Esta sopa es excelente para personas a dieta)

1 tallo de apio (con hojas), cortado en trozos
1 zanahoria, cortada en trozos
1 cebolla mediana, cortada en trozos
1/2 pimiento morrón verde, cortado en trozos (puede agregar otras verduras o substituitlas según desee — como lechuga, calabacita, pepino pelado y sin semillas, etc.)
1 diente de ajo grande, machacado
1 cucharada de salsa inglesa (Lea & Perrins)
1 cucharada de aceite de oliva (opcional — si está a dieta, omitala)
1/2 cucharadita de albahaca
4–5 tazas de jugo de tomate
Sal y pimienta al gusto

Coloque todos los ingredientes en la licuadora (si el jugo de tomate no cabe, agregue el jugo restante en un recipiente grande con los demás ingredientes después de licuarlos), licúelos a velocidad media solo hasta que los vegetales estén toscamente molidos, no hechos puré. Refrigere por lo menos 1 hora antes de servir. Sirva con cubitos de pan de ajo tostado, si desea.

MINESTRONE DIETETICO

6–8 Porciones

4 dientes de ajo, machacados
1 cebolla grande, picada
5 cucharaditas o cubitos de caldo de res, disuelto en 5 tazas de agua caliente
1 litro de jugo de tomate
1 taza de agua
1/2 cucharadita de tomillo y 1/2 cucharadita de albahaca
2 calabacitas medianas, picadas
1/4 pieza de repollo chico, picado
2 zanahorias, picadas
1/2 taza de coditos
1–2 tallos de apio, con hojas, picados
Sal y pimienta al gusto
1 chorrito de endulzante artificial líquido, o 1/8 cucharadita de endulzante artificial en polvo

Se cuecen todos los ingredientes en una olla de presión, a 15 libras de presión, durante 8 minutos. Enfríe inmediatamente. Sirva caliente con un poco de queso parmesano espolvoreado encima, si desea.

SOPA DE CHAMPIÑONES A LA SUECA

8 Porciones

3 cucharadas de mantequilla
1 libra de champiñones frescos, con tallo, finamente rebanados
1/2 cucharadita de sal
1/4 cucharadita de pimienta blanca molida
1/3 taza de harina
2 litros de caldo de pollo o res (o cubitos)
1 taza de crema espesa
1 cucharadita de jugo de limón
1/4 taza de vino blanco seco
Sal y pimienta blanca molida al gusto

En una sartén gruesa con capacidad de 3–4 litros, derrita la mantequilla a fuego lento. Agregue los champiñones y sofríalos hasta que empiecen a soltar el jugo. Vierta el jugo en un recipiente de 2 tazas de capacidad y mantenga aparte. Mezcle 1/2 cucharadita de sal, 1/4 cucharadita de pimienta blanca y la harina en los champiñones drenados. Agregue caldo al jugo de los champiñones hasta completar 2 tazas. Combine en la mezcla de champiñones. Mezcle en las 6 tazas restantes de caldo. Cueza a fuego alto y menee hasta que espese la sopa, cerca de 5 minutos. Mezcle en la crema y jugo de limón. Agregue sal y pimienta blanca al gusto. Mezcle en el vino blanco. Sirva caliente.

SOPA DE AGUACATE CON AJO (ESPAÑA)

6 Porciones

2 cucharadas de mantequilla
1 cebolla mediana, picada
4 tazas de consomé concentrado de pollo
6 dientes de ajo grandes, picados (esto parece mucho, pero despues de cocinarlos con los otros ingredientes en el caldo el sabor es exquisito)
1 aguacata grande, maduro, pelado, deshuesado y picado
Jugo de 1 limón
1 1/2–2 tazas de yogurt
Sal y pimienta recién molida al gusto

En una olla grande sofría la cebolla en la mantequilla a fuego moderado hasta que esté suave. Agregue el consomé y el ajo, tape y ponga a cocer a fuego lento durante 30 minutos. Cuando esté ligeramente frío, hágalo puré en la licuadora, en partes, y cambielo a un tazón grande. Haga puré el aguacate y el jugo de limón y añadalo al consomé. Mezclelo en el yogurt y sazone con salk y pimienta al gusto.

Sirva caliente o fria adornada con cebollita cambray picadita encima.

Esta sopa puede guardarse por varios días en el refrigerador, pero no puede ser congelada para uso futuro.

Ensaladas

ENSALADA CAESAR

6 Porciones

Hay muchas recetas con algunas variaciones de esta maravillosa ensalada la cual se invento en México, pero esta es la favorita de Marcy:

16 filetes de anchoas
1/4 cucharadita de mostaza seca
3 cucharadas de salsa inglesa (Lea & Perrins)
2 cucharadas de aceite de oliva
2 cucharadas de vinagre de vino
Jugo de un limón
1 huevo cocido a fuego lento (es muy importante que el huevo sea cocido a fuego lento, que esté menos cocido que un huevo tibio pero no crudo)
3 lechugas lizas cortadas en cuadros de 1 pulgada cuadrada
1 diente de ajo grande, machacado
2 cucharadas de queso parmesano
1 1/2 tazas de cubitos de pan de ajo tostados

En un tazón chico, mezcle los 6 primeros ingredientes, machacando las anchoas con un tenedor.

Para preparar el huevo, se coloca en una olla chica cubriéndolo con agua fría, se deja calentar el agua a fuego lento hasta que hierva. En cuanto empieze a hervir se retira del fuego. Se tapa y se deja reposar 30 segundos en el agua caliente. Luego se saca del agua caliente e inmediatamente se enfría en agua. Cuando esté frío se procede de la siguiente manera:

En un tazón grande, mezcle el huevo con la lechuga antes de agregar los demás ingredientes.

Agregue los 6 ingredientes que mezcló con anterioridad en el tazón chico. Muela suficiente pimienta entera y añadala al gusto.

Utilizando un machacador o exprimidor de ajos, agregue el diente de ajo y mezcle bien en la lechuga. Agregue el queso parmesano y mezcle de nuevo.

Añada los cubitos de pan de ajo tostados a la ensalada justo antes de servirla. Una vez que haya servido la ensalada en los platos individuales, espolvoree con más queso parmesano.

ENSALADA DE ESPINACAS

8 Porciones, o 4–6 Porciones como Platillo Principal

6 cucharadas de vinagre de vino tinto
3 cucharadas de catsup
3 dientes de ajo, machacados
1 cucharada de salsa inglesa (Lea & Perrins)
2 cucharaditas de azúcar
1/4 cucharadita de paprika
1/2 cucharadita de mostaza seca
2/3 cucharadita de sal
1/4 cucharadita de pimienta recién molida
1/2 taza de aceite vegetal
4 manojos de espinacas, sin tallos, bien lavadas y secas
1/3 taza de queso parmesano fresco rallado, o queso Roquefort desmoronado
3 huevos duros, picaditos
1/4 libra de tocino dorado hasta que esté crujiente y desmoronado

Combine los primeros 10 ingredientes y mezcle por completo. Agregue el aceite poco a poco, batiendo constantemente (ésto se hace mejor si utiliza la licuadora). Coloque 1/2 taza del aderezo en un tazón grande para ensalada (la parte inferior debe ser más chica que la parte superior). Troze las hojas de espinaca y colóquelas sobre el aderezo, distribuya queso y huevo encima de la espinaca. Espolvoree con los trocitos de tocino y revuelva.

Sirva en platos enfríados en el refrigerador.

ENSALADA DE JICAMA, NARANJA Y CEBOLLA MORADA

12 Porciones

1 lechuga liza
1 1/2 libras de jícama, pelada y rebanada al grueso del papel
6 naranjas, peladas, sin semillas y finamente rebanadas
2 cebollas moradas, finamente rebanadas y separadas en aros
1/2 taza de aceite de oliva o vegetal
1/3 taza de jugo de limón fresco
3 cucharadas de vinagre de vino tinto
3 cucharadas de mermelada de naranja
1 cucharadita de sal
Pimienta recién molida

Coloque la lechuga en un tazón para ensalada grande. Encima alterne círculos de jícama, naranja y cebolla. Cubra y refrigere. (Puede preparase 3 horas antes).

En un frasco, combine el resto de los ingredientes y agite vigorosamente. Ponga encima de la ensalada y mezcle. Sirva inmediatamente.

NOTA: Si no está disponible la cebolla morada dulce, puede substituirla con rebanadas de cebollita cambray, incluyendo parte del tallo.

NOTA: Este aderezo es un aderezo agridulce excelente para cualquier ensalada de fruta.

MOLDE DE BETABEL Y PIÑA

8–10 Porciones

1 libra de betabel, cocido, pelado y cortado en cubitos (reserve el agua en que lo coció)
1 lata de 8 onzas de piña, desmenuzada y drenada (reserve el jugo)
1 paquete de 6 onzas de gelatina sabor limón
2 tazas de agua hirviendo
1/2 taza de apio, finamente picado
3 cucharadas de jugo de limón
1 pizca de sal

Disuelva la gelatina en el agua hirviendo y agregue 1 1/2 tazas del líquido del betabel y la piña, jugo de limón y sal. Enfríe hasta que esté parcialmente cuajado. Revuelva el betabel, piña y apio. Vierta en un molde de rosca de 6 1/2 tazas de capacidad y refrigere hasta que cuaje.

Desmolde encima de un platón cubierto de lechuga y coloque una salsera pequeña en el centro del platón, que contenga una salsa hecha de mayonesa rebajada con un poco de jugo de piña y jugo de limón.

ENSALADA COBB

6 Porciones como Platillo Principal u 8–10 como Ensalada

1 lechuga china, mediana, finamente picada
2 pechugas de pollo escalfadas, sin pellejo, deshuesadas y finamente picadas
6 huevos duros, finamente picados
6 rebanadas de tocino doradas y finamente picadas
6 onzas de queso roquefort, finamente desmoronado
3 tomates medianos, finamente picados
15 aceitunas negras, deshuesadas y rebanadas (opcional)
Aderezo Vinagreta (ver sección de Aderezos)

Divida la lechuga entre el número de platos a servir. Coloque 1 capa de de pollo, huevos, tocino, queso y tomate y, si incluye, espolvoree las aceitunas negras encima.

Enfríe bien antes de servir.

ENSALADA DE POLLO ESTILO NORTEAMERICANO

10–12 Porciones

1 pollo grande, cocido, deshuesado, sin pellejo, cortado en cubitos
1 manojo de apio, picado (sin las hojas)
1 cebolla grande, toscamente picada
1 frasco mediano de pepinillos dulces, toscamente picados
4 tazas de mayonesa (o al gusto) mezclada con 1–2 cucharaditas de jugo de limón
Sal y pimienta al gusto

Hierva el pollo y todas las víceras en agua suficiente para cubrirlo. Antes de que hierva agregue lo siguiente:

3 dientes de ajo grandes, picados o machacados
1 hoja de laurel grande (ó 3 ó 4 pequeñas)
1 tallo de apio, con hojas, cortado en 4 trozos
1 zanahoria, cortada en 5 ó 6 trozos
1 cebolla, cortada en cuartos
1/4 cucharadita de tomillo y 1/4 cucharadita de romero, desmoronados unas ramitas de perejil fresco (no cilantro)
1–2 cucharadas de sal

Cuando el pollo y las víceras estén suaves, retire del fuego y enfríe (reserve el caldo para consomé concentrado de pollo para sopas u otros usos). Cuando enfríe, retire el pellejo y descartelo. Deshuese y corte la carne en cubitos. Mezcle de manera envolvente en la mayonesa, rebajada con 3 cucharadas de jugo de los pepinillos, y todos los otros ingredientes. Enfríe completamente en el refrigerador antes de servir.

Aderezos para su Ensalada Verde Favorita

ADEREZO DE YOGURT Y PEPINO PARA ENSALADAS O PESCADOS Y MARISCOS FRIOS

Rinde 2 tazas

1 taza de yogurt
1 cucharadita de jugo de limón
1 diente de ajo, machacado
1 cucharada de perejil fresco, picadito
1 cucharada de cebolla cambray, picadita
1 cucharadita de mostaza (estilo dijón de preferencia)
1 taza de pepino, pelado, sin semillas y rallado (o rebanado, si lo utiliza para pescados o mariscos fríos)
1/4 cucharadita de azúcar
Sal y pimienta al gusto

Ponga todos los ingredientes en un tazón y mezcle bien, pero cuidadosamente, con un tenedor o batidor de alambre, y guarde en el refrigerador en un recipiente con tapa de rosca.

VINAGRETA ROQUEFORT

Rinde 2 tazas aproximadamente

1/4 a 1/2 cucharadita de sal
1/2 cucharadita de pimienta blanca
1/4 cucharadita de pimienta cayena
1/2 cucharadita de sal de apio
1/4 cucharadita de mostaza seca
2 cucharadas de vinagre de vino
4 cucharadas de jugo de tomate
1 diente de ajo, machacado
1/2 taza de aceite
1/2 cucharadita de azúcar
2/3 taza de queso roquefort, desmoronado

En un frasco combine todos los ingredientes, tape y agite vigorosamente. Guarde en el refrigerador.

ADEREZO DE MENTA A LA LIBANESA

Rinde 1 taza aproximadamente

Jugo de 3 ó 4 limones
1/2 cucharadita de azúcar
1/2 a 2/3 taza de aceite
3 ó 4 ramitos de menta fresca, picada
Sal y pimienta al gusto

En un frasco combine todos los ingredientes, tape y agite vigorosamente. Guarde en el refrigerador.

ADEREZO DIOSA VERDE

Rinde 3–4 tazas

(Use solo hojas crujientes de lechuga con este aderezo)

2 dientes de ajos, machacados
1 lata de anchoas
3 cucharadas de cebolla cambray, picada
1/2 aguacate, machacado
1 cucharada de jugo de limón
3 cucharadas de vinagre de vino
1 taza de mayonesa
1/3 taza de perejil picado (no cilantro)
1 taza de crema ácida (si no está disponible, se puede substituir con yogurt)
Sal y pimienta al gusto

Mezcle todo en la licuadora hasta que esté terso.

ADEREZO DE PEPINO BABARIAN

1/2 cebolla mediana
2 pepinos, pelados
1/2 taza de crema ácida espesa
1 cucharada de vinagre de vino tinto
1 cucharadita de perejil
1 cucharadita de eneldo (fresco de ser posible)
1 diente de ajo, machacado
1 1/2 cucharadita de sal
1 cucharadita de azúcar
1/2 cucharadita de pimienta negra recién molida

Muela en la licuadora la cebolla, pepino, perejil, eneldo y ajo con el vinagre de vino tinto, hasta que esté finamente molido pero no hecho puré. Agregue los demás ingredientes y licúe solamente hasta que esté mezclado. Refrigere por lo menos 4–5 horas antes de servir. (Puede substitutir la crema ácida con yogurt, pero si utiliza yogurt, no lo agregue a la licuadora, mézclelo de manera envolvente en el aderezo después de que todos los demás ingredientes hayan sido mezclados).

ADEREZO ORIENTAL

2/3 tazas de aceite de oliva o vegetal
1/4 taza de vinagre de vino
4 cucharadas de vino blanco (muy seco)
1 diente de ajo grande, machacado
1/2 cucharadita de jengibre fresco, picado o 1/2 cucharadita de jengibre en polvo, si no está disponible el fresco
1 cucharada de salsa soya
1/2 cucharadita de azúcar

En un frasco combine todos los ingredientes, tape y agite vigorosamente. Refrigere 2 horas por lo menos antes de usar.

VINAGRETA MARCY

(Si está a dieta, omita el aceite y utilice endulzante artificial en lugar del azúcar y tendrá un aderezo casi sin calorías)

2/3 taza de aceite (no use aceite de oliva a menos que sea muy fresco y fino)
1/3 taza de vinagre de vino
1/4 taza de vino blanco seco
Jugo de un limón
1 cucharadita de mostaza seca
1 cucharadita de ajo en polvo (o, 1 diente de ajo, machacado)
1/4 cucharadita de azúcar (pruebe y ajuste el sabor después de agregar la sal si desea un aderezo con el sabor un poco dulce)
1 cucharadita de salsa inglesa (Lea & Perrins)
Sal y pimienta recién molida al gusto

En un frasco combine todos los ingredientes, tape y agite vigorosamente. Refrigere varias horas antes de servir. (Si utiliza endulzante artificial, agreguelo al último, gota por gota hasta que obtenga el sabor dulce que desea).

ADEREZO CREMOSO DE MOSTAZA — FRANCIA

2 huevos duros
1 1/2 cucharaditas de sal
1 1/2 cucharaditas de azúcar
1 cucharadita de pimienta negra, toscamente molida
1 cucharada de perejil
1 cucharada de mostaza (estilo dijón si está disponible)
1 diente de ajo grande, machacado
1/2 taza de aceite de oliva (substituya por aceite vegetal si no tiene disponible un aceite de oliva muy fino, ligero y fresco)
5 cucharadas de crema espesa
1/4 taza de vinagre de vino

Mezcle todos los ingredientes en la licuadora hasta que estén tersos.

Aderezos para Sus Frutas Frescas Favoritas

ADEREZO DE MERMELADA AGRIDULCE

(Ver receta de Ensalada de Jícama, Naranja y Cebolla Morada en este Capítulo)

1/2 taza de aceite de oliva o vegetal (use aceite vegetal si no tiene dispobinle aceite de oliva muy fresco y fino)
1/3 taza de jugo de limón fresco
3 cucharadas de vinagre de vino tinto
3 cucharadas de mermelada de naranja
1 cucharadita de sal
Pimienta recién molida al gusto

En un frasco combine todos los ingredientes y agite vigorosamente.

SALSA DE CARDAMOMO PARA FRUTA FRESCA

1/2 taza de agua
1 taza de miel de abeja (orange blossom si está disponible)
1/4 cucharadita de semilla de cardamomo, pulverizada (si no están disponibles puede usar en polvo)
2 ramitos de hojas de menta fresca, grandes (no use menta seca) picadas
1/4 cucharadita de sal
1/2 taza de vino de oporto
1/8 taza de licor benedictino, si está disponible

En una sartén combine el agua, la miel, sal, cardamomo y menta y cueza a fuego lento por 2 minutos, para combinar los sabores. Deje que se enfríe a la temperatura ambiente y agregue el vino y el licor, revolviendo bien. Refrigere durante 1 hora antes de servir sobre cualquier combinación de las siguientes frutas: Melón, Aguacate, Manzana, Naranjas, Mango, Papaya.

ADEREZO GRANADINA

1 pinta de crema ácida
2/3 taza de azúcar pulverizada
2 cucharadas de granadina
2 onzas de queso crema Philadelphia
1/4 taza de mayonesa

Mezcle todos los ingredientes en la licuadora hasta que estén tersos. Refrigere.

ENSALADA DE POLLO A LA POLINESIA

8 Porciones

3 tazas de pechuga de pollo, cocida y cortada en cubitos
3/4 taza de mayonesa
1 taza de apio finamente picado
Sal y pimienta blanca al gusto

Mezcle el pollo con 1/4 taza de mayonesa. Enfríe en el refrigerador por una hora o más. Revuelva el pollo con el apio y la mayonesa restante. Sazone con sal y pimienta. Coloque una porción de ensalada en el centro de un plato cubierto de lechuga. Adorne los platos con puntas de espárragos, tiras de zanahorias, rebanadas de piña, huevo duro partido a la mitad, aceitunas negras, gajos de tomate. Cubra la ensalada de pollo con aderezo de ron (ver receta abajo) justo antes de servir.

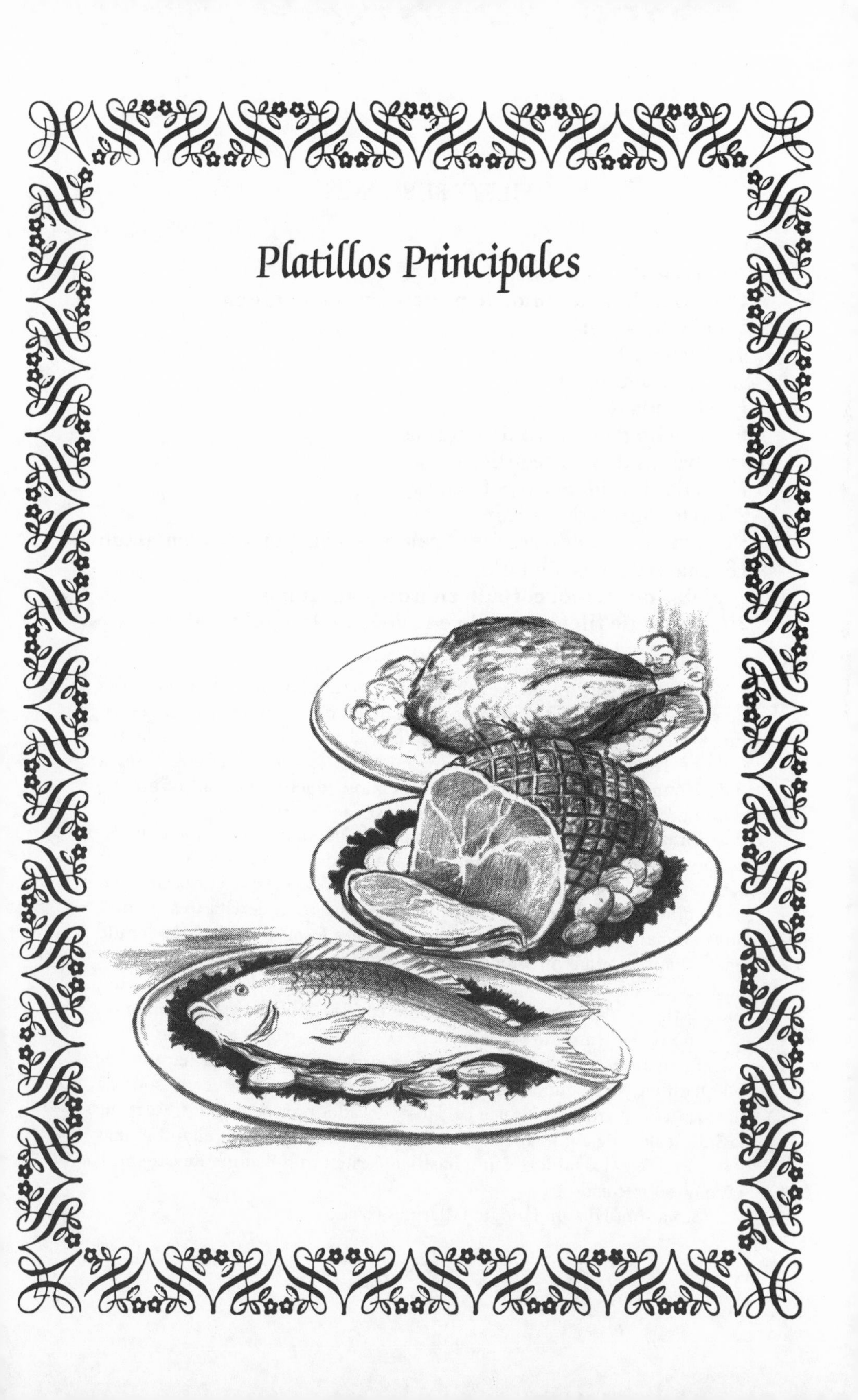

Platillos Principales

FILETE BORGOÑES

6 Porciones

$2^1/_2$ tazas de salsa café
$1^1/_2$ tazas de vino tinto, de preferencia de borgoña
1 hoja de laurel
$^1/_2$ cucharadita de tomillo
Sal y pimienta al gusto
1 rebanada de limón
1 pedacito de cáscara de naranja
$1^1/_2$ barras de mantequilla sin sal
18 cebollitas blancas, peladas
2 cucharaditas de azúcar
$^1/_4$ taza de caldo de res (ver "caldos, o consomés"), o enlatado
18 champiñones sin tallo
4 piezas de tocino, cortado en trozos pequeños
$2^1/_2$ libras de filete, cortado en cubos de $1^1/_4$ pulgada

Ponga a que llegue a hervir el vino, hoja de laurel, tomillo, 1 cucharadita de sal, 1 cucharadita de pimienta, 1 rebanada de limón, la cáscara de naranja, una vez hirviendo cueza a fuego lento hasta que se reduzca a la medida de 1 taza. Cuele esté líquido y mézclelo con la salsa café. Nuevamente haga que llegue a hervir y cueza a fuego lento, cuidadosamente, durante 25–30 minutos. Tape con un plástico y apártelo.

En una sartén caliente 4 cucharadas de mantequilla. Agregue la cebolla y sofríala a fuego moderado, espolvoreando con azúcar para glasear y dorar las cebollitas. Agregue el caldo de res, tápelas, y cueza a vapor hasta que estén tiernas pero crujientes. En otra sartén derrita tres cucharadas de mantequilla, agregue los champiñones y sofría a fuego moderado hasta que estén ligeramente dorados. Retire los champiñones, agregue 2 cucharadas de mantequilla a la sartén y sofría el tocino hasta que esté dorado y rizado. Retire, drene y combine con las cebollas y champiñones, tape con papel aluminio y apártelo.

Justo antes de servir, en una sartén gruesa caliente 5 cucharadas de mantequilla y agregue unos cuantos trozos de filete cada vez, y sofría a fuego alto hasta que estén bien cocidos y dorados por todos lados. Agregue la salsa café y deje que apenas hierva, agregue las cebollas, champiñones y tocino. Póngalos a fuego lento hasta que estén completamente calientes, pero no sobrecocidos.

Sirva sobre o a un lado de tallarines cocidos.

POLLO A LA CAZADORA

6–8 Porciones

1 pollo para freír de $2^1/_2$–3 libras cortado en piezas ó 3 pechugas de pollo grandes, cortadas en mitades y deshuesadas
2 pimientos morrones verdes, medianos cortados en cuadros de 1 pulgada
2 cebollas medianas, cortadas en cuadros de 1 pulgada
16 champiñones frescos, en rebanadas gruesas (opcional)
$^3/_4$ libra de salchicha italiana, desmoronada
3 tazas, o más, de salsa para espagueti sin carne, según desee (ver receta en la sección de "Salsas")
Sal y pimienta al gusto
$^1/_2$ taza de vino tinto seco, o más al gusto
$^1/_4$ taza de aceite vegetal
$^1/_2$ barra de mantequilla sin sal (se puede usar mantequilla con sal, sin embargo es mejor la mantequilla sin sal)

Sofría las piezas de pollo y la salchicha en la mantequilla y el aceite hasta que estén doradas por ambos lados y la salchicha esté completamente cocida. Agregue el pimiento morrón, cebolla, champiñones frescos y la sal y pimienta al gusto. Cubra todo con la salsa de espagueti y cueza a fuego lento sin tapar, agregando el vino tinto a medida que sea necesario, hasta que el pollo esté suave y las verduras cocidas, aproximadamente 15 minutos.

Sirva acompañado con espagueti cocido al dente y espolvoree con queso parmesano al gusto.

La salsa para esta receta y otras recetas italianas se puede preparar en grandes cantidades y guardar indefinidamente en el congelador en un recipiente de plástico, herméticamente cerrado.

POLLO O PAVO TETRAZZINI

6–8 Porciones

2 1/2 tazas de champiñones frescos, finamente rebanados
4–5 tazas de sobrantes de pollo o pavo, cortado en trozos pequeños, usando carne oscura o blanca, o solo blanca.
1/4 libra de rebanadas de jamón cocido, cortado en tiras estilo juliana
1/2 barra de mantequilla sin sal
1 taza de crema espesa
2 cucharadas de harina
2 tazas de caldo de pollo, de consomé concentrado de pollo cocido, o enlatado
Sal y pimienta al gusto
1 pizca de nuez moscada, o al gusto
1/4 taza de jeréz dulce
1/3–1/2 taza de queso parmesano fresco
1/2–3/4 libra de espagueti, cocido al dente

En una sartén grande derrita la mantequilla y mezcle en la harina. Gradualmente mezcle en las 2 tazas de caldo de pollo y siga cocinando a fuego lento, meneando, hasta que esté terso y espeso. Mezcle en 1 taza de crema espesa y en el 1/4 taza de jeréz dulce, sal, pimienta y nuez moscada y cueza a fuego lento 10 minutos más. Sofría en un poco de mantequilla los champiñones rebanados y apártelos. Cueza rápidamente el espagueti con agua hirviendo con sal, justo hasta que esté suave. Drene y mantenga caliente.

Agregue la mitad de la salsa cocida a los champiñones y mezcle con el espagueti cocido. Vierta la mezcla de espagueti en un platón bien engrasado con mantequilla y lo suficientemente grande para acomodar todo. Agregue la otra mitad de la salsa al jamón y pollo y póngalos al fuego hasta que estén calientes. Haga un hueco en el centro de la mezcla de espagueti y vierta la salsa con jamón y pollo en el centro. Espolvoree el queso parmesano encima y hornee a fuego moderado (350°F.) durante 10 minutos, o hasta que la parte superior esté ligeramente dorada. Sirva enseguida.

BERENJENAS A LA PARMESANA

4 Porciones

1½ libras de berenjenas, sin cáscara y cortadas en rebanadas de 1/2 pulgada, a lo largo
Sal
Harina
½ taza de aceite de oliva
2 tazas de salsa para espagueti sin carne (ver "Salsas")
8 onzas de queso Mozzarella (si no está disponible, el queso asadero, manchego o Monterrey Jack o cualquier otro queso blanco, de sabor suave, dará resultados similares)
½ taza de queso parmesano fresco

Precaliente el horno a 400°F. Engrase el fondo y los lados de una charola para hornear de 1½–2 litros de capacidad.

Espolvoree con sal ambos lados de las rebanadas de berenjena y extiéndalas en una sola capa, sobre toallas de papel, durante 20 minutos (la sal sacará el exceso de humedad). Seque con toallas de papel. Pase cada rebanada por harina y sacuda el exceso. En una sartén gruesa, ponga al fuego un poco de aceite hasta que esté caliente, y dore las berenjenas por ambos lados, pocas cada vez, añadiendo aceite a medida que sea necesario, y trabajando rápidamente. Escurra las rebanadas doradas sobre toallas de papel.

En una charola para hornear, vierta 1/4 aproximadamente de la salsa de espagueti y extienda encima, en una sola capa, la mitad de las berenjenas rebanadas. Cubralas con queso parmesano rallado. Repita con una capa de salsa, luego el resto de las berenjenas, luego queso mozzarella y parmesano. Cubra esta segunda capa con salsa y un poco más de mozzarella y parmesano.

Cubra la charola con papel aluminio bien ajustado y hornee en el centro del horno durante 20 minutos. Retire el papel aluminio y hornee sin tapar por 15 minutos más.

Para reducir las calorías de este platillo, ponga a vapor las rebanadas de berenjenas hasta que estén suaves, en lugar de freírlas, omita la harina y el aceite de oliva, y substituya el queso por queso cottage normal o desgrasado, en el cual se ha mezclado 1 huevo bien batido por el mozzarella.

HUACHINANGO ESTILO VERACRUZ

6 Porciones

2 libras de filete de huachinango
$^{1}/_{4}$ taza de aceite de oliva, muy fino y fresco (si no está disponible, use aceite vegetal)
2 cebollas grandes, toscamente picadas
2 dientes de ajo grandes, machacados
4 tomates muy grandes, pelados y toscamente picados
1 cucharada de perejil fresco, picadito (no cilantro)
2 cucharadas de vinagre de vino tinto
$^{1}/_{2}$ taza de cerveza
$^{1}/_{2}$ taza de aceitunas verdes, rebanadas
$^{1}/_{2}$ taza de alcaparras
$^{1}/_{2}$ taza de chiles jalapeños en escabeche, picados (o, si prefiere, pimientos morrones verdes)
1 hoja de laurel grande, ó 2 chicas
$^{1}/_{2}$ cucharadita de tomillo
$^{1}/_{2}$ cucharadita de mejorana
Sal y pimienta al gusto

Sofría los filetes en el aceite de oliva hasta que estén ligeramente dorados en ambos lados. Retírelos y apártelos, manteniéndolos calientes en un platón. Sofría el ajo y la cebolla hasta que estén dorados. Agregue los tomates, chiles o pimientos morrones, hoja de laurel, perejil, tomillo, mejorana y sal y pimienta al gusto, y la cerveza y vinagre. Cueza a fuego lento la salsa durante 10 minutos aproximadamente, hasta que los tomates, chiles (o pimientos) y cebollas estén cocidos. Agregue las aceitunas verdes y alcaparras y cueza un minuto más, a fuego muy lento.

Vierta esta salsa sobre los filetes de huachinango y sirva.

COQ AU VIN

6 Porciones

2 pollos para freír, cortado en piezas
Harina sazonada con sal y pimienta, y 1/2 cucharadita de jengibre en polvo
1 cucharadita de jengibre fresco, machacado, ó 2 cucharaditas de jengibre en polvo
$^{1}/_{2}$ taza de mantequilla
12 cebollitas blancas
2 dientes de ajo, machacados
1 hoja de laurel grande, ó 2 chicas
1 tallo de apio grande, incluyendo las hojas
1 taza de champiñones frescos, a la mitad o en cuartos
2 cucharadas de perejil, picado (no cilantro)
$^{1}/_{2}$ cucharadita de romero
$^{1}/_{2}$ cucharadita de mejorana
3 tazas de vino tinto seco

Limpie el pollo, córtelo en piezas como para freír y sacudalo dentro de una bolsa que contenga la harina sazonada. Asegúrese de que las piezas estén bien cubiertas. En una sartén grande o en una freidora eléctrica, derrita la mantequilla. Sacuda el exceso de harina a las piezas de pollo y dórelas en la mantequilla, por todos lados. Agregue las cebollas, ajo, hoja de laurel quebrada, perejil, apio, champiñones, jengibre, romero y mejorana. Cueza a fuego lento por 10 minutos.

Retire toda la mezcla a una caserola grande, vierta encima el vino tinto, cubra ajustadamente y cueza en la estufa a fuego muy lento, durante 1 a $1^{1}/_{2}$ horas, agregue más vino según sea necesario.

POTAJE DE POLLO SUPREMO

8 Porciones

3 tazas de pechuga de pollo (2 pechugas enteras grandes) escalfadas y cortadas en cubos
1/4 libra de jamón cocido, cortado en cubos
2 tazas de consomé concentrado de pollo (no use caldo o consomé porque no son lo suficientemente ricos)
1/4 cucharadita de mejorana
1/4 cucharadita de tomillo
2 zanahorias medianas, cocidas y cortadas en cubos
2/3–3/4 taza de chicharos frescos o congelados, cocidos
1 taza de champiñones frescos, rebanados
1/2 cebolla mediana, picada, ó 4 cebollas cambray picadas
1 papa mediana, cocida y cortada en cubos
1 1/2 tazas de crema
3 cucharadas de harina
1/4 taza de jeréz (semidulce o dulce)
1/2 barra de mantequilla
1/2 taza de queso parmesano
Sal y pimienta al gusto

Sofría la cebolla y champiñones en la mantequilla hasta que estén tiernos. Añada el pollo y apague el fuego. Agregue un poco de consomé a la harina y mezcle hasta que esté bien integrado y terso. Agregue poco a poco el resto del consomé hasta que se termine. Caliente la mezcla en una sartén pequeña. Si la mezcla parece muy espesa, agregue un poco de agua, pero solo si es necesario. Agregue la crema, sazonadores, queso parmesano y jeréz. Cuando la salsa esté espesa y tersa, agregue todos los demás ingredientes.

Vierta en un platón profundo para hornear, o en platones individuales tipo para souffle y cubra con pasta básica (ver receta en la sección de "Panes y Pastas"). Hornee a 425°F. durante 25–30 minutos, hasta que la cubierta esté dorada. Enfrie a que todo esté tibio antes de servir. (Si utiliza platos individuales, el tiempo de cocción será de 5 minutos menos).

ROLLOS DE RES

6 Porciones

6 milanesas de res grandes
Sal y pimienta recién molida al gusto
6 cucharaditas de mostaza preparada
1 libra de salchicha de puerco(puede usar chorizo Mexicano de sabor suave, quitando la tripa y desbaratando, o carne molida de ternera o res)
1 diente de ajo grande, machacado
1 cebolla grande, finamente picada
1/2 cucharadita de tomillo
1 hoja de laurel grande, ó 2 chicas
1/4 taza de cognac (puede substituirlo por un brandy menos caro)
2 tomates, pelados y picados
1/2 taza de caldo de res
2/3 taza de vino tinto seco
1 huevo, batido
3–4 rebanadas de pan, desmoronado
1/2 taza de leche

Extienda las milanesas en una superficie plana y espolvoreelas ligeramente con sal y pimienta. Unte cada milanesa con un poco de mostaza.

En un poco de aceite sofría el ajo y la cebolla hasta que estén dorados. Retire del fuego y agregue el tomillo, salchicha, cognac, huevo, leche y pan desmoronado. Un poco de sal y pimienta (pero no pruebe si está usando salchicha cruda). Mezcle bien. Extienda equitativamente la mezcla, sobre 3/4 de longitud de cada milanesa, empezando por la parte más ancha. Enrollelas y sujételas con un palillo de dientes. Espolvoree las milanesas enrolladas con un poco de harina sazonada con sal y pimienta. En la sartén, dore los rollos en un poco de aceite, baje la flama, agregue el caldo, tomates, vino tinto y hoja de laurel. Tape y cueza a fuego lento, hasta que estén suaves al probarlas con un tenedor, aproximadamente 1–1 1/2 horas. Cuando termine de cocerlas, utilize el resto de los jugos en la sartén, como salsa para vertir encima de los rollos. Si se seca la sartén, es que está demasiado alto el fuego. Reduzca la flama y agregue más vino tinto a medida que sea necesario.

CAMARONES RELLENOS AL HORNO

8–12 Porciones

24 camarones gigantes o colosales
4 1/2 tazas de cebolla picada (de preferencia cebolla morada si está disponible)
4 1/2 tazas de pimiento morrón verde, picado
1 1/2 libras de filete de pescado blanco, de sabor muy suave (de preferencia trucha) cortado en trozos de 1 pulgada
4 1/2 tazas de cubitos de pan tostado (o pan tostado cortado en piezas)
1 taza más 2 cucharadas de vino blanco
3 tazas de apio, picado
1/3 taza de mayonesa
6 dientes de ajo, machacados
2 barras de mantequilla, suavizada
Sal y pimienta blanca al gusto (aproximadamente 1 cucharadita de sal y
1/2 cucharadita de pimienta)

Precaliente el horno a 400°F.

Retire la cáscara del camarón, dejando la parte de la cola intacta. Desvene y corte el camarón en la curva interior, a lo largo. Ponga aparte.

En un recipiente a prueba de fuego, cueza a vapor el pimiento morrón verde, cebolla, pescado y apio (de preferencia en una rejilla pequeña para cocer al vapor) sobre agua hirviendo a fuego lento, durante 10 minutos (si utiliza un tazón, cúbralo con papel aluminio o plástico).

En un tazón, rocié los cubos de pan con el vino y mézclelos. Déjelos suavizar durante 10 minutos por lo menos.

En el procesador de alimentos, con la cuchilla de acero, combine los vegetales y el pescado cocidos al vapor y la mezcla de pan con la mayonesa y sal. Muela hasta que estén moderadamente molidos, no hechos puré.

En un tazón pequeño combine la mantequilla suavizada, ajo y pimienta blanca y sal al gusto.

Rellene cada camarón con una cucharadita repleta de la mezcla de vegetales, torciendo la cola del camarón encima. En una charola para hornear, acomode los camarones en una sola capa, salpíquelos con la mantequilla al ajo, y horneelos en el centro del horno durante 15 minutos (en altitudes mayores de 5000 pies hornee 20 minutos o más) hasta que estén flexibles al tacto.

MARISCADA CRIOLLA

4–6 Porciones

1/2 libra de filete de pescado blanco, de sabor suave (muy fresco), crudo, cortado en trozos de 1 pulgada
1/2 libra de camarón, de cualquier tamaño, crudo, sin cáscara y desvenado
1/4 taza de harina
1 taza de agua caliente
1 lata de puré de tomate (8 onzas)
2/3 taza de cebollitas cambray picadas y parte de las puntas
1/4 taza de perejil, picado (no cilantro)
2/3 taza de pimiento morrón verde, picado
4 dientes de ajo, machacados
1 cucharada de aceite vegetal
2 hojas de laurel grandes, o 4 chicas
1/2 cucharadita de tomillo, desmoronado
1 pizca de pimienta de cayena
1 rebanada de limón

Sofría el ajo en aceite hasta que esté dorado pero no oscuro. Agregue el agua, tomillo, hojas de laurel, rebanada de limón, pimienta de cayena y vegetales. Cueza a fuego lento hasta que estén suaves (aproximadamente 10 minutos). Haga una pasta de la harina y puré de tomate. Cuando los vegetales estén listos Agregue el agua caliente, una cucharada a la vez, a la mezcla de tomate hasta que esté lo suficientemente diluida para vertir. Luego agregue la mezcla de tomate a los vegetales y espese, meneando constantemente. Agregue el pescado y camarón, y continue cociendo a fuego muy lento, solo hasta que el camarón esté rosa y el pescado blanco (no sobrecueza). Retire las hojas de laurel y sirva caliente sobre arroz caliente.

PECHUGAS DE POLLO JACQUELINE

6 Porciones

6 pechugas de pollo chicas, ó 6 mitades grandes, deshuesadas, sin piel y ligeramente aplanadas
8 cucharadas de mantequilla
1/4 taza de almendras rebanadas (omitalas si no están disponibles)
Harina
Sal y pimienta
3/4 taza de consomé concentrado o caldo de pollo
3/4 taza de vino oporto
1 1/2 taza de crema ligera
3 manzanas ácidas, peladas, descorazonadas y cortadas en octavos

En una sartén gruesa derrita 2 cucharadas de mantequilla a fuego moderado. Agregue las almendras y menee hasta que estén doradas oscuro, 4 minutos aproximadamente. Manténgalas aparte. (Debe omitir esté paso en caso de que las almendras no estén disponibles).

Espolvoree sal y pimienta en la harina y mezcle bien. Revuelva el pollo en la harina, sacudiendo el exceso. En una sartén gruesa derrita 4 cucharadas de mantequilla a fuego modreado. Agregue el pollo y cueza hasta que esté flexible al tacto y ligeramente dorado, 4 minutos por cada lado aproximadamente. Transfiera a un platón caliente y coloque en un lugar caliente.

Agregue el consomé o caldo al oporto y vierta en la misma sartén, hierva hasta que se reduzca a la mitad, sacando cualquier resto de pechuga dorada. Agregue la crema y hierva hasta que adquiera una consistencia de salsa, meneando de vez en cuando.

Mientras tanto, en una sartén gruesa derrita las 2 cucharadas restantes de mantequilla a fuego moderado. Agregue las manzanas y cueza hasta que estén suaves, meneando con frecuencia, durante 5 ó 6 minutos. Coloque una pechuga de pollo y 4 rebanadas de manzana en cada plato. Pruebe la salsa y sazone si es necesario. Viertala sobre el pollo. Espolvoree con almendras, si las usa, y sirva.

ROLATINES DE POLLO

6 Porciones

3 pechugas de pollo, enteras, a la mitad, sin piel, deshuesadas y aplanadas hasta que estén delgadas
6 rebanadas de jamón prosciutto (puede substituirse con jamón cocido)
6 rebanadas de queso tipo mozzarella (puede substituirse con queso manchego o asadero) o gruyere
Ajo en polvo
6 cucharadas de pan, finamente desmoronado
1 cucharadita de sazonador de hierbas
Sal y pimienta al gusto
6 cucharadas de vino blanco seco
6 cucharadas de mantequilla

Precaliente el horno a 350°F. Engrase ligeramente una charola para hornear poco profunda, solo lo suficientemente grande para acomodar los 6 rolatines.

Espolvoree con ajo en polvo cada pieza de pollo. Coloque una rebanada de jamón y una de queso en cada pieza. Agregue el sazonador de hierbas, sal y pimienta al pan. Espolvoree el pan en proporciones iguales sobre cada rebanada de queso. Enrollelos, empezando con la punta más ancha de la pechuga, asegúrelas con palillos de dientes. Colóquelas en la charola para hornear.

Combine el vino blanco y mantequilla y caliente un poco, hasta que se derrita la mantequilla. Vierta encima del pollo y espolvoree con un poco de sal. Hornee 30–35 minutos aproximadamente en altitudes de 5000 pies o más, y de 20–25 minutos en altitudes más bajas.

STROGANOFF ESTILO NORTEAMERICANO

6–8 Porciones

2 libras de carne de res, sirloin o lomo, rebanado en tiras diagonales muy delgadas, (aproximadamente de 4 pulgadas de largo por 1/2–1 pulgada de ancho)
1 cebolla grande, rebanada y separada en aros
1 libra de champiñones frescos, rebanados
1/2 taza de mantequilla
Sal y pimienta al gusto
2 latas de crema de champiñones, mezclados con 1/2 lata de agua
1 1/2 cucharaditas de orégano
1 1/2 cucharadas de salsa inglesa (Lea & Perrins)
1 taza de crema ácida (o más, al gusto, si desea), o 1 taza de queso cottage y 2/3 a 1 taza de yogurt

Sofría en mantequilla los champiñones y la cebolla hasta que estén suaves. Mantenga aparte. En una sartén muy caliente sofría las tiras de carne hasta que estén doradas (no sobrecueza ya que la carne se cocerá más en la salsa). Cueza a fuego lento, agregue la crema de champiñones y agua, orégano, salsa inglesa, y los champiñones y cebolla dorados. Cueza a fuego lento durante uno o dos minutos, luego agregue la crema ácida o el queso cottage o yogurt, y sal y pimienta al gusto. Apague la flama y cubra para calentar los últimos ingredientes. Si es necesario calentar un poco, sea muy cuidadosa al hacerlo — no permita que hierva.

Sirva sobre tallarines cocidos, o, si no están disponibles, sobre arroz o puré de papa, sin embargo es mucho mejor con los tallarines.

Si desea puede preparar esté platillo con carne molida de primera calidad, sin grasa, en lugar de las tiras de res.

Si desea un sabor un poco diferente, agregue un poco de puré o pasta de tomate (no más de 1 ó 2 cucharadas) solo para darle un ligero sabor y color rosa.

CHICKEN COUNTRY CAPTAIN

8 Porciones

2 pollos para freír, aproximadamente de 2 1/2 libras cada uno, cortados en piezas
Sal y pimienta
2–3 cucharadas de mantequilla
1 cebolla grande, finamente picada
1 1/2 tazas de arroz de grano grande (long grain)
2 pimientos morrones verdes, sin semillas y toscamente picados
2 dientes de ajo grandes, picaditos
1/2 taza de pasas de uva
3 cucharaditas de curry en polvo
2 tomates grandes, pelados y picados
1 taza de puré de tomate
1 1/4 tazas de caldo de pollo, hecho en casa o enlatado
3/4 cucharaditas de tomillo seco, desmoronado
4 cucharadas de chutney (si no está disponible use la misma cantidad de mermelada de durazno o de naranja)
1/2 tazas de almendras a la mitad y rebanadas en tiritas a lo largo, blanqueadas mondando

Corte los pollos en piezas, excluyendo los espinazos, pescuezos y menudencias. Espolvoree ligeramente con sal y pimienta. En una sartén grande para freír dore las piezas de pollo por todos lados, en la mantequilla caliente, unas cuantas a la vez. Retire las piezas de pollo y manténgalas aparte. En la misma sartén mezcle la cebolla y arroz y cueza a fuego moderado hasta que la cebolla esté suave y ligeramente dorada. Mezcle en los pimientos morrones verdes, ajo, pasas de uva, chutney y curry. Continúe cociendo, meneando constantemente, durante 3–4 minutos. Agregue los tomates y puré, caldo y tomillo, meneando para mezclarlo en los pedacitos dorados de la sartén. Transfiera a un molde ancho con capacidad de 4 litros y acomode el pollo sobre el arroz, de ser posible en una sola capa, virtiendo cualquier jugo acumulado.

Tape el molde y hornee a 375°F. durante 50 minutos, hasta que el pollo esté suave. Retire las piezas de pollo y mezcle bien el arroz; coloque las piezas de pollo encima del arroz y espolvoree con las almendras. Continue horneando, sin tapar durante 15 minutos más, hasta que el pollo y las almendras estén doradas.

Si sobra, esté platillo se mantiene bien para recalentarse después.

CARBONADES FLAMANDE

8 Porciones

- **½ libra de tocino con poca grasa, cortado en cubos**
- **1 cucharada de sal y 4 pizcas de pimienta recién molida**
- **4 cucharadas de mantequilla**
- **5–6 cebollas grandes, finamente rebanadas**
- **3 libras de chuck o retazo de res sin grasa, deshuesado, cortado en trozos de 2 pulgadas**
- **1 hoja de laurel**
- **1 cucharadita de ajo, picadito**
- **1 cucharada de vinagre**
- **1½ cucharaditas de azúcar**
- **1 cucharadita de tomillo seco, desmoronado**
- **2 cucharadas de perejil fresco, finamente picado**
- **3 cucharadas de harina**
- **2 botellas de cerveza oscura (12 onzas cada una)**
- **1 cucharada de mostaza preparada, untada en uno de los lados de**
- **2 rebanadas de pan**

Caliente el horno a 325°F. Engrase una charola grande con tapa, para hornear.

En una sartén gruesa, cueza el tocino hasta que haya soltado la mayor parte de la grasa. Transfiera las piezas a la charola. Retire la grasa, de la sartén pero deje 3 ó 4 cucharadas. Agregue la mantequilla y ponga al fuego hasta que esté caliente pero no humeante. Dore las cebollas, retírelas y póngalas aparte. Espolvoree los cubos de carne con la harina sazonada con sal y pimienta, sacuda el exceso y dorelos en la sartén. Agregue el tomillo, ajo, azúcar, hoja de laurel quebrada en pedacitos, el perejil y vinagre, y menee hasta que esté bien mezclado. Transfiera la carne a la charola. Cubra con la cebolla dorada. Coloque las rebanadas de pan, con el lado de la mostaza hacia abajo, encima de las cebollas. Vierta la cerveza sobre el pan. Ponga a que hierva la charola en la flama de la estufa, luego transfiera al horno caliente, tape y hornee durante 45 minutos. Mezcle el pan en la carne y cebollas y continue horneando durante 1½ horas, o hasta que la carne esté suave. Después de una hora, pruebe de vez en cuando.

Sirva con papas cocidas o tallarines.

PESCADO CON RELLENO DE JAIBA

6 Porciones

Elija cualquier tipo de pescado pleuronecto de sabor suave, con pocas espinas, tales como huachinango o lenguado, aumente el tamaño del estómago del pescado después de haberlo abierto, limpiado y destripado, para acomodar el siguiente relleno. Este relleno también puede usarse encima de cualquier filete deshuesado de cualquier pescado blanco, de sabor suave. También es excelente encima de filetes de pechuga de pollo, o rebanadas de pechuga de pavo.

Precaliente el horno a 375°F. elija una charola de hornear lo suficientemente grande para acomodar un pescado, o varios, o los filetes en una sola capa, y engrase con mantequilla la charola. Seque completamente el interior del pescado o pescados con toallas de papel.

1/2 a 3/4 libra de pulpa de jaiba (también la imitación de pulpa de jaiba sirve muy bien)
1/2 taza de vino blanco seco
1/3 taza de mantequilla
2 cucharadas de apio, finamente picado
2 cucharadas de pimientos morrones verdes, finamente picados
2 cucharadas de cebolla, finamente picada
1 cucharada de chives, o, si no está disponible, use cebollita cambray
1 diente de ajo grande ó 2 chicos, picadito
1 cucharada de salsa inglesa (Lea & Perrins)
1 cucharada de mostaza preparada
1/2 cucharadita de sal
Varias pizcas de pimienta negra
1 huevo, bien batido
1 1/2 tazas de pan, finamente desmoronado
1 cucharadita de perejil, picado
1 taza de salsa bechamel (ver sección de "Salsas")

En mantequilla derretida, sofría el apio, pimiento morrón verde, cebolla y ajo hasta que estén dorado oscuro. Agregue la salsa bechamel. Mezcle la pulpa de jaiba con la salsa inglesa, mostaza, sal y pimienta, huevo batido y pan desmoronado. Agregue la mezcla de jaiba a la salsa y vegetales, mezclando muy bien. Ponga a cucharadas en el pescado preparado, o, si utiliza filetes, amontone el relleno encima de cada filete. Colóquelos en el plato preparado, tape el pescado, o cada pescado o filete con una poca de mantequilla, vierta el vino con sumo cuidado en el fondo del platón sin mojar los pescados. Hornee sin tapar durante 20–30 minutos aproximadamente para un pescado de 4 libras, o 15–20 minutos para los pescados pequeños rellenos individualmente, o durante 15 minutos para los filetes cubiertos de relleno. Use el vino blanco como salsa para bañar, poniendo a cucharadas sobre el pescado de vez en cuando, según sea necesario. Pruebe cada pescado antes de sacarlos del horno. Si ya está listo, el pescado se deshace fácilmente con el tenedor.

Adorne con rebanadas de limón y ramitos de perejil.

CORDERO AL CURRY

6 Porciones

(Esta receta parece complicada debido a la larga lista de ingredientes, pero en realidad es muy sencilla de preparar y hace una salsa al curry soberbia).

1/2 barra de mantequilla
3 cebollas medianas, picaditas
2 dientes de ajo, machacados
2 zanahorias, picaditas
1 tallo de apio, picadito
1/2 pimiento morrón verde, sin semillas y picadito
2 cucharadas de perejil, picadito
2 cucharadas de harina
1 1/2 tazas de caldo de pollo o consomé en polvo
1/2 taza de vino tinto o blanco, seco
1/2 taza de tomate fresco, sin cáscara y picado
1/2 taza de leche de coco (puede substituirse por leche normal)
1/4 taza de jugo de limón
3 cucharadas de chutney (o mermelada de naranja, o de chabacano, o de durazno)
2 1/2 cucharadas de azúcar mascabado
2 cucharadas de pasa güeras (pueden substituirse con pasas oscuras) bouquet garni (2 clavos de olor enteros y 1 hoja de laurel chica, amarrados en una tela)
3 cucharaditas de curry en polvo humedecido con un poco de agua fría para mezclar
2 cucharaditas de jengibre fresco, molido (ó 4 cucharaditas de jengibre en polvo, si no está disponible)
1/2 cucharadita de canela
2 cucharaditas de curcuma
2 cucharaditas de cilantro
4 semillas de cardamomo, machadadas
1/8 cucharadita de nuez moscada
1/4 cucharadita de pimienta cayena (o 1/2 cucharadita de pimienta blanca si no está disponible)
4 tazas de cubos de cordero cocido (los cubos no deben ser más grandes de 1 pulgada) mondar toda la grasa
2 manzanas ácidas grandes, peladas, descorazonadas y en cubos
1/2 taza de yogurt natural

En una sartén gruesa con capacidad de 5 litros, derrita la mantequilla a fuego medio. Agregue la cebolla, ajo, zanahoria, apio, pimiento morrón verde y perejil y sofría hasta que la cebolla esté dorada.

En un tazón pequeño combine la harina con un poco de caldo, meneando hasta que la harina esté disuelta y la mezcla esté tersa. Agregue los vegetales y tomate y mezcle bien. Mezcle en el resto del caldo, vino y todas las especies y cueza tapado, a fuego muy lento, durante 45 minutos, meneando ocasionalmente. Agregue la leche (agua) de coco o leche normal, jugo de limón y chutney o mermelada y cueza a fuego lento 10 minutos más. Agregue el cordero y cueza 15 minutos más. Cuidadosamente mezcle en la manzana y yogurt. Apague el fuego. Sirva en el centro de una rosca de arroz o sobre arroz.

Si utiliza la salsa para servir sobre pollo o camarón, no agregue los cubos de cordero, de manzana y el yogurt, pero sirva cualquier tipo de los siguientes platillos acompañantes ya sea alrededor del platón con el pollo o camarón cubierto con la salsa en el centro, o en pequeños tazones encima de cada porción individual de pollo o camarón y salsa:

"SAMBALS"

Cacahuates picados
Coco rallado, tostado
Piña picada o en cubos (fresca de preferencia)
Yogurt natural
Cebollita cambray, picada
Manzana picada
Pepino, con cáscara, picado
Chutney

Está salsa es deliciosa servida sobre pechugas de pollo escalfadas, o sobre camarón recién hervido, tanto mediano como grande, y puede ser preparada con 2 ó 3 días de anticipación o congelarse. Si va a ser congelada es mejor doblar o triplicar la receta, ya que se mantiene de maravilla en el congelador durante 1 ó 2 meses.

TURBANTES DE FILETE DE PESCADO A LA NEWBURG

6 Porciones

2 libras de filete de pescado crudo (cualquier tipo de pescado blanco de sabor suave)
1 cucharadita de sal
1/4 cucharadita de pimienta
1/4 taza de mantequilla derretida
3 tazas de arroz cocido
Salsa Newburg

Espolvoree los filetes con sal y pimienta. Enrolle cada filete empezando con la parte más ancha y terminando con la puntiaguda. En un plato para hornear engrasado con mantequilla, coloque los rollos de pescado en una sola capa, barnice con mantequilla derretida y nornee a 350°F. durante 15–20 minutos, o hasta que el pescado se desprenda al probarse con un tenedor. Coloque los rollos en sus lados. Estilo turbante, en una cama de arroz cocido y vierta encima la siguiente salsa:

1/2 taza de mantequilla
1/4 taza de harina
1/2 cucharadita de sal
1 pizca de pimienta cayena
1 1/2 tazas de crema espesa
1 1/2 tazas de leche, escaldada
6 yemas de huevo
1/3 taza de vino de madera (si no está disponible, use jeréz medio o vino blanco)

Derrita la mantequilla. Mezcle en la harina, sal y pimienta de cayena. Retire del fuego y agregue poco a poco la leche escaldada, mezclando hasta que esté terso. Agregue la crema. Cueza hasta que espese, meneando constantemente. Mezcle un poco de la salsa caliente en las yemás de huevo, previamente batidas con el vino. Agregue la mezcla a la sartén con el resto de la salsa y caliente lentamente hasta que espese. Vierta encima del pescado y sirva de inmediato.

LOMO DE PUERCO CON SALSA DE MANGO

6 Porciones

2–3 libras de lomo de puerco en rebanadas de 1 pulgada de grueso y golpeadas hasta que queden de 1/2 pulgada, aproximadamente
4 rebanadas de jengibre fresco (ó 2 cucharaditas de jengibre en polvo si no está disponible)
5 tiras de cáscara de limón
2/3 taza de vino blanco seco
1/2 taza de azúcar mascabado
Jugo de 2 limones
1/2 taza de crema dulce (aproximadamente)
1/2 taza de jalea de grosellas (si no está disponible, puede substiruirla con mermelada de naranja)
4 mangos chicos, ó 2 grandes, frescos, pelados, sin hueso y rebanados
4 cucharadas de mantequilla
Harina sazonada con sal y pimienta
3 dientes de ajo, machacados
1 cebolla rebanada

Espolvoree ligeramente cada rebanada de lomo con la harina sazonada y dore en mantequilla caliente, por ambos lados. Retire y mantenga aparte. En la misma sartén, con la mantequilla sobrante (si la sartén está muy seca, agregue más mantequilla) sofría el ajo y la cebolla hasta que estén dorados. Regrese las rebanadas de puerco a la sartén, desechando del fondo de la sartén cualquier resto de ajo, cebolla o harina. Agregue el vino y caliente a que hierva. Agregue el jengibre y cáscara de limón. Tape y cueza a fuego lento hasta que el puerco esté cocido completamente y suave (cerca de 25 minutos en altitudes bajas, 40 minutos en altitudes superiores a 5000 pies). Retire del fuego y mantenga aparte en un platón precalentado. Agregue el azúcar mascabado y el jugo de limón al líquido. Agregue la crema y la jalea o mermelada, poco a poco, probando para evitar que esté muy cremoso o muy dulce. Cueza un poco, cuidadosamente, a fuego lento, para espesar la crema. Mezcle de manera envolvente en la rebanadas de mango y caliente bien. Vierta encima del puerco y sirva.

LOMO DE RES CON CHAMPIÑONES EN ALCARAVEA

8 Porciones

1 lomo de res de 4 libras
2 tazas de vino blanco seco
2 barras de mantequilla sin sal
1 taza de semillas de alcaravea
1 libra de champiñones frescos, rebanados

Marine el lomo con 1 taza de vino blanco seco, por lo menos durante 2 horas, a la temperatura ambiente, volteándolo con frecuencia para asegurarse que se cubra por completo.

Caliente el horno a 300°F.

Retire la carne del vino (reserve el vino para bañarlo), unte generosamente con una barra de mantequilla suavizada pero no derretida. Cubra el lomo por completo, incluyendo la parte inferior, con las semillas de alcaravea, presionando ligeramente para asegurar que las semillas se adhieran. Las semillas deben parecer una cubierta como pasta — por esa razón no tema utilizar la cantidad requerida. Hornee a 350°F. durante 30 minutos para llegar a término crudo, para término medio, hornee de 40 a 45 minutos. (Es muy importante no sobrecocer el lomo). Bañe con el vino reservado.

Mientras está horneando el lomo, sofría ligeramente los champiñones con la otra barra de mantequilla. Agregue una taza de vino blanco y cueza a fuego lento hasta que se reduzca a la mitad.

Después de que el lomo esté horneado, retirelo a un platón de servicio precalentado y vierta los jugos y el resto del vino en la sartén con los champiñones. Cueza la salsa a fuego lento, durante 10 minutos, manteniendo el lomo caliente.

Rebane fina y diagonalmente la carne y sirvala en un platón con la salsa aparte.

Este platillo es excelente acompañado de tallarines hervidos, mezclados con mantequilla y espolvoreado con un poco de perejil picado.

LOMO DE PUERCO ORIENTAL AGRIDULCE

8–10 Porciones

4–6 libras de lomo de puerco
2 tazas de azúcar
1 taza de vinagre (de preferencia blanco)
1 pimiento morrón verde entreo, chico, sin semillas y picado
1 cucharadita de sal
1 taza de agua
4 cucharaditas de fécula de maíz (mezclada en 2 cucharadas de agua)
4 cucharadas de salsa soya
1 cucharada de jengibre fresco, machacado (ó 3–4 cucharaditas en polvo)
2 dientes de ajo grandes, machacados y sofritos en un poco de aceite hasta que estén dorados
2 cucharadas de perejil fresco, picadito (no cilantro)

En una sartén pequeña, en un poco de aceite, sofría el ajo (y el jengibre si utiliza fresco). Aprátelos. En una sartén lo suficientemente grande para acomodar el lomo, dórelo en un poco de aceite por todos lados. Retire el lomo y colóquelo en una charola profunda para hornear.

En una sartén mezcle el azúcar, vinagre, pimiento morrón, sal, salsa soya, y la mezcla de fécula de maíz, agua, ajo y jengibre. Cueza a fuego lento hasta que espese. Añada el perejil.

Vierta la salsa sobre el lomo en el molde profundo, sin tapar. Hornee a 300°F. durante 2 1/2 horas, o hasta que la carne esté suave. Bañe ocasionalmente.

Retire el lomo del molde. Sirvalo acompañado por la salsa a un lado, o aparte.

También puede utilizar esta receta para asar pollos enteros, solo ajuste la temperatura y tiempo de horneado. Hornee el pollo a 350°F. durante 1 a 1 1/2 horas, hasta que al introducir un tenedor esté suave.

PESCADO HORNEADO A LA FLORENTINA

6 Porciones

1 huachinango de 4–5 libras (ó 2 o más huachinangos más pequeños, ó 6 truchas de 3/4 a 1 de libra, ó 12 filetes de lenguado, trucha, ó de otro pescado blanco, de sabor suave y carne firme)

(Si utiliza huachinango grande, es aconsejable quitarle el esqueleto para facilitar el rebanarlo. Sin embargo, es un proceso difícil y no absolutamente necesario. Si no retira el esqueleto, corte rebanadas horizontales y saque una cucharada de relleno por porción).

Sin importar el tamaño del pescado, si está utilizando uno entero, límpielo y quitele las escamas y aletas, pero deje intacta la cabeza y la cola. Abra y agrande el estómago para acomodar el relleno.

Si utiliza filetes, extienda el relleno (aproximadamente 1 cucharada), al final de la parte grande de cada filete, enróllelo y asegúrelo con un palillo de dientes.

4 cucharadas de mantequilla
2 dientes de ajo, machacado
3 cebollas cambray, finamente picadas (solo la parte blanca)
3/4 taza de espinaca cocida, finamente picada
2 tazas de pan, finamente desmoronado
3–4 cucharadas de crema espesa
1/2 cucharadita de sal
Pimienta recién molida
1/4 cucharadita de jugo de limón

PARA EL PESCADO

5 cucharadas de mantequilla derretida
1 taza de vino blanco seco

Precaliente el horno a 400°F.

Si utiliza pescado entero, lávelo bien por dentro y fuera en el chorro de agua corriendo y séquelo completamente.

En una sartén gruesa derrita a fuego moderado 4 cucharadas de mantequilla, sofría la cebolla y el ajo hasta que estén suaves pero no dorados. Exprima la espinaca para quitar tola la humedad posible y agreguela a la sartén. Cueza a fuego alto, menenado constantemente hasta que esté casi seco. Transfieralo a un tazón grande y agregue el pan, crema, sal, pimienta, jugo de limón y mezcle bien.

Con una brocha, unte 1 cucharada de mantequilla derretida en el fondo de una charola de hornear poco profunda, pero lo suficientemente grande para acomodar todo el pescado. (En caso de utilizar filetes o pescados pequeños, acomódelos en una sola capa sin traslapar o empalmar). Llene el pescado con el relleno y cierre con palillos de dientes, en caso necesario. Coloque el pescado en la charola preparada, unte con una brocha 2 cucharadas de mantequilla derretida, encima de cada pescado y sazone con sal y pimienta. Combine las 2 cucharadas de mantequilla derretida en el vino y vierta la mezcla alrededor, no encima del pescado.

Hornee, sin tapar, en el centro del horno, bañando frecuentemente, durante 30–40 minutos en el caso de usar pescado entero o durante 20 minutos en el caso de usar pescados pequeños o filetes. No sobrecueza, hornee solo hasta que el pescado esté firme al presionarlo ligeramente con la yema del dedo. Si se seca el líquido, agregue un poco más de vino.

Retire los jugos y sirvalos aparte.

NOTA: Este relleno es muy versátil, y puede ser utilizado para rellenar pechugas de pollo, deshuesadas o escalopas delgadas de ternera. Utilice las mismas técnicas de preparación, y aproximadamente el mismo tiempo de horneado. También es excelente para rellenar tomates o champiñones (ver receta en la sección de vegetales).

CAMARONES SCAMPI

6 Porciones

2 libras (aproximadamente 36) de camarones grandes, crudos, pelados, desvenados, con las colas intactas
1 1/2 barras de mantequilla
3 cucharadas de vino blanco seco
1 cucharada de ajo, machacado
1/4 taza de cebolla cambray, finamente picada, usando un poco de la parte verde
1 cucharada de jugo de limón
Sal y pimienta al gusto

Sofría el ajo y la cebolla cambray en mantequilla, agregue el camarón y sofría rápidamente, volteando constantemente solo hasta que el camarón esté rosado (no sobrecueza). Retire el camarón de la sartén y reservelo en un platillo caliente, dejando la mayor cantidad de mantequilla posible en la sartén. En la misma sartén agregue el jugo de limón y vino a la mantequilla y cueza durante 1 minuto. Regrese los camarones a la sartén y apague la flama. Sazone al gusto y sirva inmediatamente con la salsa encima. Sirva con arroz blanco, o pasta a la mantequilla, o bien para una ocasión muy elegante, se puede servir con fettuccine alfredo (ver receta en la sección de "Panes y Pastas").

Tradicionalmente, este platillo de camarones se clabora cocinándolos a la parrilla, acompañados con la misma salsa, pero el restaurante Marcy prefiere este metodo, debido a la facilidad e preparación y mayor impregnación del sabor de la salsa de ajo al camarón.

TERNERA CORDON BLEU

6 Porciones

12 escalopas de ternera de 3–4 onzas (de preferencia de un corte de pierna)
Sal y pimienta recién molida
6 rebanadas redondas, delgadas de jamón prosciutto (puede substituirlo con jamón cocido, si no está disponible)
6 rebanadas redondas, delgadas de queso gruyere
2 huevos, ligeramente batidos
1 cucharadita de agua
1½ tazas de pan recién desmoronado
½ taza de mantequilla
Harina

Sazone la harina con sal y pimienta. Coloque cada escalopa entre dos pedazos de papel encerado y golpéelas con un mazo liso o con el fondo de una sartén pesada hasta que estén delgadas. Coloque una rebanada de jamón en el centro de 6 de las escalopas y cúbralas con una rebanada de queso. Bata los huevos y el agua juntos. Barnice con la mezcla de huevo la parte de abajo de la escalopa donde puso el jamón y queso. Coloque las otras 6 escalopas encima del queso y barnice la parte superior con la mezcla de huevo. Con cuidado espolvorée en ambos lados, cada escalopa con la harina sazonada. Bañe las piezas en el huevo batido y luego en el pan desmoronado hasta que estén bien cubiertas. Golóee suavemente las piezas con el lado de un cuchillo de cocina grueso, para ayudar a que se adhiera el pan.

Ponga la carne empanizada en una rejilla y refrigere durante 1 ó 2 horas. (Esto ayuda a que el empanizado se adhiera a la escalopa cuando se está cociendo).

En una sartén grande caliente la mantequilla y, cuando esté caliente pero no dorada o quemada, sofría las escalopas hasta que estén doradas en ambos lados y el queso derretido.

Si desea, puede servir las escalopas con una salsa. La preferida del restaurante Marcy es:

$1/2$ barra de mantequilla con sal, rebanada
Jugo de 2 limones
1 taza de vino blanco seco
2 cucharaditas de fécula de máiz

En una sarten mezcle todos los ingredientes y cueza hasta que espese. También, en el Marcy agregamos una cucharadita de queso roquefort o bleu desmoronado encima de cada rebanada de queso antes de agregar la otra rebanada de carne, para obtener un sabor diferente y único. Delicioso!

Vegetales

TIMBALES DE VEGETALES

8 Porciones

NATILLA BASICA PARA TIMBALES:

4 huevos, bien batidos
$^1/_2$ cucharadita de mostaza seca
$^1/_2$ taza de crema espesa
1 cucharada de aceite vegetal ligero
3 cucharadas de queso parmesano, rallado (opcional)
$^1/_2$ cucharadita de sal

Combine todos los ingredientes y cueza a baño maría, meneando, sobre agua hirviendo a fuego lento, hasta que empiezen a espesar. Retire del fuego hasta que la mezcla empieze a cuajar, y mezcle de manera envolvente en cualquier combinación de vegetales, como las siguientes:

1. 3 tazas de combinado de cubitos de zanahoria, nabos, ejotes y chicharos, todo cocido.
2. 3 tazas de brocoli, picado chiquito, cocido y secado entre toallas de papel; agregue 1/4 cucharadita de albahaca desmoronada.
3. 3 tazas de calabacita en cubitos, cocida y secada entre toallas de papel; agregue 1/4 cucharadita de tomillo, desmoronado.
4. 3 tazas de coliflor, picada chiquito, cocida y secada entre toallas de papel; agregue 1 cucharadita de pimiento morrón rojo, enlatado picado.
5. $1^1/_2$ libras de espinaca, bien lavada, finamente picada, cocida y exprimida.
6. 3 tazas de champiñones, toscamente picados o rebanados finito, sofritos en un poquito de mantequilla y bien drenados.
7. 2 tazas de papas cocidas en cubitos, 1/2 taza de cebolla picada, ligeramente sofrita, una pizca de tomillo.

Vierta la mezcla en un molde para hornear con capacidad de $1^1/_2$ litros o en 8 platos para flan, engrasados con mantequilla. Coloque en un recipiente grande, lleno de agua caliente hasta cubrir la mitad del molde o los platos para flan. Hornee a 350°F. durante 25 ó 30 minutos para el molde de $1^1/_2$ litros, ó 20 minutos para los platos individuales. Sirva caliente.

Si desea, puede agregar una salsa, pero deberá servirse por separado, de manera que los invitados puedan vertir la cantidad que deseen. Sugerimos la salsa de tomate ligera, holandesa o de champiñones.

ACELGAS SUIZAS U HOJAS DE LECHUGA RELLENAS

6 Porciones

Si utiliza acelga suiza, corte la parte gruesa del tallo, asegurándose de seleccionar las hojas más grandes y perfectas. Si utiliza lechuga, seleccione las hojas más grandes y perfectas de la parte exterior de la lechuga china. Remoje brevemente las hojas en agua hirviendo. Seque por completo y extiéndalas en una superficie plana o en una tabla para picar. Rellene con cualquiera de las siguientes combinaciones:

A.

3 huevos, revueltos
1 diente de ajo, picadito, sofrito en un poquito de mantequilla
6 champiñones frescos, picados y sofritos en la mantequilla con el ajo
1/2 cebolla mediana, picada finito y sofrita con el ajo y los champiñones
6–8 hojas de espinaca, picadas y sin tallo, luego secadas en toallas de papel
1/2 taza de queso gruyere, rallado
Sal y pimienta al gusto

Mezcle por completo todos los ingredientes de arriba y colóquelos en montoncitos en el centro de la raíz puntiaguda de cada hoja. Enrolle una vez y luego doble las orillas hacia el centro y enrolle toda la hoja. Asegure con un palillo de dientes, si es necesario. Colóquelas en una sola capa en una charola para hornear, engrasada con mantequilla, cubra con papel aluminio y hornee a 350°F. durante 30 minutos.

B.

1/2 cebolla mediana, sofrita en un poco de mantequilla
1 diente de ajo, picadito y sofrito con la cebolla
2/3 taza de pan fresco, finamente desmoronado
1 tomate, pelado y picado
1 calabacita chica, picada finito
6 champiñones frescos, picados finito
3 cucharadas de queso parmesano, rallado

Mezcle por completo todos los ingredientes de arriba y siga las mismas instrucciones del A.

C.

Use 10 hojas — 10 Porciones

2 dientes de ajo, picaditos y sofritos en un poco de mantequilla
1 cebolla mediana, picada y sofrita con el ajo
1 taza de repollo, finamente rallado, sofrito en un poco más de mantequilla, hasta que esté dorado
2 tomates pequeños, pelados y picados finito
1 pimiento morrón verde, picado y sofrito hasta que esté dorado
1/2 taza de pan fresco, desmoronado
2 cucharaditas de mostaza preparada
1 taza de granos de elote enteros
1/4 cucharadita de cada una de mejorana, albahaca, perifollo y tomillo desmoronados y mezclados
3 cucharadas de queso parmesano
Sal y pimienta al gusto

Mezcle por completo todos los ingredientes y siga las mismas instrucciones del A y B.

CLAFOUTI DE VEGETALES

6–8 Porciones

PASTA BASICA PARA CLAFOUTI:

2 cucharadas de pan seco, desmoronado
6 cucharadas de queso parmesano fresco, rallado
3 huevos
1/3 taza de harina integral
2 tazas de leche o crema ligera
1/2 cucharadita de sal
1 pizca de pimienta cayena

Engrase una charola para hornear, poco profunda de 10–12 pulgadas, o un molde para pay o tarta. Espolvoree con una mezcla de pan desmoronado y 2 cucharadas de queso parmesano. Bata los huevos hasta que estén esponjosos. Agregue la harina y mezcle bien. Añada leche o crema, el queso restante y sal y pimienta y bata bien durante 3 minutos. Agregue uno de los siguientes rellenos (o invente el suyo propio) y hornee a 375°F. durante 45 minutos, o hasta que la cubierta esté un poco dorada y esponjada, y cuando al insertar un palillo de dientes en el centro, salga limpio. Corte en 6 u 8 rebanadas y sirva caliente.

RELLENOS DE VEGETALES PARA PASTA CLAFOUTI:

1. Pique toscamente 1/4 taza de cebolla, 1/4 libra de calabacita, 1/4 taza de pimiento morrón rojo. Agregue 1 cucharadita de ajo fresco, machacado y 1/4 cucharadita de tomillo seco.
2. Corte toscamente 2 tomates grandes y drene. Agregue 1 cucharadita de albahaca y 1/2 cucharadita de ajo, machacado. Pique finito 1 cucharada de perejil fresco y agregue la mezcla total a la pasta.
3. Agregue 2 cucharaditas de mostaza seca y 1/2 cucharadita de nuez moscada recién molida a la pasta básica. Ponga 2 tazas de flores de brocoli cocidas (pero todavía un poco crujientes), ó 1 taza de coliflor y 1 taza de brocoli, en el fondo del molde para hornear. Vierta la pasta encima y espolvoree la cubierta con 1/4 taza de queso parmesano fresco, rallado.
4. Agregue 1 cucharadita de curry en polvo (ó 2 cucharaditas si desea un sabor definido de curry) a la pasta básica. Extienda 1½ a 2 tazas de granos de elote en el molde de hornear preparado. Espolvoree con 1/4 taza de cebollita cambray, finamente picada. Agregue la pasta.

PAPAS AL GRATIN

6–8 Porciones

1½ libras de papas sin pelar
2 cucharadas de mantequilla
2 cucharadas de harina
1½ tazas de leche caliente
½ taza de queso fuerte, rallado (de preferencia cheddar, puede substituirlo con queso manchego, pero solo si es necesario)
1 cucharada de queso parmesano fresco, rallado
2 dientes de ajo, machacados (opcional)
Sal y pimienta recién molida al gusto
Queso fuerte rallado (de preferencia cheddar), queso Parmesano rallado y paprika para la cubierta.

Hierva las papas en agua ligeramente salada hasta que estén suaves. Enfríe, pélelas, y córtelas en rebanadas de 1/4 de pulgada. Alinie las rebanadas en una cacerola o molde engrasado con mantequilla.

En una sartén mediana, derrita la mantequilla, sofría el ajo (si lo usa) y mezcle con la harina hasta que esté tersa. Poco a poco, agregue la leche caliente, meneando con frecuencia. Mezcle con el queso fuerte y el parmesano y continúe cociendo justo hasta que se derrita. Sazone al gusto con sal y pimienta. Mezcle el queso fuerte, parmesano y paprika y vierta encima de la capa de papas. Hornee durante 20–30 minutos a 350°F., luego meta el molde al asador justo hasta que estén doradas y burbujeantes. Sirva inmediatamente.

CHAMPIÑONES O TOMATES CON RELLENO A LA FLORENTINA

6 a 8 Porciones

Si va a rellenar tomates, seleccione de 6 a 8 tomates medianos y maduros, con una cuchara saque la pulpa del tomate hasta dejar 1/4 de pulgada en los lados, espolvoree sal dentro y volteelos encima de toallas de papel para drenarlos. En una sartén cueza a fuego lento la pulpa hasta que espese y esté casi seca. Mezcle con el relleno preparado y rellene los tomates. Hornee sin tapar en el horno precalentado a 400°F., en una charola bien engrasada con mantequilla, durante 35 minutos. Cerca de 15 minutos antes de que los tomates estén cocidos, coloque una pequeña rebanadita de mantequilla encima de cada tomate. Cuando las conchas estén suaves y la punta dorada, los tomates están listos para servirse. Sirvalos calientes como acompañamiento.

Si va a rellenar champiñones, seleccione 3 champiñones grandes ó 4 medianos por persona. Limpie muy bien, retire los cabos y píquelos. Mezcle los cabos picados con el relleno preparado y rellene los champiñones, redondeando el relleno; colóquelos en un platón para hornear o en una charola de alumino, engrasado con mantequilla, lo suficientemente grande para colocarlos en una sola capa. No los amontone. En una sartén derrita 1/2 taza de mantequilla y agregue 1/2 taza de vino blanco; cuando esté bien incorporado y caliente, veírtala con sumo cuidado alrededor de los champiñones, ponga solo un poquito encima de cada champiñón. Hornee sin tapar a 400°F. durante 20 minutos o hasta que estén dorados, bañándolos a medida que sea necesario con el líquido en la charola. Sírvalos calientes como acompañamiento.

RELLENO A LA FLORENTINA

4 cucharadas de mantequilla
3 dientes de ajo, machacados
3/4 taza de espinaca fresca o congelada, picada, cocida y presionada para sacar todo el jugo
2 1/2 tazas de pan integral fresco desmoronado
4 cucharadas de crema espesa
1/2 cucharadita de sal
1/2 cucharadita de jugo de limón
Pimienta recién molida

Derrita la mantequilla a fuego moderado y sofría el ajo solo un momento para darle sabor, luego agregue la espinaca bien exprimida, y siga cocinando hasta que esté razonablemente seca. Apague la flama y agregue todos los demás ingredientes, mezcle bien y rellene.

HOJUELAS DE PAPA HORNEADAS

6 Porciones

4 libras de papas medianas, con cáscara, bien lavadas
6–7 cucharadas de mantequilla, derretida
Sal y pimienta al gusto

Precaliente el horno a 500°F. y engrase ligeramente 2–3 hojas para hornear. Corte las papas, con cáscara, en rebanadas de 1/8 de pulgada de grueso. Acomode las rebanadas en capas sencillas en las dos o tres hojas. unte generosamente con la mantequilla derretida. Hornee 7 minutos con las hojas en las parrillas superiores e inferiores del horno. Después de 7 minutos cambie la posición de las charolas, la charola de arriba a la parrilla de abajo y las charolas de abajo a la parrilla superior, y siga horneando hasta que las papas estén crujientes y doradas alrededor, cerca de 7–9 minutos. Pongalas en un platón precalentado y espolvoree con sal y pimienta. Sirva inmediatamente.

Si prefiere puede pelar las papas antes de rebanarlas, pero nos gusta el sabor que adquiere la papa al dejarle la cáscara.

FRITURAS DE PAPA

6 Porciones

1 libra de papas, horneadas a 400°F. hasta que al introducir un tenedor estén suaves
1 huevo grande, batido
3 cucharadas de crema ligera
2 cucharadas de cebolla, picadita
2 cucharadas de mantequilla
2 rebanadas de tocino, cocido hasta que esté crujiente, drenado y desmoronado
1½ onzas de queso de sabor suave, rallado (como Americano)
1 huevo grande, batido
2–3 cucharadas de leche
½ taza de harina
1½ tazas de migajas de pan suaves
Aceite para freído profundo

Enfríe ligeramente las papas y saque la pulpa a cucharadas y machaque bien. Sazone con sal y pimienta al gusto. Agregue 1 huevo batido y suficiente crema para mantener la pulpa junta sin permitir que llegue a estar muy húmeda. No mezcle demasiado.

Sofría la cebolla en mantequilla y mezclela con el tocino y queso. Agregue a la mezcla de papa, y haga pequeñas bolitas, de 1 a 1½ pulgadas de diámetro.

Combine el otro huevo batido con la leche. Cubra las bolitas con harina, luego con la mezcla de huevo y leche, y después en las migajas de pan, unas cuantas a la vez, y fría en un recipiente o sartén profundo, en aceite caliente a 375°F., hasta que estén doradas, cerca de 3–4 minutos. Tenga cuidado de no amontonar las frituras, friendo 6 ó 7 cada vez. Mantengalas calientes en una charola para galletas, cubierta con toallas de papel, en el horno a 400°F., hasta que todas estén cocidas. Luego retire las toallas de papel y hornee 5 ó 6 minutos en el horno caliente, hasta que la cubierta esté crujiente.

Sirva caliente.

CACEROLA DE CAMOTE Y MANZANA

6–8 Porciones

7 camotes medianos, pelados y rebanados en trozos de 1/2 pulgada, ó 2 latas (1 libra) de camote, drenado
2 ó 3 manzanas medianas, ácidas, peladas, descorazonadas y cortadas en rebanadas de 1/2 pulgada
8 cucharadas de mantequilla, derretida
1/2 taza de miel de maíz oscura
1/2 taza de azúcar mascabado, bien presionada
2 cucharadas de jeréz seco (si no está disponible, use vino blanco)
1 cucharadita de canela
1/8 cucharadita de sal

Si utiliza camotes frescos, cuezalos en suficiente agua para cubrirlos. Cuando estén tiernos, drene y hágalos puré junto con la mantequilla, miel de maíz, azúcar mascabado, vino, canela y sal. Si utiliza camotes enlatados, siga el mismo procedimiento.

Cueza las manzanas, en agua suficiente para cubrirlas, hasta que estén apenas tiernas. Drene y reserve el agua de manzana.

En el fondo de un molde redondo para hornear de 10 pulgadas, engrasado con mantequilla, extienda la mitad de la mezcla de camote. Extienda encima las rebanadas de manzana y luego extienda el resto del puré sobre las rebanadas de manzana. Vierta encima 3 cucharadas del agua de manzana, salpique con mantequilla y espolvoree un poco de azúcar blanca o mascabado en toda la parte superior. Hornee, sin tapar, a 350°F., durante 35 minutos.

ZANAHORIAS AL JENGIBRE

4–6 Porciones

12 zanahorias medianas, peladas y cortadas en rebanadas de 1/2 pulgada de grueso
1/4 taza de mantequilla
1/2 taza de crema o leche evaporada
1/4 cucharadita de jengibre
2 cucharadas de azúcar mascabado
1/4 taza de almendras rebanadas tostadas o almendras en trocitos (opcional)
Sal y pimienta al gusto

Sofría las zanahorias en la mantequilla hasta que estén tiernas y crujientes. Agregue todos los demás ingredientes, exceptuando las almendras. Tape y cueza a fuego lento durante 10–15 minutos más, hasta que estén tiernas. Destape y cueza otros 5 minutos. Espolvoree con las almendras tostadas.

BETABEL GLAZEADO

6–8 Porciones

2 1/2 tazas de néctar de pera
2 1/2 tazas de agua
3 cucharadas de mantequilla
1 1/2 libras de betabeles tiernos, pelados y cortados en tiras estilo juliana
2 cucharadas de azúcar
1/2 cucharadita de mostaza seca
1/2 cucharadita de sal
1/4 cucharadita de jengibre molido

Ponga a hervir rápido el néctar de pera y el agua. En una sartén, lo suficientemente grande para que quepan todos los ingredientes, derrita la mantequilla y agregue el resto de los ingredientes, mezcle bien. Vierta la mezcla de agua y néctar sobre los betabeles y ponga a hervir. Cueza lentamente, sin tapar, hasta que los betabeles estén suaves, meneando con frecuencia (cerca de 40 minutos, agregando el agua restante a medida que sea necesario). Sirva caliente.

CEBOLLAS AGRIDULCES

8 Porciones

2 libras de cebollitas blancas, sin pelar (1 a 1 1/2 pulgadas de diámetro)
1 cucharada de aceite de oliva
1 cucharada de mantequilla
1/8 cucharadita de pimienta dulce, en polvo
1/2 a 3/4 taza de vino blanco seco
2–4 cucharadas de vinagre de vino tinto
2 cucharaditas de azúcar
Sal al gusto

Hierva 3–4 litros de agua, y cuando esté hirviendo mucho, agregue las cebollas enjuagadas en sus cáscaras y hierva de nuevo cocinando durante 3 minutos. Drene y enjuage las cebollas en agua fría y quite la cáscara.

En una sartén grande, gruesa, que no sea de aluminio, caliente el aceite y mantequilla. Agregue las cebollas y la pimienta dulce y sofría hasta que empiezen a ponerse un poco doradas, cerca de 4 minutos, meneando de vez en cuando. Rocíe con 1/2 taza de vino, 2 cucharadas de vinagre y 2 cucharaditas de azúcar. Sazone con la sal.

Hornee a 375°F. durante 30 minutos, meneando con frecuencia, hasta que las cebollas estén doradas y todavía un poco firmes al pincharlas con un cuchillo. Retire las cebollas del líquido y colóquelas en un platón, y agregue el suficiente vinagre restante a la sartén para conseguir el balance agridulce. Vierta la salsa encima de las cebollas y sirva a la temperatura ambiente.

CHAMPIÑONES CREMOSOS

6–8 Porciones

2 libras de champiñones frescos, rebanados
2 cucharadas de cebolla picadita
4 cucharadas de mantequilla
4 cucharadas de vino blanco seco
1 1/2 tazas de salsa bechamel caliente (ver "Salsas")
1/2 cucharadita de mejorana
1–2 cucharaditas de perejil fresco, picadito (opcional)

Sofría en la mantequilla los champiñones y la cebolla, hasta que la cebolla esté dorada y los champiñones café pero no tanto para que se quemen o tuesten. Agregue el vino y siga cociendo, meneando constantemente, cerca de 2 minutos. Agregue la salsa bechamel caliente y las especias, y mantenga en el fuego hasta que esté bien mezclado, meneando con frecuencia. Si es necesario, ajuste el sazón con un poco de sal y pimienta blanca. Sirva caliente.

PEPINOS CON ENELDO

6 Porciones

3 pepinos grandes
2–3 cucharadas de mantequilla
2–3 cucharadas de eneldo fresco, picadito, ó 1 cucharadita de semilla de eneldo seco, machacada, con 1 cucharada de perejil fresco, picadito
Sal y pimienta blanca al gusto

Pele los pepinos y rebánelos a la mitad, por lo largo. Sazue las semillas con una cuchara, luego corte de nuevo cada mitad a la mitad a lo largo. Luego corte cada trozo en triángulos, cortando diagonalmente, primero a la derecha y luego a la izquierda. Derrita la mantequilla, agregue los pepinos y mézclelos sobre fuego moderadamente alto, sazonando al gusto con sal y pimienta, hasta que los pepinos estén casi cocidos, pero un poco crujientes. Mezcle en el eneldo y perejil y sirva al momento.

Esté platillo es el acompañamiento perfecto para platillos de pescado.

CALABACITAS FRITAS ESTILO ITALIANO

6 Porciones

9 calabacitas medianas, finamente rebanadas
4 cucharadas de aceite de oliva, muy fino y fresco
1/2 cucharadita de albahaca, desmoronado
1/2 cucharadita de tomillo, desmoronado
Sal y pimienta al gusto

En una sartén grande, sofría todos los ingredientes a fuego medio alto, hasta que las rebanadas de calabacita estén doradas y tiernas. Sirva inmediatamente.

CACEROLA DE BERENJENAS

6 Porciones

2 1/2 tazas de berenjenas, pelada y cortada en cubos
18 galletas saladas, desmoronadas
1/2 taza de queso fuerte, rallado, de preferencia cheddar (puede substituirlo con queso manchego)
1/4 taza de apio, finamente picado
2 cucharadas de pimiento morrón verde, picado
1 cucharada de mantequilla derretida
1/2 cucharadita de sal
1/8 cucharadita de pimienta
1 taza de crema ligera o leche evaporada
1 diente de ajo grande, machacado
1 cebolla mediana, picadita

Cueza la berenjena en agua salada hirviendo, durante 10 minutos. Drene. Sofría el ajo y la cebolla en un poco de aceite hasta que estén tiernos. Cambine la berenjena, ajo, cebolla y todos los otros ingredientes y póngalos en un molde para hornear con capacidad de 1 litro, engrasado con mantequilla. Hornee a temperatura moderada (350°F.) durante 45 minutos. Sirva caliente.

PAPAS HASH BROWN ESPECIALES

6 Porciones

8 rebanadas de tocino, finamente picadas
2 cebollas grandes, picaditas
1 libra de papas, peladas y ralladas
Sal y pimienta al gusto

Seque la papa rallada con toallas de papel. En una sartén grande sofría el tocino hasta que esté crujiente. Agregue la cebolla y sofría hasta que la cebolla esté suave y dorada. Agregue las papas y fríalas hasta que estén doradas, volteando solo una o dos veces con una espátula ancha. Mantenga el calor en la sartén a fuego medio alto, y si se doran muy rápidamente y las papas aún no están cocidas, cubra la sartén con una tapa parte del tiempo. Sazone con sal y pimienta al gusto y sirva inmediatamente.

ZANAHORIAS GLAZEADAS

4–6 Porciones

1 libra de zanahorias frescas, peladas y cortadas estilo juliana
1 1/2 tazas de jugo de naranja fresco
1/2 taza de azucar mascabado
1 1/2 cucharadas de mantequilla
1 cucharada de fecula de maiz mezclada en 1/4 taza de agua fría
1 pizca de jengibre molido

Cueza las zanahorias a vapor hasta que están tiernas. Cámbielas a un platón de servicio y manténgalas calientes. Combine el jugo de naranja, azucar y mantequilla, luego agregue la férula de maiz en agua. Cueza a fuego moderado hasta que esté claro y espeso. Agregue el jengibre. Vierta sobre las zanahorias y revuelva para cubrirlas bien. Si desea, adorne con hojas de menta frescas.

Panes

PALITOS DE PAN ITALIANOS

Rinde 80 aproximadamente

1 paquete (1 cucharada) de levadura activa en polvo
1 lata de cerveza de 12 onzas, tibia y sin efervescencia
3/4 taza de aceite vegetal
1 1/2 cucharaditas de sal
4 3/4 a 5 1/4 tazas de harina
1 diente de ajo grande, machacado
1 cucharadita de cada uno, de albahaca, orégano y tomillo secos, molidos juntos en el molcajete/mortero
1/2 taza de queso parmesano, rallado
1 huevo batido con una cucharada de agua para barnizar, si desea

En un tazón grande disuelva la levadura en la cerveza. Déjela reposar hasta que esté espumosa, cerca de 10 minutos. Agregue el aceite, sal y 3 tazas de harina, junto con el ajo, hierbas y queso parmesano. Si utiliza batidora eléctrica, bata a velocidad media, durante 2 minutos, o bata a mano vigorosamente 200 veces. Mezcle en la harina restante suficiente para hacer una masa suave. Póngala en una superficie ligeramente enharinada. Engrase un tazón lo suficientemente grande para acomodar toda la masa. Amase durante 8 minutos o hasta que la masa esté tersa y elástica, y pongala en el tazón engrasado, cubra con una toalla un poquito húmeda y déjela reposar en un lugar tibio, libre de corrientes de aire, para que se levante hasta que doble su tamaño, cerca de 1 hora.

Divida la masa en 2 partes. Cubra 1 pieza y extienda la otra con un rodillo para formar un rectángulo de 22 x 8 pulgadas. Corte transversalmente en tiras aproximadamente, de 1/2 pulgada de ancho. Acomódelas en charolas de hornear engrasadas, estirando las tiras a 6–7 pulgadas. Barnícelas con el huevo. Repita con el resto de la masa. Deje que se levante, sin tapar, durante 30 minutos. Precaliente el horno a 350°F. y hornee cerca de 25 minutos o hasta que estén dorado oscuro. Enfríe en parrilas.

PAN BLIZBROT (PAN NEGRO — ALEMAN)

Rinde 2 panes grandes ó 4 chicos

2.2 libras de harina integral
1 1/2 onzas de levadura fresca, o 1 1/2 cucharadas de levadura en polvo
2 cucharadas rasas de sal
3/4 litro de agua tibia (110°F. ó 45°C.)
1 ó 2 yemas de huevo (para glazear)

Mezcle el agua, levadura y sal en un tazón grande. Deje reposar 10 minutos o hasta que la levadura esté completamente disuelta y empezando a hacer espuma. Agregue la harina y mezcle bien. Deje el tazón en un lugar tibio y deje que la masa se levante (cerca de 20–30 minutos).

Amase y divida la masa en 2 porciones iguales (o en 4 si va a hacer panes pequeños). Engrase los moldes de pan con margarina. Ponga la mitad de la masa en cada molde, o, si está haciendo 4 panes chicos, forme bolas con la masa y horneelas en una hoja para hornear galletas. Barnice con la yema de huevo para glazear.

Coloque en medio del horno frío a 375°F. coloque un molde con agua en la última parrilla del horno para mantener la humedad. Hornee 40–50 minutos, o hasta que el pan suene hueco al tocar la cubierta.

Nos gusta esté pan porque no tiene azúcar. Si desea puede dividir la receta a la mitad.

PAN DE QUESO Y CALABACITA

Rinde 1 pan

2 huevos
2 tazas de harina
2 cucharaditas de polvo de hornear
1/2 cucharadita de bicarbonato de sodio
3/4 cucharadita de sal
1/8 cucharadita de paprika
1/4 cucharadita de tomillo seco)
1/4 cucharadita de albahaca seca)
1/2 cucharadita de mejorana) machacados en el molcajete
1 diente de ajo grande, machacado
2 cucharadas de cebolla, picadita
1 cucharada de azúcar
3/4 taza de queso de sabor fuerte, rallado (de preferencia cheddar, pero si no está disponible, puede substituirlo con manchego)
1 taza de calabacita sin pelar, rallada
1/2 taza de yogurt
1/4 taza de aceite vegetal

Bata los huevos hasta que estén ligeros y esponjosos. Agregue el yogurt y mezcle bien. En un tazón grande combine todos los ingredientes secos, luego mezclelos en el queso y calabacita, el ajo y la cebolla. Por último, agregue la mezcla de yogurt y huevo junto con el aceite. Mezcle completamente hasta que esté bien integrado. Vierta en un molde para panqué de 8 x 4 pulgadas, engrasado. Precaliente el horno a 350°F. y hornee durante 50 minutos, o hasta que al introducir un palillo de dientes en el centro, salga limpio. Puede servirlo caliente o a la temperatura ambiente.

ROLES DE CANELA

Rinde 4 docenas

2 paquetes de levadura en polvo
1/2 taza de agua tibia
2 tazas de leche escaldada
1/2 taza de azúcar
6 cucharadas de manteca vegetal
2 cucharaditas de sal
2 huevos, batidos
7–8 tazas de harina
Azúcar, canela y pasas de uva

CUBIERTA BUTTERSCOTCH:

1 taza de azúcar mascabado, bien presionada
2 tazas de miel de maíz clara
2 barras de mantequilla

Disuelva la levadura en agua tibia. Escalde la leche con el azúcar (por ejemplo, caliente a que casi hierva pero no por completo). Agregue la manteca vegetal a la mezcla de leche y azúcar mientras está todavia caliente. Enfríe cerca de 3 minutos. Luego agregue la sal y los huevos batidos y la mezcla de levadura. En un tazón lo suficientemente grande para acomodar toda la masa, mezcle gradualmente en las 7–8 tazas de harina. Deje de agregar harina cuando la mezcla esté dura y pegajosa. Cambie la masa a un tazón engrasado, cubra con una tela un poco húmeda y ponga la masa en un lugar tibio, lejos de corrientes de aire, hasta que doble su tamaño.

Divida la masa en dos partes iguales para facilitar el extenderla. En una superficie bien enharinada, extienda cada mitad, con un rodillo, hasta formar un rectángulo grande (cerca de 15 x 11 pulgadas) de 1/2 pulgada de grueso. Unte con un poco de mantequilla derretida, espolvoree con azúcar y canela y cubra con pasas. Enrolle de uno de los lados largos al otro, corte en rebanadas de 2 pulgadas de grueso y colóquelos en el butterscotch que virtío en el fondo de un molde de hornear de 18 x 12 x 2 pulgadas, o en dos moldes de 13 x 9 x 2 pulgadas. Tápelos con una tela limpia y colóquelos en un lugar tibio lejos de corrientes de aire y permita que se levante de nuevo hasta que doble su tamaño. Precaliente el horno a 400°F. y hornee 25–30 minutos, hasta que la parte superior esté ligeramente dorada. Enfrié en una parrilla.

Para el Butterscotch: Derrita la mantequilla en una sartén pequeña. Agregue el azúcar mascabado y la miel de maíz y mezcle bien, pero no caliente. Vierta en el fondo de un molde o moldes de hornear.

BOLLOS "BISCUITS" FRITOS

Rinde 4 docenas, aproximadamente

3 1/2 cucharaditas de levadura activa en polvo
2 tazas de leche tibia — no caliente
1/4 taza de manteca vegetal
3 1/2 a 4 1/2 tazas de harina
2 cucharadas de azúcar
2 cucharaditas de sal

Disuelva la levadura en la leche y deje reposar hasta que esté espumosa (cerca de 10 minutos). Mezcle en la manteca. Mezcle hasta que la manteca esté casi derretida. Agregue, poco a poco, la harina, azúcar y sal y mezcle hasta que esté tersa. Tape con una toalla un poco húmeda y deje reposar en un lugar tibio hasta que doble su tamaño, cerca de 2 horas.

En una superficie ligeramente enharinada, extienda la masa para formar un rectángulo de 1/2 pulgada de grueso. Caliente el aceite a 375°F. en una freidora profunda. Corte la masa con un molde para bollos (biscuits) y fría, unos cuantos a la vez, en el aceite caliente. Cuando los bollos estén esponjados y dorados, volteelos para dorar el otro lado. Sáquelos con una cuchara ranurada, drénelos en toallas de papel y sírvalos de inmediato.

PIZZA VOLTEADA

4 Porciones

1/4 taza de cebolla, picada
1/4 taza de pimiento morrón verde, picado
10 champiñones frescos, rebanados
1/4 libra de cualquier carne — res, salchicha o jamón — picado o rebanado, cocida antes de usarla si utiliza carne de res molida o salchicha cruda
1 taza de queso mozzarella, rallado (si no está disponible, el queso Manchego es un buen substituto del mozzarella)
1 taza de salsa marinara (ver receta en la sección de "Salsas")
1 3/4 tazas de mezcla de hornear (ver receta en esta sección)
3/4 taza de agua
1 huevo, batido
2 cucharadas de queso parmesano, rallado

Engrase un molde redondo para pan de 9 pulgadas. Espolvoree la cebolla y pimiento morrón verde en el fondo del molde. Ponga una capa con los champiñones rebanados y agregue la carne que esté usando, encima de todo lo anterior y extienda el queso rallado encima de la carne. Por último, extienda la salsa, en forma pareja, sobre el queso. En un tazón mezcle el agua y el huevo, agregue la mezcla de hornear y mezcle hasta que esté integrado. No mezcle de más. Espolvoree el queso parmesano en toda la cubierta. Precaliente el horno a 350°F. y hornee durante 35 minutos, o hasta que la cubierta esté dorada oscura. Vierta en un platón precalentado, rebane y sirva.

BEIGNETS SIN RELLENAR COMO UN PAN

Rinde 40

3/4 taza de agua
1/4 taza de mantequilla sin sal
2 cucharadas de azúcar
1/8 cucharadita de sal
1 taza de harina
4 huevos grandes
1 cucharadita de vanilla
1/2 taza de azúcar
1/4 cucharadita de canela
Aceite para freído profundo

Mezcle la mantequilla, agua, azúcar y sal, y derrita a fuego lento. Cuando la mezcla esté líquida e hirviendo lentamente, retire del fuego e inmediatamente agregue la harina de una sola vez, como cuando está preparando chous cremosos, batiendo con una cuchara hasta que la mezcla se despegue de los lados de la sartén y forme una bola. Regrese al fuego y, a fuego lento, siga batiendo hasta que se vea el fondo de la sartén (cerca de 2 minutos). Retire del fuego y deje reposar por 5 minutos. Transfiera la masa al procesador o a un tazón grande de batidora eléctrica y bata unos cuantos segundos. gregue los huevos, uno a uno, mientras sigue batiendo. Agregue la vainilla. Si usa procesador, para de vez en cuando para quitar la masa de los lados del tazón.

Caliente el aceite a 375°F., en una freidora o un recipiente para freído profundo, por lo menos 3 pulgadas de profundidad. Usando cerca de 2 cucharaditas de masa para cada bollo, fríalos en pequeñas tandas, volteando una o dos veces, hasta que estén esponjados y dorados en todos lados. Asegúrese de no amontonarlos. Retire los bollos y drene en toallas de papel. Si desea, revuelque los bollos en azúcar mezclada con canela y manténgalos calientes en el horno a 200°F. hasta que estén listos para usarse. Estos bollos pueden, al igual que los bollos (biscuits) fritos en este capítulo, recalentarse para uso posterior.

MEZCLA PARA HORNEAR

Rinde 12 tazas

9 tazas de harina
10 cucharaditas de polvo de hornear
2 cucharaditas de sal
10 cucharadas de manteca vegetal
6 cucharadas de mantequilla, fría, picada

Cuidadosamente mezcle la harina, polvo de hornear y sal. Cuando estén bien integrados, agregue la manteca vegetal y la mantequilla. Mezcle con un mezclador de pastas o con batidora eléctrica a baja velocidad o con los dedos, hasta que la mezcla parezca que tiene granitos de arroz. No amase. Coloque la mezcla en un recipiente o varios recipientes herméticamente cerrados, y guarde en el refrigerador, o congélela indefinidamente en el congelador. Saque y mida de acuerdo a la receta que va a preparar.

Puede usar está mezcla para bollos (biscuits), hotcakes, shortcakes, etc., así como para los "Bisquick" comerciales.

MANTEQUILLA DE MIEL DE FRUTAS

Rinde casi 1 taza

2/3 taza de mantequilla, suavizada a la temperatura ambiente
1/3 taza de miel de abeja
2 cucharadas de jugo de limón o naranja Y
2 cucharaditas de ralladura de cáscara de limón o naranja
O
1/4 taza de la mermelada o jalea de su elección CON
1 cucharada de jugo de limón Y
1 cucharadita de ralladura de cáscara de limón

Mezcle todos los ingredientes en la licuadora, procesador o batidora eléctrica hasta que estén tersos y cremosos. Tape y refrigere hasta que esté lista para usar. Deje a la temperatura ambiente durante 30 minutos antes de servir.

QUESO CREMA DE NARANJA UNTABLE

Rinde 1 taza aproximadamente

1 paquete de queso crema (8 onzas), a la temperatura ambiente
1/4 taza de jugo de naranja
2 cucharadas de azúcar pulverizada
2 cucharaditas de ralladura de cáscara de naranja, fresca

En una licuadora, procesador o batidora eléctrica mezcle todos los ingredientes hasta que estén tersos y esponjosos. Tape y refrigere hasta que esté listo para usarse, pero póngalo a la temperatura ambiente (cerca de 30 minutos) antes de usarlo para untar en rollos o panes dulces.

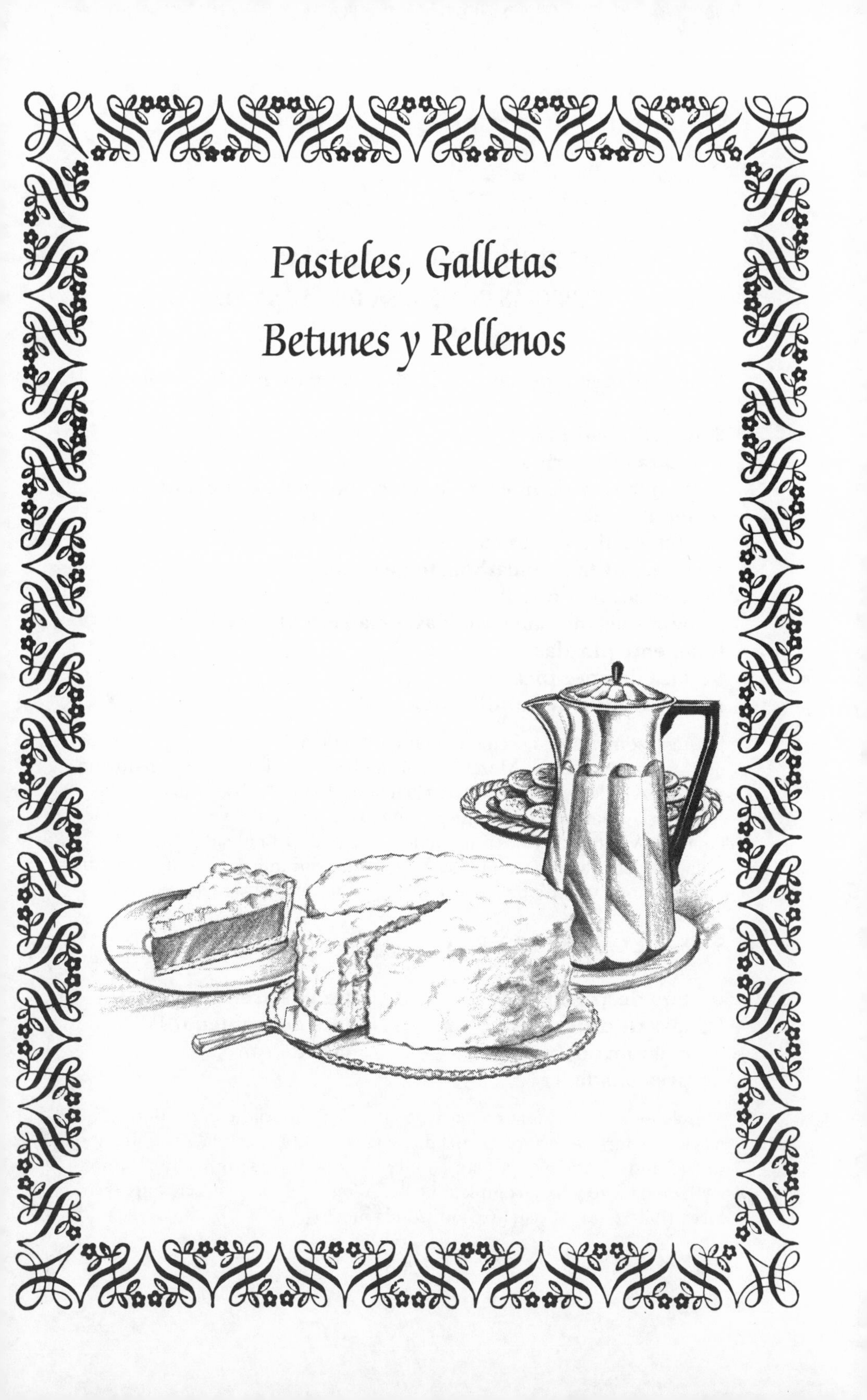

Pasteles, Galletas Betunes y Rellenos

PASTEL ESCANDINAVO DE MANZANA Y ESPECIAS CON SALSA DE CARAMELO

8 Porciones

1 taza de mantequilla, suavizada a la temperatura ambiente
1 taza de azúcar
2 huevos, batidos
1 1/2 tazas de harina
1 cucharadita de nuez moscada en polvo (si es posible, recién molida)
1 cucharadita de canela
1 cucharadita de bicarbonato de sodio
1/2 cucharadita de sal
3 manzanas medianas, ácidas, peladas, sin corazón y finamente picadas
3/4 taza de nuez picada
1 cucharadita de vainilla

En un tazón grande acreme la mantequilla con el azúcar y agregue los huevos, batiendo bien. Mezcle la harina, las especias, el bicarbonato y la sal, y mezcle de manera envolvente en la mezcla de azúcar y mantequilla. Agregue las manzanas y las nueces junto con la vainilla, y mezcle completamente. Vierta la masa en un molde de pay de 10 pulgadas bien engrasado, precaliente el horno a 350°F. y hornee durante 45 minutos aproximadamente. Sirva tibio con o sin nieve y cubra con la siguente salsa.

SALSA DE CARAMELO Y RON

1/2 taza de azúcar
1/2 taza de azúcar mascabado, bien presionada
1/2 taza de crema espesa
1/2 taza de mantequilla
1/4 taza de ron

Mezcle los azúcares y la crema y ponga a baño maría. Cueza sobre agua hirviendo durante 1 hora, poniendo agua en el otra cacerola a medida que sea necesario. Agregue la mantequilla y cueza durante otros 30 minutos. Retire del fuego y bata completamente. Agregue el ron y mezcle muy bien. Sirva tibia sobre el pastel y, si utiliza, la nieve.

PASTEL DE CHOCOLATE CELESTIAL

10–12 Porciones

1 caja de harina para pastel devil's food de 18 onzas (o una caja de harina para pastel de chocolate)
1 caja de pudín de chocolate instantáneo de 4 onzas (o 1 caja de pudín regular)
4 huevos, a la temperatura ambiente
3/4 taza de crema ácida
1/2 taza de aceite vegetal
1/2 taza de agua
1/4 taza de mayonesa
3 cucharadas de kahlúa
1 taza de chispas de chocolate semi-dulce
1/2 taza de almendras tostadas, picadas (pueden sustituirse con nueces)
Cocoa amarga en polvo

Engrase el molde "bundt" de 10 pulgadas y espolvoree con la cocoa. En un tazón grande combine la harina de pastel, el pudín, los huevos, la crema ácida, el aceite, el agua, la mayonesa y el kahlúa. Bata hasta que esté terso. Agregue las chispas de chocolate y las almedras (o nueces). Vierta la masa en el molde preparado, precaliente el horno a 350°F. y hornee cerca de 1 hora, o hasta que al insertar un palillo de dientes o una pajilla, salga limpio. Enfríe en el molde sobre una parrilla y deje que se enfríe ligeramente antes de retirar el molde. Espolvoree con azúcar pulverizada y permita que se enfire antes de servir. Si desea adorne con crema batida.

Si usa una caja de harina para pastel de chocolate, la cual es más fácil de encontrar que la caja de harina para pastel devil's food indicada, agregue 1 cucharada de cocoa a la masa. Si la caja de harina para pastel de chocolate es de 500 gramos, o sea cerca de 1/2 onza menos que la de 18 onzas, también agregue 1 cucharada de harina a la mezcla.

EXQUISITO PASTEL DE ZANAHORIA

12 Porciones

2 tazas de azúcar
1 1/2 tazas de aceite vegetal
3 huevos, batidos
2 tazas de zanahoria rallada
1 taza de nuez, picada
1 taza de dátiles, picados (opcional)
1 1/2 tazas de harina
1 taza de piña desmenuzada, enlatada, drenada
1 cucharadita de vainilla
1 cucharadita de bicarbonato de sodio
1/2 cucharadita de sal
1 cucharadita de canela

Combine el azúcar y el aceite. Agregue los huevos, batiendo bien. Mezcle con los otros ingredientes. Precaliente el horno a 350°F., ponga la masa en un molde para hornear de 9 x 13 x 2 pulgadas, engrasado. Hornee de 40 a 45 minutos, o hasta que el centro del pastel esté firme. Si desea, embetune el pastel con el betún de queso crema.

BETUN DE QUESO CREMA

1/4 taza de mantequilla suavizada
3 onzas de queso crema
1/2 libra de azúcar pulverizada
1 cucharadita de vainilla

Mezcle completamente todos los ingredientes y embetune el pastel.

PASTEL DE PIÑA Y NUEZ

12–15 Porciones

2 huevos
2 tazas de azúcar
1 cucharadita de vainilla
2 tazas de harina
2 cucharaditas de bicarbonato de sodio
1 taza de piña desmenuzada, enlatada
1 taza de nuez, toscamente picada

En un tazón grande bata los huevos, azúcar y vainilla; mezcle con la harina, bicarbonato y piña. Añada las nueces. Vierta la masa en un molde para hornear de 13 x 9 x 2 pulgadas bien engrasado y enharinado. Precaliente el horno a 350°F. y hornee durante 60 minutos aproximadamente. Enfríelo y fórrelo con su betún favorito.

VOLTEADO DE MANZANA Y ESPECIES

6 Porciones

1/4 taza de manteca vegetal
1/2 cucharadita de sal
1/2 cucharadita de canela
1/4 cucharadita de nuez moscada
1/4 cucharadita de pimienta dulce
3/4 taza de azúcar
1 huevo, sin batir
1 1/4 tazas de harina
1 1/2 cucharaditas de polvo de hornear
1/2 taza de leche
2 manzanas medianas, ácidas, peladas, sin corazón y rebanadas
4 cucharadas de mantequilla
1/2 taza de azúcar mascabado, bien presionada
2 cucharadas de leche

Acreme la manteca, sal, especies y azúcar hasta que esté ligera y esponjosa. Agregue el huevo y bata completamente. Cierna la harina y el polvo de hornear y agregue en pequeñas cantidades a la mezcla cremosa, alternando con la leche y batiendo después de cada adición, hasta que esté tersa. Engrase un molde o plato de hornear de 8 x 8 pulgadas y arregle las manzanas sobre el fondo. En una cacerola, derrita la mantequilla, el azúcar mascabado y leche, mezclando bien. Extienda sobre las manzanas y vierta la masa encima de todo. Precaliente el horno a 350°F. y hornee durante 60 minutos, aproximadamente. Volteelo y sírvalo con crema batida.

PASTEL AMARILLO

8–10 Porciones

1/2 taza de manteca vegetal
1 cucharadita de vainilla
1 taza de leche
2 1/4 tazas de harina
1 1/2 tazas de azúcar
3 cucharaditas de polvo de hornear
1/2 cucharadita de sal
2 huevos

Bata la manteca, vainilla y azúcar hasta que esté cremosa. Agregue los huevos y siga batiendo hasta que esté tersa. Mezcle la harina, polvo de hornear y sal. Añada la mezcla seca, poco a poco, a la mezcla cremosa, alternando con la leche, batiendo hasta que esté tersa. Engrase y enharine 2 moldes para pastel de 8 pulgadas. Ponga la masa en porciones iguales en los dos moldes y hornee en el horno precalentado a 350°F., durante 25 a 30 minutos o hasta que los centros de los pasteles estén flexibles al tocarlos con la yema del dedo. Rellene y ponga el betún de su elección.

POUND CAKE FACIL Y RAPIDO

12 ó Más Porciones

1 caja de harina para pastel blanco
4 huevos
2/3 taza de aceite
2/3 taza de agua
1 caja de gelatina en polvo (limón o naranja)
1/2 cucharadita de macia en polvo

Ponga todos los ingredientes en un tazón grande de batidora eléctrica y bata a velocidad media alta, durante 5 minutos. O bata a mano durante 7 minutos. Precaliente el horno a 375°F., engrase un molde tube con mantequilla o manteca vegetal. Vierta la masa y hornee de 45 a 55 minutos hasta que el pastel esté firme y dorado en la parte superior.

CASSATA ITALIANA

12 ó Mas Porciones

1 pound cake de 9 x 5 pulgadas en forma de rectángulo (ver receta para "pound cake" èn esta sección)

2 tazas de queso ricotta (para esté pastel el queso es muy importante de manera que si no tiene queso ricotta, use queso llamado "requesón" o queso cottage, y mezcle 1 1/4 tazas de requesón o queso cottage con 3/4 taza de queso crema. El queso crema suavizará el otro para hacer que pueda untarse mejor, pero manteniendo su sabor correcto.
2/3 taza de nueces o almendras picadas, tostadas (opcional)
4 onzas de chispas de chocolate semi-dulce, picadas
2 onzas de licor de naranja o crema de cacao
1 1/4 tazas de jalea de frambuesa sin semillas (pueden substituirse con jalea de naranja o chabacano, pero la frambuesa es mejor, o puede usar fruta confitada picada, al verdadero estilo italiano, pero pensamos que la jalea o mermelada es mejor)
Betún de chocolate o crema batida, o más queso en una manga de duya pastelera o cualquier combinación para la cubierta.

Enfríe el pastel de 1 a 2 horas. Rebane el pastel horizontalmente en 4 capas. Pique las chispas de chocolate en la licuadora o en el procesador de alimentos con el licor. No pique mucho o perderá la textura. En un tazón mezcle el chocolate en la jalea y mantenga aparte. Si usa dos quesos mézclelos hasta que estén bien integrados y listos para untar. Si usa ricotta mezclelo para obtener una consistencia untable. Extienda 1/3 del queso en la capa del fondo del pastel. Extienda 1/3 de la mezcla de jalea encima de la capa de queso. Enseguida agregue 1/3 de las nueces o almendras picadas, si la está utilizando, y luego repita este procedimiento dos veces más, colocando la cuarta capa del pastel encima. Con cuidado, presione el pastel relleno y nìvele los lados con una espátula. Cubra con plástico o papel aluminio y refrigere toda la noche o más. Embetune con betún cremoso de chocolate y si desea adorne las orillas del pastel con más queso con duya pastelera, embetune con crema batida dulce. Refrigere otros 30 minutos o más antes de rebanarlo y servirlo.

Estes es un delicioso postre que llena mucho, por lo tanto rendirá.

POUND CAKE

6–8 Porciones

Incluimos esté pastel debido a su versatilidad de uso. Los sabores pueden cambiar y adaptarse para incluir casi cualquier sabor, y su textura lo hace una base excelente para pasteles de nieve, siempre favorito de los niños y para fiestas especiales.

1/2 taza de manteca vegetal
1/4 taza de mantequilla, suavizada a la temperatura ambiente
3/4 cucharadita de sal
1/2 cucharadita de macia
1/2 cucharadita de ralladura de limón fresco
1 1/4 tazas de azúcar
3 huevos, sin batir
2 3/4 tazas de harina cernida
1 1/2 cucharaditas de polvo de hornear
1/2 taza de leche

Bata la manteca, sal, mantequilla, macia y ralladura de limón con el azúcar, hasta que esté esponjosa. Agregue los huevos, uno a la vez, batiendo bien después de cada adición. Cierna varias veces la harina con el polvo de hornear hasta que esté ligera y esponjosa. Agreguela a la mezcla cremosa, alternando con la leche, mezclando muy bien después de cada adición hasta que esté tersa. Forre un molde de pan de 9 x 5 x 3 pulgadas, con el papel encerado o pergamino engrasado en la qarte superior. Vierta la masa en el molde, precaliente el horno y hornee a 300°F. (baja) durante 1 hora, luego aumente la temperatura a 325°F. y hornee de 45–50 minutos más, hasta que el centro del pastel esté flexible al presionarlo con la yema del dedo, o hasta que al introducir un palillo de dientes o una pajilla, salga limpio. Invierta en una parrilla de alambre y retire el papel mientras está tibio.

Si va a utilizar el pastel para nieve, permita que se enfríe por completo y rebane horizontalmente en 3 ó 4 capas, luego suavice cualquier sabor deseado o combinación de sabores de nieve, hasta que esté untable, extienda entre las capas y cubra con papel aluminio y regrese al molde y congele. Si desea, antes de servir cuando esté congelado el pastel, puede cubrirlo con crema batida dulce. Desmolde en un platón de servicio, embetune con la crema o cualquier tipo de betún, o más nieve, luego rebane y sírvalo.

1 cucharadita de extracto de limón, o cualquier otro sabor que guste, puede substituir la 1/2 cucharadita de macia requerida arriba, para cambiar el sabor de las capas del pastel y relleno de cualquier sabor, puede substituir la nieve.

DELICIOSO Y ELEGANTE PASTEL DE NARANJA RELLENO

12–16 Porciones

Para este pastel tenga todos los ingredientes a la temperatura ambiente.

3 tazas de harina
3/4 cucharadita de sal
3 1/2 cucharaditas de polvo de hornear
Ralladura de 1 cáscara de naranja
1 1/2 tazas de azúcar
3/4 taza de mantequilla
3 huevos
1/2 taza de jugo de naranja
1/2 taza de agua
2 cucharadas de limón fresco

Acreme el azúcar y la mantequilla hasta que estén cremosas. Agregue los huevos, uno a uno, batiendo todo el tiempo hasta que esté terso. Agregue los ingredientes secos cernidos, alternando con los jugos y el agua que mezcló previamente, batiendo cada vez que agregue ingredientes hasta que esté terso. Engrase y enharine el fondo de 3 moldes para pan de 9 pulgadas, redondos. Precaliente el horno a 375°F. ponga la masa en los tres moldes en porciones iguales y hornee 30–35 minutos, o cuando los centros estén flexibles al tocarlos ligeramente con la yema del dedo. Saque los pasteles de los moldes y cuando estén fríos extienda entre las capas el siguiente relleno cremoso de naranja:

RELLENO CREMOSO DE NARANJA

1 cucharadita de gelatina sin sabor, remojada en 1 cucharada de agua durante 5 minutos
2 cucharadas de maicena
2 cucharadas de harina
3/4 taza de azúcar
3/4 taza de agua
1 cucharada de mantequilla
2 yemas de huevo, batidas
Ralladura de 1 cáscara de naranja
3 cucharadas de jugo de naranja
3 cucharadas de jugo de limón
1/2 taza de crema para batir

Mezcle todos los ingredientes secos, y póngalos a baño maría. Agregue el agua y cuezalos hasta que espesen, sin dejar de menear (cerca de 12 minutos) agregue la mantequilla. Agregue un poco de la mezcla hasta que las yemas estén tibias. Luego agregue las yemas a la mezcla y caliente a que esté a punto de hervir meneando constantemente. No hierva. Añada la gelatina remojada. Revuelva hasta que se disuelva y retire del fuego. Agregue la ralladura de naranja y los jugos. Enfríe. Bata la 1/2 taza de crema hasta que esté firme y añadala, poco a poco a la mezcla. Refrigere una hora y extienda entre las capas del pastel despues embetune con lo siguente:

BETUN ESPONJOSO DE NARANJA SIETE MINUTOS

2 claras de huevo, sin batir
1 1/2 tazas de azúcar
5 cucharadas de jugo de naranja
1/4 cucharadita de cremor tártaro o
1 1/2 cucharaditas de miel de maíz clara

Mezcle todos los ingredientes en un recipiente, a baño maría, sobre agua hirviendo. Con un batidor giratorio, bata la mezcla continuamente sobre el agua hirviendo, hasta que se formen picos húmedos (cerca de 8 minutos). Retire del fuego y agregue:

1 cucharadita de ralladura de naranja

Siga batiendo hasta que el betún tenga la consistencia adecuada para untarlo en el pastel.

Mantenga refrigerado el pastel hasta el momento de servir.

DELICIOSO PASTEL DE COCOA DEVIL'S FOOD

12 Porciones

2/3 taza de manteca vegetal
1 1/4 tazas de azúcar
2 huevos
1 cucharadita de vainilla
1 1/2 tazas de harina
1/2 taza de cocoa
3/4 cucharadita de sal
1 1/4 cucharaditas de bicarbonato
1 taza de leche agria o leche cortada (la leche agria se puede hacer agregando 1 cucharadita de vinagre a la leche)
1 cucharadita de canela en polvo
1/2 cucharadita de pimienta dulce en polvo

Bata la manteca con el azúcar hasta que esté cremosa. Agregue los huevos y la vainilla. Mezcle la harina, la cocoa, la sal y todas las especies juntas. Mezcle el bicarbonato con la leche agria. Agregue los ingredientes secos, alternando con la mezcla de leche, a la mezcla de manteca, azúcar, huevo y siga batiendo hasta que esté terso. Engrase y enharine, ligeramente, dos moldes para pastel de 9 pulgadas y vierta la masa en ellos. Precaliente el horno y hornee a 350°F. durante 35 minutos. El pastel está listo cuando está flexible al tocarlo. Enfríe en una parrilla antes de desmoldar. Embetune con betún esponjoso 7 minutos.

BROWNIES DE CHOCOLATE-FUDGE

Rinde cerca de 30

Favoritas de todos los americanos, las brownies parecen muy fáciles. *Son fáciles* de preparar, pero como se hacen es importante. Para lograr esa textura de chocolate chicloso, muy admirada en una buena brownie, el tamaño del molde para la cantidad de masa es muy importante. Esta receta requiere un molde de pastel de 13 x 9 x 2 pulgadas. Si no quiere hacer una cantidad tan grande, corte la receta a la mitad y use un molde cuadrado de 8 x 8 pulgadas.

1/2 taza de manteca vegetal o mantequilla
4 onzas de chocolate amargo
4 huevos, a la temperatura ambiente
1/4 cucharadita de sal
2 tazas de azúcar
1 cucharadita de vainilla
1 taza de harina
1 taza de nuez picada (opcional)

Derrita la mantequilla o manteca y el chocolate a baño maría, sobre agua hirviendo, mantenga aparte hasta que se enfríe. (No lo use hasta que se enfríe porque es importante no derretir el azúcar con el que será mezclado). Bata los huevos junto con la sal hasta que estén claros de color y espesos. Gradualmente agregue el azúcar y vainilla y siga batiendo hasta que esté bien integrado. A mano bata la mezcla de chocolate en la mezcla de huevo y azúcar y, entonces, justo hasta que estén casi mezclados agregue la taza de harina y bata la masa completa, hasta que esté bien integrada. Si usa las nueces agreguelas en esté punto, justo antes de vertir la masa en el molde bien engrasado y enharinado. Precaliente el horno a 350°F. y hornee cerca de 25 a 30 minutos, hasta que el centro esté firme. Enfríe completamente antes de cortar en cuadros. Sirvalas solas o con betún, o con un poco de crema batida dulce o nieve.

Galletas

GALLETAS DE REFRIGERADOR

Rinde cerca de 3 1/2 docenas

Estas galletas son maravillosas rellenas, vea abajo

1/2 taza de mantequilla, a la temperatuta ambiente
1 taza de azúcar
1 huevo, batido
1 cucharadita de vainilla
1/2 cucharadita de ralladura de limón
1/4 cucharadita de sal
1 1/2 cucharaditas de polvo de hornear
1 1/4 a 1 1/2 tazas de harina

Acreme la mantequilla, azúcar, huevo, vainilla y ralladura juntos hasta que esté esponjoso. Agregue la sal y polvo de hornear, y luego la harina y mezcle completamente, agregando solo la harina suficiente para hacer una bola firme. Ponga la bola de masa en un pedazo de papel encerado o aluminio grande y dele forma de un rollo largo. Enrolle el papel alrededor y enfríe en el refrigerador por varias horas o toda la noche, hasta que esté firme. Corte las rebanadas de 1/4 de pulgada y póngalas en hojas de hornear engrasadas. Precaliente el horno a 400°F. y nornee de 8 a 10 minutos, o hasta que estén doradas. Enfríe sobre papel o aluminio en una parrilla de alambre.

Para rellenar estas galletas, coloque una galleta en una hoja de hornear, ponga cerca de 1/2 cucharadita de relleno o un trozo de fruta seca encima, cubra con otra galleta y haga cortes con un tenedor todo alrededor para sellar. Puede utilizar cualquier tipo de mermelada como relleno, o fruta seca picada, mezclela con un poco de licor de naranja, o, si tiene disponible, rellene con 1/2 mezclada cucharadita de mincemeat.

GALLETAS DE REFRIGERADOR BUTTERSCOTCH

Siga la receta de arriba, a excepción de que tiene que substituir 1 1/4 taza de azúcar mascabado por la taza de azúcar blanca, y agregue un poco de nueces picadas a la masa antes de enrollarla.

MOLLETES DE NUEZ

Rinde cerca de 3 1/2 docenas

1 taza de mantequilla a la temperatura ambiente
2 cucharadas de azúcar
1 cucharadita de vainilla
1 taza de nueces, toscamente molidas
1 taza de harina
Azúcar pulverizada

Acreme la mantequilla, azúcar y vainilla juntos hasta que esté esponjoso. Mezcle en la harina y menee o amase hasta que esté bien integrado. Amase en las nueces molidas. Forme pequeñas bolitas con la masa y colóquelas en una hoja de hornear galletas, engrasada. Precaliente el horno a 300°F. y hornee cerca de 30 minutos. Mientras los molletes están aún calientes, revuelquelos en el azúcar pulverizada. Enfríelos bien antes de servirlos. Puede guardar estos molletes por algún tiempo en el refrigerador en recipientes de tapa hermética.

GALLETAS BROWN RIM

Rinde cerca de 4 docenas

1 taza de manteca vegetal
1 cucharadita de sal
1 cucharadita de vainilla
2/3 taza de azúcar + 2 cucharadas
2 huevos, bien batidos
2 1/2 tazas de harina

Acreme el azúcar, manteca, sal y vainilla hasta que esté esponjoso. Agregue los huevos y siga batiendo hasta que esté terso. Agregue la harina y mezcle bien. Deje caer de la punta de una cuchara, o haga pequeñas bolitas con las manos, en una charola para hornear galletas, engrasada. Humedezca muy ligeramente una tela limpia y tersa, y colóquela sobre el fondo ancho de un vaso de fondo plano. Sosteniendo la tela ajustada encima del vaso, presione cada bolita para hacerla plana. Precaliente el horno a 375°F. y hornee cerca de 8 a 10 minutos hasta que estén delicadamente doradas. Volteelas de una sola vez, a una superfivcie plana cubierta de papel encerado, de preferencia a una parrilla de alambre.

Puede cambiar el sabor de estas galletas con tan solo usar 1/2 cucharadita de extracto de almendra con 1/2 cucharadita de vainilla, o usando 1/2 cucharadita de extracto de limón con la ralladura de un limón.

Esta receta hace galletas crujientes y delicadas, adecuadas para la tarde con té o café.

GALLETAS DE AZUCAR

Rinde 3 docenas

2 tazas de harina cernida
1/2 cucharadita de polvo de hornear
1/4 cucharadita de sal
1/2 taza de mantequilla
1/2 cucharadita de ralladura de limón
1/2 cucharadita de nuez moscada
3/4 taza de azúcar + 2 cucharadas
1 huevo
1 cucharada de leche

Amase todos los ingredientes juntos hasta que pueda formar una bola tersa. Enfríe durante 30 minutos aproximadamente, antes de extenderla con un rodillo en una superficie enharinada, extienda cerca de una cuarta parte de la masa cada vez. Corte en las formas que desee. Ponga las galletas en hojas para hornear engrasadas; precaliente el horno a 400°F. y hornee durante 12 a 15 minutos, hasta que doren. Si desea, embetune las galletas después de que se hayan enfriado.

BETUN ESPONJOSO SIETE MINUTOS

2 claras de huevo
1 1/2 tazas de azúcar
1 1/2 cucharaditas de miel de maíz clara ó 1/4 cucharadita de cremor tártaro
1/3 taza de agua fría
1 pizca de sal
1 cucharadita de extracto de vainilla

Coloque todos los ingredientes, excepto la vainilla, a baño maría. Mezcle bien, cueza sin dejar de batir con batidor giratorio o batidora eléctrica, sobre agua hirviendo hasta que la mezcla forme picos, cerca de 7–8 minutos. Retire del fuego y agregue la vainilla. Siga batiendo hasta que espese lo suficiente para mantenerse después de untado.

BETUN CREMOSO DE MANTEQUILLA

1/3 taza de mantequilla suavizada
2 1/2 a 3 tazas (1 libra) de azúcar pulverizada
1/4 taza de crema, leche evaporada o leche
2 yemas de huevo o un huevo entero
1 cucharadita de extracto de vainilla

En un tazón de mezclar bata bien la mantequilla, sal y cerca de 1/3 del azúcar pulverizada. Alternadamente agregue la crema o leche, yemas de huevo o huevo y el resto del azúcar. Bata hasta que esté terso, esponjoso y con una consistencia para untar. Agregue el extracto de vainilla. Si está muy aguado, agregue un poco más de azúcar pulverizada. Si está muy espeso, agregue unas gotas de leche.

BETUN CREMOSO DE MANTEQUILLA SABOR LIMON

Use la receta de arriba, agregue 3 1/2 cucharadas de jugo de limón en lugar de la vainilla, y mezcle la ralladura de un limón. También use solo las yemas de huevo no huevo entero.

BETUN DE CHOCOLATE FUDGE

3 onzas de chocolate amargo
3 cucharadas de mantequilla
1/4 taza de crema o leche evaporada
1 cucharadita de vainilla
2 a 2 1/2 tazas de azúcar pulverizada

En un sartén a fuego lento derrita la mantequilla y chocolate. Retire del fuego, enfríe durante 3 minutos y agregue la crema o leche. Bata en el azúcar con batidor de mano o batidora eléctrica y agregue la vainilla. Si está muy aguado, agregue un poco más de azúcar. Si está muy espeso. Agregue un poco más de leche, hasta que éste tenga una consistencia para untar.

BETUN HORNEADO

6 cucharadas de mantequilla derretida
2/3 taza de azúcar mascabado, bien presionada
1/4 taza de leche evaporada
1 taza de granola, nueces picadas o coco rallado, según prefiera

En un tazón mezcle todos los ingredientes juntos. Cuando el pastel esté horneado, retírelo del horno y rápidamente extiéndalo en el pastel caliente. Regrese al horno y cuézalo bajo el asador, tan retirado de la flama como sea posible, durante 5 minutos. También puede untar el betún en el pastel frío y colocarlo bajo el asador (parrilla) hasta que haga burbujas.

RELLENO DE NATILLA (FLAN) ALMENDRA

3/4 tazas de azúcar
3 cucharadas de fécula de maíz
1/4 cucharadita de sal
2 tazas de leche
2 huevos, batidos
3/4 cucharadita de extracto de vainilla
3/4 cucharadita de extracto de almendra
1 taza de crema para batir, batida (opcional)

Mezcle juntos el azúcar, fécula de maíz y sal. Agregue la leche y mezcle hasta que esté terso. Ponga a que hierva lentamente, meneando con frecuencia. Mezcle un poco en los huevos batidos y luego regrese los huevos y la mezcla a la sartén principal y siga cocinando a fuego muy lento hasta que la natilla esté caliente pero no hirviendo todavía, cerca de 2 a 3 minutos durante esté tiempo, menee la mezcla vigorosamente. Retire del fuego y agregue los extractos. Enfríe y mezcle de forma envolvente en la crema batida, si la usa.

RELLENO DE NATILLA DE VAINILLA

Siga exactamente la receta de arriba, a exepción de omitir el extracto de almendras y usar 1 1/2 cucharaditas de vainilla.

RELLENO DE NATILLA DE CHOCOLATE

Use la receta de relleno de natilla almendrada de arriba, pero agregue 2 onzas de chocolate amargo y 2 cucharadas de mantequilla, los cuales derritió juntos, a la leche antes de agregarlos a los ingredientes secos y substituya 1 1/2 cucharaditas de extracto de vainilla por los 3/4 de cucharadita de vainilla y omita el extracto de almendras.

RELLENO RAPIDO DE LIMON

1/4 taza de azúcar
1 1/2 cucharadas de fécula de maíz
1/2 taza de agua
3 cucharadas de jugo de limón
1/2 cucharadita de ralladura de limón
1 cucharada de mantequilla
1 yema de huevo, batido con 1 cucharadita de leche

En una sartén mediana mezcle el azúcar, fécula de maíz y sal juntos. Mezcle en agua, jugo y ralladura de limón y mantequilla. Cueza a fuego moderado hasta que hierva mucho, meneando constantemente cera de 2 minutos saque una pequeña cantidad y agreguela a la mezcla de yema de huevo, y luego regrese a la sartén. Ponga a que casi hierva de nuevo, meneando constantemente. Enfríe. Bata con batidor de mano hasta que esté espeso y terso.

Pays

PAY CHIFON DE LIMON AGRIDULCE

6–8 Porciones

1 pizca de sal
1 taza de azúcar
1 1/4 tazas de agua
1 cucharada de mantequilla
1/3 taza de fécula de maíz
6 cucharadas de jugo de limón
1 cucharadita de ralladura de limón
3 huevos, separados
1 concha de pay de 9 pulgadas, horneada (ver receta para "Pasta Básica" en el glosario al final de la sección)
2 cucharadas de leche

En una cacerola combine muy bien el azúcar, sal, mantequilla y fécula de maíz. Agregue el agua y mezcle bien, cueza, meneando constantemente, a fuego lento hasta que espese. Agregue las 6 cucharadas de jugo y la ralladura de limón. Bata las yemas de huevo con la leche hasta que estén esponjosas. Lentamente, agregue un poco de la mezcla de fécula de maíz a las yemas de huevo y luego regréselas a la sartén. Ponga a que casi llegue a hervir, pero no hierva, y retire del fuego cuando espese para enfriar.

Bata las claras de huevo hasta que estén duras pero no secas. Mezcle de manera envolvente 1/3 de las claras batidas en el relleno de limón. Extienda el relleno en la concha de pay, horneada, y prepare la cubierta de merengue esponjoso, de la siguiente manera:

1/2 taza de azúcar
1/8 cucharadita de sal
1/4 taza de agua
1/8 cucharadita de cremor tártaro

En una cacerola chica combine todos los ingredientes anteriores, cuézalos a fuego lento, sin dejar de menear, hasta que haga hebras. Gradualmente vierta sobre las claras restantes, sin dejar de batir. Siga batiendo hasta que la mezcla mantenga su forma, 3 ó 4 minutos. Agregue 1 cucharadita de jugo de limón ó 1/8 cucharadita de vainilla y extienda sobre el pay. Refrigere por lo menos 2 horas antes de servir.

PAY DE PIÑA FRESCA

8 Porciones

1 ó 1 1/2 taza de azúcar (dependiendo de que tan ácida o dulce esté la piña fresca)
3 cucharadas de harina
1/2 cucharadita de nuez moscada
1 cucharadita de canela
1 cucharada de mantequilla
2 huevos, batidos
4 tazas de piña, cortada en trozos de 1 pulgada
1 concha para pay de 9 pulgadas, sin hornear (ver receta para "Pasta Básica" en el glosario al final de la sección) + la mitad de 1 receta para la cubierta

Mezcle el azúcar, harina, nuez moscada y canela y una pequeña pizca de sal. Corte la mantequilla en la mezcla hasta que parezca harina de maíz. Coloque la piña en trozos en el fondo de la concha de pay, sin hornear. Combine los dos huevos en la mezcla de azúcar, harina, mantequilla y mezcle bien. Ponga encima de la piña, asegurándose de cubrir todos los trozos. Extienda con un rodillo la otra mitad de la receta para pasta básica, en forma de oblongo, de 1/4 de pulgada de grueso aproximadamente y corte tiras de 1/2 pulgada de ancho. Coloque las tiras, atravesándolas, para formar una cubierta de rejilla. Presione las tiras alrededor de las orillas de la concha de pay. Precaliente el horno a 450°F., hornee durante 10 minutos, luego reduzca la temperatura a 350°F. y siga horneando durante 30 a 40 minutos, o más si es necesario, hasta que el relleno esté firme y la cubierta dorada. Sirva tibio o a la temperatura ambiente.

PAY DE LIMON CARIBEÑO

8–10 Porciones

1/2 taza de jugo de limón fresco
2 sobres de gelatina sin sabor
5 yemas de huevo
1 taza de azúcar
1/4 taza de ron
1 cucharada de licor de naranja
Ralladura de 2 limones
5 claras de huevo, batidas con 1/2 taza de azúcar
3 ó 4 gotas de colorante vegetal color verde
1 taza de crema para batir, batida
Rebanadas de limón y 1/2 taza de crema para batir, batida con 1 cucharada de azúcar pulverizada para adornar (opcional)
1 concha de coco para pay (vea abajo)

En una cacerola pequeña mezcle la gelatina y el jugo de limón, póngalos a fuego lento hasta que se haya derretido completamente la gelatina. Bata las yemas de huevo con 1/2 taza de azúcar, a baño maría, hasta que estén bien mezcladas. Agregue la mezcla de gelatina y continúe batiendo sobre agua hirviendo a fuego lento, hasta que esté lo suficientemente espeso para cubrir bien una cuchara (cerca de 10–15 minutos). Retire del fuego y enfríe. Agregue el ron, licor de naranja y ralladura de limón.

En un tazón grande de batidora eléctrica, bata las claras con el colorante vegetal, hasta que estén duras pero no secas, añada el azúcar poco a poco, tan pronto como las claras estén espumosas, pero antes de que empiecen a endurecerse. Con cuidado agregue de manera envolvente la mezcla anterior en las claras, solo hasta que logre un efecto veteado. No mezcle demasiado. Cuidadosamente mezcle en la crema batida. Coloque a cucharadas el relleno en la concha y, si desea, refrigere o congele.

Justo antes de servir extienda la otra taza de crema batida encima del relleno y espolvoree con el resto de coco tostado que reservó y ribetee con rebanadas de limón.

CONCHA DE COCO

3 tazas de coco fresco rallado
6 cucharadas de mantequilla derretida

Extienda el coco, en una capa delgada, sobre una hoja para hornear galletas, o en un recipiente grande poco profundo y tueste un poco en el horno precalentado a 350°F., durante 8 minutos aproximadamente.

Reserve 1/2 taza del coco tostado para adorno, combine el resto del coco con la mantequilla derretida y revuelva ligeramente, hasta que esté bien mezclado. Presione firmemente en un molde para pay de 9 pulgadas, cubra cuidadosamente con papel aluminio y refrigere hasta que esté listo para utilizarse.

Si tiene invitados a los que no les gusta el coco, puede substituir por una concha de galletas de harina de trigo entero (ver receta de "Pastel de Queso Sencillo" en la sección de postres) o una concha de galletas de chocolate (usando las mismas proporciones que en la receta de galletas de harina de trigo entero, pero omitiendo la canela y refrigerando la concha en lugar de hornearla).

PAY DE NUEZ CON KAHLUA

8 Porciones

1 concha para pay de 9 pulgadas, sin hornear (ver receta para "Pasta Básica" en el glosario al final de la sección)
1/4 taza de mantequilla (suavizada pero no derretida)
3/4 taza de azúcar
1 cucharadita de vainilla
2 cucharadas de harina
3 huevos
1/2 taza de kahlúa
1/2 taza de miel de maíz oscura
3/4 taza de leche evaporada
1 taza de nuez, toscamente picada

Bata la mantequilla, azúcar, vainilla y harina. Mezcle bien. Agregue los huevos enteros, uno a uno. Mezcle con el kahlúa, miel de maíz, leche evaporada y nuez. Mezcle bien y ponga encima de la concha de pay. Precaliente el horno a 400°F., hornee durante 15 minutos, luego reduzca la temperatura a 325°F., dejando la puerta del horno abierta por 3 ó 4 minutos, para bajar la temperatura de 400°F. a 325°F., después cierre la puerta y hornee 45 minutos más o hasta que esté firme. Refrigere antes de servir y, si desea, adorne con crema batida y mitades de nuez.

TORTA DE LIMON "ANGEL"

6–8 Porciones

4 huevos, a la temperatura ambiente, separados
3/4 taza de azúcar
1/4 cucharadita de sal
1/4 cucharadita de cremor tártaro
1 taza de crema espesa, batida
1 receta de relleno de limón (ver receta abajo)

Bata con la batidora a velocidad alta las claras de huevo con el azúcar, sal y cremor tártaro, hasta que se formen picos muy duros. Extiéndala en un molde de pay de 9 pulgadas, bien engrasado, Precaliente el horno a 225°F. y hornee durante 1 1/2 a 2 horas, hasta que la concha esté firme al tacto y ligeramente dorada. Enfríe.

Rellene la concha con la mitad de la crema batida, luego extienda encima el relleno de limón, con mucho cuidado, y extienda encima la otra mitad de la crema batida. Enfríe bien antes de servir.

RELLENO DE LIMON

Bata las 4 yemas de huevo y colorante vegetal color limón hasta que espesen. Poco a poco batalas en 1/2 taza de azúcar, una pizca de sal, 1 cucharada de ralladura de limón, y 3 cucharadas de jugo de limón. Cueza a fuego lento hasta que espese (cerca de 6 minutos). Enfríe antes de extenderla sobre la crema batida en el merengue.

Puede adornar la parte superior del pay con ralladura de limón.

PAY DE MANZANA Y YOGURT

8 Porciones

1 concha de pay de 9 pulgadas, sin hornear (ver receta para "Pasta Básica" en el glosario al final de la sección)
1/4 taza de azúcar
1/4 taza de azúcar mascabado, bien presionada
2 cucharadas de fécula de maíz
1/4 cucharadita de sal
1/2 cucharadita de canela
4–5 tazas de manzana, pelada, finamente rebanada y ácida de preferencia
1/2 cucharadita de jugo de limón
1 taza de yogurt
1 huevo
1/2 cucharadita de vainilla
1/4 taza de almendras picadas y tostadas)
1/2 taza de azúcar mascabado, bien presionada)
1 cucharadita de canela)

Combine los azúcares, canela, fécula de maíz y sal. Agregue las manzanas. Revuelva en el jugo de limón. Ponga la mezcla de manzanas en la concha de pay, distribuyéndola de forma pareja. Precaliente el horno a 400°F. y hornee 30 minutos.

Bata el huevo hasta que esté esponjoso. Agregue el yogurt y la vainilla, mezcle bien. Reduzca la temperatura del horno a 350°F. permita que el horno se enfríe durante 2 minutos, con la puerta abierta, antes de meter de nuevo el pay, después de haber puesto la mezcla de yogurt sobre las manzanas, distribuyendo muy bien. Continue horneando durante 40 minutos más, hasta que tenga una consistencia de flan y las manzanas estén cocidas.

Enfríe el pay durante 10 minutos y espolvoree sobre el pay las almendras, y la otra 1/2 taza de azúcar mascabado y canela, los cuales mezcló previamente. Sirva tibio o a la temperatura ambiente.

PAY DE FRUTA FRESCA DE DOS CAPAS

8 Porciones

1 concha de pay de 9 pulgadas, horneada (ver receta para "Pasta Básica" en el glosario al final de la sección)
1/2 taza de azúcar pulverizada
1/2 cucharadita de vainilla
1/2 cucharadita de extracto de almendras
1 paquete grande (6 onzas) de queso crema
1/2 taza de crema espesa batida (si es necesario, puede usar 1 taza de crema artificial pre-batida como crema chantilly, si usa crema dulce pre-batida, reduzca a 1/4 de taza el azúcar pulverizada)
1/3 taza de azúcar
3 cucharadas de fécula de maíz
1/3 taza de agua
1/3 taza de miel de maíz clara
1 cucharada de jugo de limón
2 tazas de fruta fresca (fresas enteras, duraznos rebanados, mango rebanado o en cubitos, piña rebanada o en cubitos, ciruelas rebanadas, etc.)
Varias gotas de colorante vegetal, un color que combine con la fruta que está utilizando.

Agregue el azúcar pulverizado, vainilla y extracto de almendras al queso y bata hasta que esté terso y cremoso. Mezcle con la crema batida. Extienda sobre el fondo de la concha de pay horneada. Refrigere durante varias horas.

En un recipiente combine 1/3 taza de azúcar y la fécula de maíz. Lentamente agregue el agua, meneando para obtener una mezcla tersa.

Añada la miel y el jugo de limón y el colorante. Cueza meneando constantemente, hasta que esté espesa y clara. Enfríe.

Agregue a la fruta, meneando para cubrir con el glaseado. Extienda encima de la capa de crema. Refrigere completamente antes de servir. si desea, sirva con un chopito de crema batida dulce en cada rebanada.

PAY DE MERMELADA ITALIANO
CROSTATA DI MARMALADA

8 Porciones

Use la receta en el Glosario de Pastas para Crostata Italiana. Extienda el resto con un rodillo, sobre una superficie enharinada hasta tener el tamaño de un plato de 10 pulgadas. Pellisque u ondule las orillas de la concha con los dedos y pinche con un tenedor el fondo y los lados de la concha. Hornee a 400°F. durante 10 minutos y retire. Mantenga aparte. Extienda con un rodillo el resto de la pasta, en forma oblonga y corte de 8 a 10 tiras de 3/4 de pulgada de ancho, para formar una rejilla para la cubierta del pay. Extienda el relleno de mermelada sobre el fondo de la concha de pay, ponga la mitad de las tiras encima del relleno, dejando 1 pulgada entre cada tira. Entrelace el resto de las tiras en dirección opuesta, en forma de diamante o cuadrado. Espolvoree con azúcar y hornee durante 20–25 minutos, hasta que las tiras estén doradas. Déjelo estar 2 ó 3 horas, a la temperatura ambiente, antes de servir.

RELLENO DE MERMELADA

1 libra (aproximadamente) de mermelada de naranja agria, o cualquier otra mermelada de su sabor favorito
1/4 taza de agua tibia

Mezcle la mermelada con el agua hasta que tenga una consistencia para untar (si la mermelada que está usando tiene una consistencia adecuada para untar, sin adelgazar, omita el agua).

TARTALETAS O PAY DE RON Y MANGO

8 Porciones

1 concha de pay de 9 pulgadas, horneada, u 8 conchas para tartaletas de 4 pulgadas, horneadas (ver receta para "Pasta Básica" en el glosario al final de la sección)
3 mangos grandes, sin cáscara, maduros, finamente rebanados
1/2 taza de azúcar
1/4 taza de ron oscuro
2 cucharadas de fécula de maíz
1 cucharadita de jugo de lima o limón
2 yemas de huevo
1/4 cucharadita de jengibre en polvo
Crema batida dulce con dos cucharadas de ron, ó 1 cucharadita de saborizante de ron

Rebane los mangos y póngalos en una sartén. Agregue el azúcar y el ron. Cueza a fuego lento durante 10 minutos, meneando constantemente. Combine la fécula de maíz con el jugo y 1 cucharada de agua, mezclando hasta que esté tersa. Añada las yemas batidas. Agregue un poco de la fruta caliente a la mezcla de huevo y luego vacíe la mezcla de huevo en la sartén. Siga cociendo a fuego lento, meneando constantemente, hasta que espese y esté tersa. Mezcle en el jengibre. Enfríe y ponga en la concha de pay o en las conchas de tartaletas. Sirva con la crema batida dulce, con sabor a ron.

PAY CHIFON DE CALABAZA

8 Porciones

3 yemas de huevo
1/2 taza de azúcar
1 1/4 taza de calabaza fresca, cocida, o calabaza enlatada
1/2 taza de leche
1/2 cucharadita de jengibre
1/2 cucharadita de canela
1/2 cucharadita de nuez moscada
1 cucharada (1 sobre) de gelatina sin sabor
1/4 taza de agua fría
1/2 cucharadita de sal
3 claras de huevo, batidas hasta que estén duras
1/2 taza de azúcar
1 concha de pay de 9 pulgadas, horneada (ver receta para "Pasta Básica" en el glosario al final de la sección)

Bata las yemas de huevo y 1/2 taza de azúcar hasta que espese. Agregue la calabaza, leche, sal y especies. Cueza a fuego lento, meneando constantemente hasta que espese. Disuelva la gelatina en el agua fría y agréguela a la calabaza, meneando hasta que se disuelva la gelatina. Agregue las claras batidas con la 1/2 taza de azúcar restante. Ponga la mezcla en la concha de pay horneada y refrigere. Si desea, adorne la cubierta con crema dulce batida.

PAY "DEL HOSTELERO" COLONIAL

8–10 Porciones

2 onzas de chocolate amargo
2/3 taza de agua
2/3 taza de azúcar
8 cucharadas de mantequilla, suavizada pero no derretida
2 cucharaditas de vainilla
1 taza de harina
3/4 taza de azúcar
1 cucharadita de polvo de hornear
1/2 cucharadita de sal
1/2 taza de leche
1 huevo
1/2 taza de nuez, picada (opcional)
1 taza de crema para batir, batida
1 concha de pay de 9 pulgadas, sin hornear (ver "Pasta Básica" en el glosario al final de la sección)

A fuego muy bajo, derrita el chocolate en el agua, meneando constantemente. Cuando se haya derretido y mezclado, agregue 4 cucharadas de mantequilla y el azúcar y déjelo hervir, meneando constantemente. Agregue 1/2 de la vainilla y coloque la mezcla aparte.

Mezcle muy bien la harina, 3/4 taza de azúcar, polvo de hornear y sal. Colóquelos en un tazón grande de batidora eléctrica, o en un tazón lo suficientemente grande para batir a mano. Agregue la leche, las 4 cucharadas de mantequilla restantes y la vainilla. Bata hasta que esté bien mezclado. Agregue el huevo y bata durante 2 ó 3 minutos hasta que esté mezclado por completo. Ponga la masa sobre la concha de pay. Revuelva la mezcla de chocolate y con mucho cuidado póngala encima de la masa. Si desea, espolvoree con nueces. Precaliente el horno y hornee a 350°F. durante 55 minutos a una hora, hasta que al insertar un probador en el centro, salga limpio. (Un palillo de dientes, un cuchillo pequeño, o una pajita — son magníficos probadores).

Sirva tibio o a la temperatura ambiente — no refrigere — con la crema batida encima.

PAY DE CHOCOLATE ANGEL

6–8 Porciones

2 claras de huevo (a la temperatura ambiente)
1/8 cucharadita de sal
1/8 cucharadita de cremor tartaro
1/2 taza de azucar
1/2 taza de nuez picada
1/2 cucharadita de vainilla
2 cucharadas de azucar
1 paquete de 8-onzas, de chispas de chocolate semi-dulce
3 cucharadas de leche
4 huevos, separados (a la temperatura ambiente)

Bata las 2 claras de huevo hasta que estén espumosas, luego agregue la sal, el cremor tartaro y el azucar. Siga batiendo hasta que estén duras pero no secas. Mezcle de manera envolvente en las nueces y vainilla. Engrase un molde de pay de 9 pulgadas, extienda el merengue en el molde engrasado, arreglando las orillas de tal manera que el merengue esté 1/2 pulgada arriba de los lados. Precaliente el horno y hornée a 225°F. por 1 1/2 a 2 horas, hasta que el merengue esté ligeramente dorado y firme. Apague el horno, abra la puerta, pero no saque el pay antes 10–15 minutos por lo menos. Enfrie.

En una cacerola, derrita 2 cucharadas de azucar, las chispas de chocolate y 3 cucharadas de leche. Bata las 4 yemas de huevo con 1 cucharadita de vainilla o, si desea, con una cucharada de ron o kahlua. Bata hasta que esté bien mezclado. Enfrie un poco la mezcla de chocolate y agregue la mezcla de huevo lentamente, batiendo muy bien. Recaliente hasta que el chocolate y la mezcla de huevo estén calientes pero no hirviendo. Ponga aparte. Bata las claras hasta que estén duras pero no secas, luego agreguelas de manera envolvente, con mucho cuidado en la mezcla de chocolate. Rellene el merengue con el relleno y refrigere muy bien.

Cubra con crema batida ligeramente endulzada, y rizos de chocolate, o chispas de chocolate o nueces picadas.

Glosario de Pastas

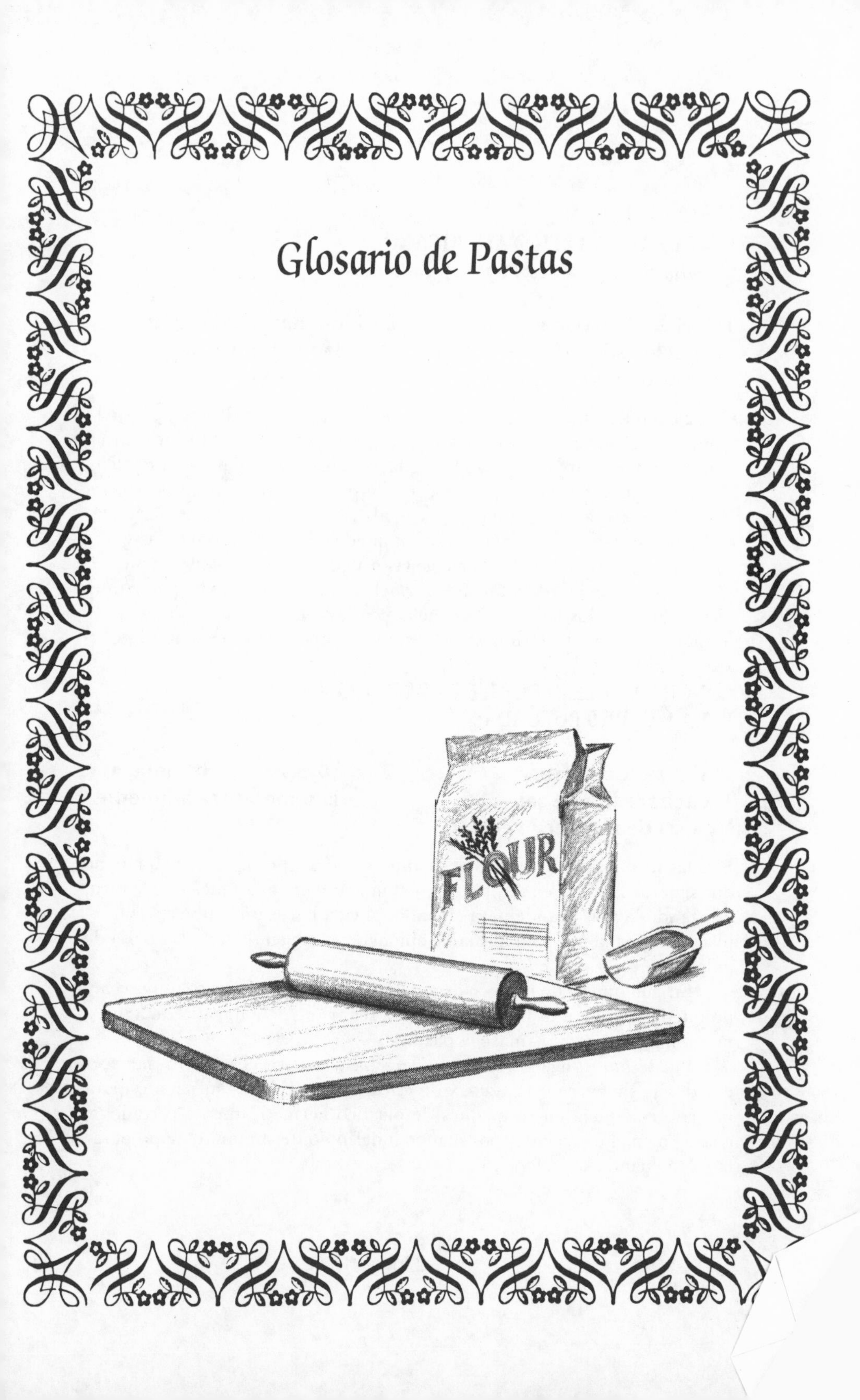

PASTA BASICA ESTILO AMERICANO
Concha Sencilla Para Pay de 9 Pulgadas:

$1^1/_4$ taza de harina
$^1/_2$ cucharadita de sal
$^1/_3$ taza de manteca vegetal
2–3 cucharadas de agua, a la temperatura ambiente

Con 2 cuchillos, uno en cada mano, o con un mezclador de pasta, corte la manteca en la mezcla de harina y sal, hasta que la mezcla parezca que tiene granitos de arroz. Agregue el agua, 1 cucharada cada vez y mezcle la masa para juntarla con las manos, solo hasta que forme una masa suave. (Es muy importante no amasar la pasta!) En una superficie enharinada, extienda un círculo para que cubra un molde de pay de 9 pulgadas y que sobre un poquito alrededor. Arregle las orillas con los dedos y rellene. O, si va a cocer parcial o totalmente la concha antes de rellenarla, pique muy bien el fondo y los lados de la concha con un tenedor para evitar que se levante o se formen burbujas al estarla horneando. Hornee a 400°F. durante 10 minutos.

CONCHA DOBLE, O CUBIERTA DE REJILLA PARA PAY DE 9 PULGADAS:

$2^1/_2$ tazas de harina
1 cucharadita de sal
$^3/_4$ taza de manteca vegetal
4–6 cucharadas de agua, a la temeratura ambiente

Siga las mismas instrucciones de la anterior, a excepción de que aquí tiene que separar la masa en dos partes, una ligeramente más chica que la otra, utilizando la más grande para el fondo. Si va a hacer una cubierta con rejilla, extienda la masa en forma de oblongo y corte en tiras de 1/2 ó 3/4 de pulgada.

En cualquiera de las recetas anteriores, si la masa parece muy seca y no puede fromar una bola, no tema agregar otra cucharada de agua o más. Sin embargo, no amase la pasta.

Puede multiplicar está receta para pasta básica el número de veces que desee, sin agregar el agua, y dividiendo en porciones suficientes para un pay, colóquela en recipientes de plástico herméticamente cerrados y guardela en el congelador por tiempo indefinido, terminando de preparar la masa cuando sea necesario.

PASTA FRANCESA, O PATE BRISEE:
Concha Sencilla Para Pay de 9 Pulgadas u 8–10
Conchas Para Tartaletas de 2–3 Pulgadas

1½ tazas de harina
¼ cucharadita de sal
6 cucharadas de mantequilla sin sal, enfriada en el refrigerador y cortada en trocitos de 1/4 de pulgada
2 cucharadas de manteca vegetal, enfriada en el refrigerador y cortada en trocitos de 1/4 de pulgada
3–4 cucharadas de agua, enfriada en el refrigerador

En un tazón grande enfriado, combine la harina, sal, 6 cucharadas de mantequilla en trocitos y manteca vegetal. Con las yemas de los dedos desbarate la grasa en la harina hasta que parezca que tiene granitos de arroz. Agregue el agua, 1 cucharada a la vez, rociandola sobre la mezcla de manera que se distribuya bien entre la mezcla. Forme una bola con la masa cuidando de no amasarla. Cubra la pasta con una tela un poco húmeda y déjela reposar en el refrigerador durante 2 horas, por lo menos. Extienda la masa en una superficie ligeramente enharinada, solo la harina necesaria para evitar que se pegue.

Use esta pasta para platillos de pay principales.

PASTA FRANCESA, O PATE SUCREE:

Use la misma receta de arriba, agregando 4 cucharaditas de azúcar a la harina y mezcla de grasa antes de agregar el agua.

Esta receta es para usarla como pasta para postres de pays de crema y tartas o fruta.

PASTA ITALIANA DE HUEVO, O CROSTATA:
(Concha para pay de 10 pulgadas más cubierta de rejilla)

2 tazas de harina
¾ taza de mantequilla, a la temperatura ambiente
½ taza de azúcar
½ cucharadita de sal
2 huevos enteros
2 cucharaditas de vainilla
2 cucharaditas de ralladura de limón fresco

En un tazón, combine la harina, mantequila, azúcar, sal, huevos, vainilla y ralladura de limón. Trabaje la mezcla con las manos hasta que esté bien integrada, forme una bola tersa, cubra bien y refrigere durante 30 minutos por lo menos. Separe parte de la masa para la cubierta de rejilla y extienda el resto en un círculo suficientemente grande para cubrir un pay de

10 pulgadas. Extienda la otra parte más pequeña en forma de oblongo y corte tiras de 1/2 a 3/4 de pulgada para la cubierta de rejilla. Rellene con el relleno que desee.

Si hace esta pasta para utilizarla con rellenos de vegetales o carne, omita el azúcar, vainilla y ralladura de limón y prosiga de la misma forma que arriba.

PASTA ESCANDINAVA DE QUESO COTTAGE:
Concha doble para pay de 9 pulgadas

1 taza de mantequilla fría, firme
2 tazas de harina
1 taza de queso cottage
1–2 cucharadas de agua fría, si es necesario

En un tazón grande, corte la mantequilla en la harina hasta que la mezcla parezca desmoronada o como con granitos de arroz. Mezcle en el queso cottage hasta que la mezcla parezca una masa desmoronada. Amase ligeramente para formar una bola, agregando agua en pequeñas gotas y solo la necesaria para formar la bola. Enfríe en el refrigerador por lo menos 30 minutos antes de extenderla.

Esta receta hace una pasta firme, que puede utilizar para forrar carnes, o pescado, o mezclas de vegetales o queso, pero también es una pasta deliciosa para todo tipo de rellenos, para platillos principales, platillos de acompañamiento o postres.

Postres

MOUSSE DE CHOCOLATE

6–8 Porciones

9 cuadros de chocolate semidulce, ó 9 onzas de chispas de chocolate
1/4 taza de café fuerte, caliente
6 huevos
3/4 taza más 2 cucharadas de azúcar
1 cucharada de ron oscuro

En una sartén pequeña, agregue el chocolate al café caliente y cueza a fuego muy lento, hasta que se derrita el chocolate. Separe las yemas de las claras y deje aparte las claras de huevo. Bata las yemas con la mitad del azúcar hasta que estén cremosas. Agregue el ron a las yemas y luego combine con la mezcla caliente de chocolate, agregando un poco de la mezcla de chocolate a los huevos y luego recombinando todo. Bata las claras de huevo hasta que estén espumosas. Agregue el resto del azúcar y bata hasta que las claras formen picos suaves. Cuidadosamente, mezcle de forma envolvente en la mezcla de chocolate. Vierta el mousse a cucharadas en copas con base alta o tazones para postre. Enfríe hasta que esté firme. Cubra con crema batida dulce justo antes de servir.

CREMA DE NARANJA BAVARIAN

10–12 Porciones

7 yemas de huevo
2 naranjas grandes
3/4 taza de azúcar
2 cucharaditas de fécula de maíz
1 1/2 tazas de leche tibia
2 cucharadas de gelatina sin sabor
5 claras de huevo
2 cucharadas de azúcar
1 taza de crema para batir
2–3 cucharadas de licor de naranja

Ralle las cáscaras de naranja y manténgalas aparte. Exprima el jugo y manténgalo aparte. Bata las yemas con batidora eléctrica o batidor de mano, hasta que estén esponjosas y ligeras. Agregue la fécula de maíz y el azúcar y mezcle bien. Gradualmente agregue 3/4 taza de azúcar a las yemas de huevo y bata constantemente hasta que la mezcla esté espesa. Agregue la leche tibia y mezcle bien. Cambiela a una sartén gruesa y agregue el jugo de naranja y la gelatina suavizada en un poco del jugo de naranja. Caliente con cuidado, meneando con frecuencia hasta que espese la mezcla y cubra una cuchara, pero *no hierva*. Retire del fuego y deje que repose para que se enfríe un poco.

En un tazón grande bata las claras de huevo hasta que formen picos suaves. Gradualmente agregue 2 cucharadas de azúcar y siga batiendo hasta que forme picos duros. Mezcle la natilla en un chorro delgado en la mezcla de claras, incorporando de forma envolvente hasta que esté bien mezclado. Refrigere, menee ocasionalmente, hasta que la natilla esté ligeramente espesa y forme un montoncito en la cuchara (cerca de 1 1/2 horas — no permita que se haga muy firme). Bata la crema hasta que esté dura. Agregue el licor de naranja, mezclando de manera envolvente con cuidado. Luego incorpore de forma envolvente la crema en la natilla, mezclando bien. Vierta la mezcla en vasos, copas o platos para postre y refrigere durante varias horas. Adorne con crema batida o decore con un poquito de fruta fresca.

Puede congelar esté postre y puede cambiar el sabor a cualquiera que desee, agregando la misma cantidad de jugo a otra fruta, y/o ralladura de otra fruta. Y puede hacer chocolate o moka bavarian substituyendo 1/2 taza de agua por el jugo, omitiendo la ralladura y agregando 2–3 onzas de chocolate dulce derretido y/o 3 cucharaditas de café instántaneo, más 1 cucharadita de vainilla a la leche, antes de agregarla a las huevos.

MOUSSE DE FRESA

10 Porciones

2 claras de huevo, a la temperatura ambiente
1/4 cucharadita de cremor tártaro
1 pizca de sal
2 tazas de crema para batir
1 1/4 tazas de azúcar pulverizada, cernida
2 tazas de fresas, lavadas, secas, sin cabo, hechas puré, y enfriadas en el refrigerador antes de usarse

En un tazón pequeño, bata las claras de huevo junto con el cremor tártaro y sal hasta que estén duras y brillantes. En un tazón chico bata la crema y el azúcar hasta que esté dura. Bata el puré de fresas, con cuidado, en la crema. Cuidadosamente, mezcle de manera envolvente en las claras de huevo, incorporando bien. Vierta el mousse a cucharadas en copas con base alta para postre. Refrigere 1 hora, por lo menos, antes de servir. Adorne cada copa con crema batida adicional, justo antes de servir y, si desea, coloque una fresa entera encima.

Puede adaptar esta receta para usarla con cualquier fruta fresca que pueda hacerse puré, tal como, duraznos, chabacanos, piña.

PASTEL DE QUESO SENCILLO

6–8 Porciones

8 onzas de queso crema, suavizado a la temperatura ambiente
2 cucharadas de mantequilla, suavizada a la temperatura ambiente
1/2 taza de azúcar
1 huevo entero
2 cucharadas de harina
2/3 taza de leche
1/4 taza de jugo de limón
2 cucharadas de ralladura de limón

Acreme el queso y la mantequilla hasta que estén bien incorporados. Agregue el azúcar y el huevo, luego la harina y leche y mezcle bien. Mezcle en el jugo y ralladura de limón. Cuando la mezcla esté completamente integrada viertala en una concha de galleta de harina de trigo entero sin hornear, de 9 pulgadas, Precaliente el horno a 350°F. y hornee durante 35 minutos. Enfríe bien antes de servir. Si desea, puede servir fruta fresca endulzada encima de cada rebanada.

CONCHA DE GALLETAS DE TRIGO ENTERO

1 1/2 tazas de galletas de harina de trigo entero desmoronadas
1/3 taza de azúcar
1/2 cucharadita de canela
1/2 taza de mantequilla derretida

Mezcle muy bien las galletas desmoronadas, azúcar y canela. Agregue la mantequilla derretida y mezcle todo hasta que esté bien incorporado. Presione bien está mezcla en un molde de pay de 9 pulgadas y rellene con la mezcla de arriba.

CARLOTA

12 Porciones

Forre un molde de carlota o un tazón con los lados inclinados, con soletas, (las cuales puede comprar en la mayoría de las pastelerías o puede encontrarlas en la sección de galletas en la mayoría de los supermeracados — hacer las soletas es un trabajo extra e innecesario, ya que, en mi opinión, las soletas hechas en casa saben igual que las de pastelería).

Llene el interior del molde con cualquiera de las recetas de mousses de está sección, o con cualquier variación de crema Bavarian que se ha proporcionado, rellenando el molde directamente después del último paso antes de enfriar en el refrigerador el platillo final. Enfríe completamente antes de desmoldar en el platón de servicio.

Para variar la carlota, puede salpicar o remojar ligeramente las soletas en otros licores, o brandy, dependiendo del sabor del relleno, y después desmoldar, adornar alrededor de las orillas, con una manga de duya, con crema batida.

SOLETAS

Hace 15 aproximadamente

Todos los ingredientes deben estar a la temperatura ambiente.

- **1/3 taza de harina, cernida varias veces hasta que esté muy ligera**
- **1/3 taza de azúcar pulverizada, bien cernida**
- **1/8 cucharadita de sal**
- **1 huevo entero**
- **2 yemas de huevo**
- **1/2 cucharadita de vainilla**
- **2 claras de huevo, batidas hasta que estén duras pero no secas**

Bata 2 yemas de huevo, vainilla y 1 huevo entero, hasta que espesen y tengan un color amarillo limón. Mezcle de manera envolvente el azúcar y la sal, poco a poco, en las claras de huevo, que previamente batió hasta que estuvieran duras pero no secas. Siga batiendo hasta que esta mezcla esté muy espesa de nuevo. Combine en forma envolvente con la mezcla de yemas de huevo y luego en la harina. Forme tiras, de 3 1/2 pulgadas de largo por 1 1/4 de ancho, con la masa (para está operación es muy necesario utilizar una manga de duya, a menos que tenga un molde para soletas) en una hoja para hornear forrada con papel. Precaliente el horno a 375°F. y hornee de 12 a 15 minutos, hasta que estén doradas. Cuando se enfríen, espolvoree con azúcar pulverizada y mantengalas en un recipiente herméticamente cerrado, si las reserva para utilizarlas posteriormente.

MOUSSE DE MANGO

12 Porciones

- **5 mangos medianos, maduros, pelados, deshuesados, cortados a la mitad (cerca de 2 1/2 libras)**
- **1/3 taza de jugo de limón fresco**
- **3 claras de huevo, a la temperatura ambiente**
- **1 pizca de sal**
- **1/3 taza de azúcar**
- **1 taza de crema para batir**

Haga puré los mangos con el jugo de limón. En un tazón grande, con batidora eléctrica o batidor de mano, bata las claras de huevo hasta que formen picos suaves. Poco a poco agregue el azúcar y continue batiendo hasta que estén duras pero no secas. En otro tazón grande bata la crema hasta que forme picos suaves. Con cuidado mezcle las claras de manera envolvente en la crema, luego de igual forma mezcle el puré de mango. Vierta en vasos o copas con base alta para postre. Enfríe en el refrigerador durante 6 horas, por lo menos, antes de servir.

Esta receta es más fuerte en la fruta que la receta para mousse de fresa, como puede ver, y es mejor para usarla con una fruta dulce, menos ácida.

CHOUS CREMOSOS O ECLAIRS

Hace 15 chous medianos

1 taza de agua hirviendo
1/2 taza de manteca vegetal
1/4 cucharadita de sal
1 taza de harina
4 huevos

Antes de empezar, precaliente el horno a 450°F. y engrase generosamente una o dos charolas para galletas.

En una sartén mediana mezcle el agua hirviendo, manteca y sal. Cuando la manteca se haya derretido, agregue la harina, toda a la vez y mezcle vigorosamente, siga cociendo a fuego lento y menee constantemente, hasta que la mezcla esté húmeda y sólida, y se despegue de los lados de la sartén. Retire del fuego y enfríe 1 minuto. Agregue los huevos sin batir, uno a la vez, batiendo constantemente, hasta que la masa esté tersa. Ponga la masa a cucharadas, en un solo montoncito, de un solo golpe, dejando 2 pulgadas entre cada montoncito. Si va a hacer eclairs, amontone la masa en montoncitos alargados para cada eclair.

Hornee a 450°F. durante 15 minutos. Reduzca la temperatura del horno a 400°F. y siga horneando durante 15–20 minutos más. Los chous están listos cuando al probar con un chous no se baja al sacarlo del horno, y cuando las puntas están doradas. Enfríe completamente. Con un cuchillo filoso corte las puntas y rellene con flan, fruta o nieve, o crema batida dulce.

Puede hacer estos chous más grandes con solo aumentar el tamaño de la cucharada en la charola y aumentando el tiempo de horneado por solo 2 minutos o más. Los chous más grandes son ideales para rellenarlos con vegetales acremados, o carne acremada, o pescado, o para rellenarlos con ensalada de carne o pescado. Use su imaginación. Los chous cremosos son deliciosos y muy versátiles.

Salsas, Aderezos, Caldos Platillos de Acompañamiento y Consomés

SALSA BASICA PARA ESPAGUETI SIN CARNE

Rinde $1^1/_2$ litros

10–15 tomates medianos, muy maduros, pelados, picados
1 pinta de puré de tomate
1 pimineto morrón verde muy grande, ó 2 pequeños, picados
2 cebollas grandes, picadas
3–4 dientes de ajo, machacados
1 hoja de laurel grande, ó 2 pequeñas
1–2 cucharaditas de cada uno, de romero y tomillo, molidos en el molcajete
$^3/_4$ cucharadita de orégano, molido con el tomillo y romero en el molcajete
Sal al gusto
1 cucharadita de pimienta blanca
2 cucharaditas de azúcar (o al gusto)
1 taza (o más, si es necesario) de vino tinto seco
2 tazas de champiñones frescos, rebanados (opcional)

Sofría el ajo machacado en un poco de aceite hasta que esté transparente (de preferencia aceite de oliva, pero si no tiene disponible un aceite de oliva muy fresco y fino, es mejor usar aceite vegetal que aceite de oliva fuerte). Agregue las cebollas y sofría un minuto o dos, junto con los champiñones si los usa. Agregue los pimientos, hoja u hojas de laurel, hierbas, pimienta, azúcar, tomates, puré de tomate y sal al gusto (después de 10 minutos aproximadamente, saque una cuchara y pruebe el sabor). Deje que llegue a hervir, agregue la taza de vino tinto y baje la flama a fuego muy lento. Cueza, sin tapar, agregando vino de vez en cuando si la mezcla empieza a espesar mucho, por lo menos durante 4 horas, pero de preferencia 5–6 horas, meneando de vez en cuando con una cuchara de madera.

Si utiliza carne, ya sea carne de res molida, o salchicha estilo italiano. Sofría la carne hasta que esté bien cocida y agréguela a la salsa 1 hora antes de usarla para permitir que los sabores se combinen. Use la cantidad de carne deseada, pero no menos de 1/2 libra para esta receta.

Puede doblar, cuadruplicar, etc. esta receta y congelarla en recipientes de plástico de 1 litro de capacidad, herméticamente cerrados, por un período de tiempo indefinido, al menos durante 6 meses. Debido a que toma tantas horas preparar adecuadamente está salsa, recomendamos, siempre que sea posible, hacerla en grandes cantidades y guardarla hasta que se necesite.

SALSA MARINARA
(PARA PASTAS O CARNES)

Rinde 6 tazas aproximadamente

$^1/_2$ taza de aceite de oliva fresco y suave
8 dientes de ajo, machacados
8 tazas de tomates, pelados, picados y cocidos a fuego lento, ó $1^1/_2$ litros de puré de tomate más 2 tazas de tomates frescos, pelados y picados
$^1/_2$ cucharadita de orégano, pulverizado en el molcajete
Sal y pimienta al gusto

Sofría el ajo en el aceite a fuego alto, hasta que el ajo esté ligeramente dorado. Reduzca la flama a fuego lento y agregue los tomates frescos, o puré de tomate, y el orégano. Tape la sartén y cueza durante 30 minutos o hasta que la salsa espese. Es importante que se noten unos trocitos de tomate en la salsa final, por lo tanto no despedace todos los tomates a manera que no se noten.

SALSA CARBONARA PARA ESPAGETI

4 Porciones

5 cucharadas de mantequilla
8 rebanadas de tocino
$^3/_4$ taza de media crema
2 huevos enteros
1 yema de huevo
1 taza de queso Parmesano fresco, rallado
1 cucharadita de pedacitos de pimienta roja seca (opcional)
1 libra de espagueti

Corte transversalmente las rebanadas de tocino en tiras de 1/4 de pulgada. Cueza lentamente a fuego moderado hasta que estén crujientes. Retire el tocino y escurra en toallas de papel, luego desmóronelo en un tazón y mantengalo aparte. Drene toda la grasa de la sartén, pero deje una cucharada en la sartén y mezcle la crema en esa grasa. Caliente con cuidado de que no hierva. Enfríe 2 minutos. Mientras tanto, bata los huevos y la yema de huevo, agregue el queso, pimientas rojas, si las usa, y sal al gusto. Luego agregue la crema y regrese la mezcla completa a la sartén y caliente, cuidando de que no hierva.

Derrita 5 cucharadas de mantequilla y mantenga aparte. Cueza el espagueti al dente y drene. Mazcle la salsa, mantequilla derretida y los trocitos de tocino en espagueti caliente.

SALSA ESTILO TRATORIA

(También conocida como Al Burro, o en Estados Unidos Alfredo)

6 Porciones

1 1/2 libras de fettucine, cocido al dente
8 cucharadas de mantequilla
2 tazas de crema espesa
3 yemas de huevo
2 tazas de queso Parmesano fresco, rallado
Sal y pimienta al gusto

Después de cocer el fettucine, drénelo bien y póngalo en un tazón de servicio caliente y mezclelos con cuidado en 2 cucharadas de la mantequilla, derretida. Mantenga caliente.

En una sartén, derrita la mantequilla restante y mezcle en la crema. Caliente bien la mezcla. En un tazón bata ligeramente las yemas y mezclelas en la mantequilla y crema, poco a poco. Regrese la mezcla a la sartén y recaliente, pero no permita que hierva. Mezcle en una taza de queso y agregue la sal y pimienta. Vierta la salsa sobre la pasta y mezcle, junto con el resto del queso. Sirva de inmediato.

SALSA BECHAMEL O "SALSA BLANCA"

Rinde 3 tazas

2 tazas de leche
1 hoja de laurel
3 cucharadas de mantequilla
4 cucharadas de harina
1 pizca de pimienta blanca y sal al gusto
1 yema de huevo, muy bien mezclada en 2 cucharadas de crema ligera 1 1/4 cucharadas de jeréz dulce

En una sartén pequeña derrita la mantequilla. Retire del fuego y agregue la harina. Mezcle hasta que esté bien integrada. Gradualmente agregue la leche, luego la hoja de laurel y la pizca de pimineta blanca y sal al gusto. Cueza, moviendo constantemente, a fuego moderado hasta que espese. Apague la flama y tape. Enfríe 3–4 minutos por lo menos, para permitir que la hoja de laurel de su sabor a la salsa. Mientras tanto, bata la yema de huevo y la crema hasta que estén bien mezcladas. Agregue el jeréz dulce. Combine toda la mezcla en la salsa hasta que casi, pero no completamente, hierva y espese. Retire la hoja de laurel. Enfríe. Si no la va a utilizar de inmediato, tape bien y refrigere. Se mantiene bien durante un día o dos en el refrigerador.

Esta salsa es llamada "salsa blanca," lo cual no es. La salsa blanca no se cueze. No hay nada igual que está deliciosa y exquisita salsa.

SALSA NEWBURG

Rinde 1 taza

1/2 taza de mantequilla
1 diente de ajo mediano, machacado
1/4 taza de vino dulce de madera (si no está disponible puede substituirlo con jeréz dulce, sin embargo el vino de madera es mucho mejor)
1 taza de crema
3 yemas de huevo

Derrita lamantequilla y sofría el ajo hasta que esté transparente pero no dorado. Retire del fuego. Bata las yemas de huevo hasta que espesen y estén amarillo limón. Agregue la crema y el vino y mezcle bien. Vierta está mezcla en la mantequilla y cueza a fuego lento justo hasta antes de hervir — no hierva o los huevos se cuajarán — y la salsa haya espesado. Use de inmediato.

Usela para jaiba y langosta.

Si necesita guardar la salsa por un poco de tiempo, puede substituir leche y harina por la crema, de la siguiente manera:

Agregue 2 1/2 cucharadas de harina a la mantequilla derretida y ajo. Luego vierta en 1 1/4 tazas de leche y mezcle bien.

Cueza hasta que espese. Bata las yemas de huevo y vino y agreguelas a la mezcla espesa y caliente justo hasta antes de hervir. Puede enfriar esta salsa y mantenerla refrigerada hasta que la use, luego recaliéntela.

SALSA MORNAY

Rinde 4 tazas aproximadamente

Esta salsa depende mucho del tipo de queso que se utilice. Básicamente, esta salsa requiere un queso muy añejo, fuerte y que se derrita. Si la receta pide "salsa mornay" ningún otro queso lo hará como el requerido la hará.

2 tazas de salsa bechamel (ver receta)
2 tazas de crema ligera
2 tazas de queso cheddar muy fuerte, rallado
1 cucharadita de salsa inglesa (Lea & Perrins)
1 cucharada de jeréz dulce
1 pizca de pimienta cayena

Caliente las 2 tazas de salsa bechamel. Agregue la crema y el queso, la salsa inglesa, el jeréz y la pizca de pimienta cayena y, cueza, meneando constantemente, solo hasta que se haya derrerido el queso y todos los ingredientes estén bien incorporados.

Esta salsa, igual que la bechamel, puede guardarla, bien tapada, en el refrigerador por varios días o una semana.

SALSA BLANCA DE ALMEJAS PARA LINGUINE

4–6 Porciones

1/3 taza de aceite de oliva (muy fresco, muy fino)
3 dientes de ajo grandes, machacados
1/2 taza de jugo de almejas, embotelladas, reservando de las almejas frescas o enlatadas, o ambas
1/4 cucharadita de sal
Pimienta recién molida
1 pizca grande de orégano seco, molido en el molcajete
1 pizca grande de tomillo seco, molido en el molcajete
10 1/2 onzas de almejas enlatadas, picaditas, o el equivalente
2 cucharadas de perejil fresco, picado
1/2 taza de zanahoria, picadita
1/2 taza de apio, picadito
1/2 taza de pimiento morrón verde, picadito
1/2 taza de cebolla, picadita
1/2 taza de vino blanco seco
2 cucharadas de harina
1 libra de linguine

En una sartén gruesa, caliente el aceite. Sofría el ajo hasta que esté amarillo pálido. Agregue el jugo de almejas, sal, pimiento morrón, especies, hierbas y vegetales picaditos. Cueza, tapado, a fuego lento durante 10 minutos, hasta que los vegetales estén suaves. Con sumo cuidado, mezcle la harina con el vino. Mezcle las almejas en el jugo de los vegetales junto con la mezcla de vino y harina y cueza, sin tapar, durante 2 minutos, hasta que la harina haya espesado ligeramente la salsa. Mezcle en el perejil y apague la flama.

Cueza el linguine solo al dente, drene y pongalo en un tazón caliente. Agregue la mitad de la salsa y mezcle bien. Sirva en tazones calientes y vierta encima la salsa restante.

SALSA ROJA DE ALMEJAS PARA LINGUINE

4–6 Porciones

1/4 taza de aceite de oliva
2 cebollas medianas, picadas
2 dientes de ajo, machacados
3 tazas de tomates picados, cocidos a fuego lento, ó 4 tazas de puré de tomate
3/4 cucharadita de sal
Pimienta recién molida al gusto
1/2 cucharadita de trocitos de pimienta roja
1 cucharadita de orégano seco
10 1/2 onzas de almejas enlatadas picaditas, ó 15 almejas frescas, reserve el jugo
3/4 taza de jugo de almejas, embotellado o del reservado de las almejas
4 filetes de anchoas, picados
1 libra de linguine

En una sartén grande y gruesa, caliente el aceite. Sofría las cebollas y ajos hasta que estén suaves. Agregue los tomates o puré, sal, pimienta negra y roja, orégano y anchoas. Haga que llegue a hervir y cueza poco a poco, sin tapar, durante 10 minutos, meneando unas dos veces. Agregue las almejas y sus jugos, mezclando bien y cociendo a fuego lento, sin tapar, durante 3–4 minutos, meneando con frecuencia. Si esta salsa le parece muy aguada, puede espesarla con 2–3 cucharadas de harina, mezcladas con un poco de vino tinto.

Cueza el linguine al dente, drene y pongalo en un tazón grande, caliente. Agregue la mitad de la salsa de almeja, mezcle bien, sirva en tazones calientes y ponga encima la salsa restante.

SALSA DE VINO BLANCO

Rinde 2 tazas

3 cucharadas de mantequilla
3 cucharadas de harina
1 taza de consomé concentrado de pescado
1/4 taza de vino blanco seco sal y pimienta al gusto
1/2 taza de crema espesa mezclada con 2 yemas de huevo

En una sartén derrita la mantequilla. Mezcle en la harina. Retire del fuego y agregue poco a poco el consomé de pescado y el vino, y mezcle hasta que esté bien integrado. Cueza, meneando con frecuencia, hasta que espese y esté terso. Sazone al gusto con sal y pimienta. Vierta un poco de la salsa caliente en la mezcla del huevo y crema y mezcle. Agréguelo a la salsa en la sartén y cueza a fuego lento hasta que espese. No permita que hierva o los huevos se cuajarán.

Sirva sobre platillos de pescado, en particular, con pescado escalfado caliente.

SALSA DE CHAMPIÑONES

8 Porciones

3 tazas de cebolla, finamente rebanada
5–6 cucharadas de mantequilla
1 libra de champiñones frescos, finamente rebanados
1 cucharada de base de res como bovril, dos cubitos de caldo de res ó 1 cucharada de caldo de res en polvo
1/4 cucharadita de mejorana, desmoronada
1/4 cucharadita de albahaca, desmoronada
1 pizca de tomillo, desmoronado
1/2 taza de leche
1 taza de salsa bechamel (ver receta)
1 1/2 tazas de crema ácida

Dore la cebolla en la mantequilla, agregue los champiñones y sofría 2–3 minutos. Mezcle en el bovril o los cubitos y las hierbas, junto con la leche. Cueza a fuego lento 2 ó 3 minutos meneando constantemente. Agregue la salsa bechamel y caliente pero no hierva. Agregue la crema ácida y mezcle hasta que esté bien integrada y caliente pero, una vez más, que no hierva.

Puede refrigerar está salsa y recalentarla, pero igual que arriba, que no hierva o la salsa se cuajará.

Es deliciosa servida como salsa sobre medallones de filete de res, o cualquier carne asada.

SALSA DE PEPINO

Rinde 2 tazas

2 pepinos grandes
1 cucharadita de sal
1 taza de crema ácida
1 taza de mayonesa
1 cucharada de crema estilo horseradish (puede omitirla si no está disponible)
1 cucharadita de cebolla rallada
1 cuchardada de vinagre de estragón (agregue una cucharada de estragón fresco, picado o estragón seco, a 1 taza de vinagre de vino tinot o blanco y permita que repose por unas cuantas horas, luego cuele, para hacer el vinagre con sabor al estragón si no está disponible)
1/4 cucharadita de pimienta blanca

Pele los pepinos y córtelos en rebanadas muy delgaditas. Colóquelos en un tazón para mezclar con capacidad de 2 litros y cubra con agua fría. Agregue 1 cucharadita de sal y mezcle bien. Permita que repose durante 30 minutos y luego drene y seque con toallas de papel. Combine en un tazón la crema ácida, mayonesa y horseradish (si usa), cebolla rallada y vinagre. Agregue los pepinos y mezcle con cuidado. Sazone con un poco más de sal, si desea, y la pimienta blanca.

Esta salsa es deliciosa en pescado frío o caliente, cocido a fuego lento, en pescado horneado, en especial con salmón y trucha.

SALSA PICANTE DE MOSTAZA

Rinde 1 taza

1/4 taza de mostaza seca
2 cucharadas de aceite vegetal
2 cucharadas de agua
1/4 taza de azúcar
1 cucharada de fécula de maíz
1/2 cucharadita de sal
1/2 taza de agua
1/4 taza de vinagre blanco

En una sartén mediana mezcle el azúcar, fécula de maíz, sal, 1/2 taza de agua y 1/4 taza de vinagre. Cueza a fuego lento hasta que espese la mezcla. Combine la mostaza, aceite y 2 cucharadas de agua y menee hasta que esté tersa; agréguela a la sartén y mezcle completamente. Sirva a la temperatura ambiente.

Use para frituras, rumaki y tostadas de camarón (ver recetas en "Entremeses").

SALSA HOLANDESA RAPIDA

Rinde 1 taza

3 huevos enteros, a la temperatura ambiente
5 cucharaditas de jugo de limón
3 cucharadas de agua
7 cucharadas de mantequilla
1/2 cuchardadita de sal
1 pizca de pimienta blanca
1/8 cucharadita de mejorana, molida
1/8 cucharadita de tomillo, molido

En una sartén mediana derrita la mantequilla. Agregue el jugo y el agua a la mantequila derretida y mezcle. En un tazón chico de batidora eléctrica bata los huevos, o con un batidor de alambre, hasta que estén esponjosos y amarillos. Caliente la mantequilla derretida y el jugo y agua hasta que estén a punto de hervir y, luego, mientras está batiendo, vierta en un hilo constante del líquido, en los huevos. Bata hasta que espese, agregue la mejorana, tomillo, sal y pimienta, mezcle por completo y regrese la mezcla al sartén. Caliente lentamente sobre fuego muy bajo, moviendo con frecuencia hasta que espese. (Si está muy espesa para vertir, agregue un poco más de agua). Cuando espese, retire del fuego y tápela hasta que la utilice.

Está salsa mantendrá su forma, a diferencia de la salsa holandesa tradicional, y podrá guardarla uno o dos días en el refrigerador, y recalentarla para servirla posteriormente.

SALSA CHINA AGRIDULCE

Rinde 1 1/4 tazas

1/2 taza de jugo de piña
1/2 taza de vinagre de vino blanco
2 cucharadas de aceite vegetal
2 cucharadas de azúcar mascabado, bien presionada
1 cuchardada de salsa de soya
1/2 cucharadita de pimienta blanca
2 cucharadas de fécula de maíz, mezclada con suficiente agua para diluirla (2 cucharadas aproximadamente)

En una sartén mediana, mezcle todos los ingredientes excepto la fécula de maíz, y pongalos a hervir. Combine en la mezcla de fécula de maíz y cueza hasta que la salsa esté clara y espesa.

Usela para tostadas de camarón o para cualquier tipo de frituras (ver recetas en "Entremeses").

SALSA A LAS HIERBAS

Rinde 1 1/2 tazas aproximadamente

1/2 taza de vino blanco seco
1/2 taza de perejil fresco, picado (no cilantro)
1/4 taza de vinagre blanco
1 cebolla chica, en cuartos
2 dientes de ajo grandes, cortados en cuartos
2 1/2 cucharaditas de hojas de estragón seco, machacado
1/4 cucharadita de hojas de perifollo seco, machacado
1/8 cucharadita de pimienta blanca
1 taza de mayonesa

Mezcle en la licuadora a la velocidad alta, todos los ingredientes, excepto la mayonesa, hasta que estén hechos puré. Cámbielos a una sartén chica y cueza a fuego lento hasta que se reduzca a la mitad, cerca de 1/3 de taza. Cuele y regrese el líquido a la sartén. Mezcle en la mayonesa y caliente justo hasta que esté tibio.

Usela con carnes rojas o pescado como salsa bearnaise.

MAYONESA VERDE

Rinde 2 tazas

1 manojo grande de espinacas, lavadas, sin tallos
1/2 taza de perejil, estragón, perifollo y eneldo, frescos, finamente picados; ó 1 cucharadita de cada uno, si utiliza secos
1 cucharadita de cebollita cambray, picadita
2 tazas de mayonesa
Sal y pimienta recién molida al gusto

Sumerja la espinaca en agua hirviendo durante 1 minuto, rápidamente póngala en agua fría y drene. Luego córtela muy finito. Mezcle en las hierbas y pique todo junto. Si utiliza hierbas secas, asegúrese de que la mezcla esté bien incorporada. Mezcle en la mayonesa y sazone con sal y pimienta al gusto. Deje que se enfríe en el refrigerador durante una o dos horas, antes de usarla, para que se incorporen los sabores.

Use está mayonesa como acompañamiento de cualquier platillo de pescado, pero en especial es buena con pescado frío o escalfado.

DELICIOSA SALSA DE FUDGE CALIENTE

Rinde 1 1/2 tazas aproximadamente

1 lata de 14 onzas de leche condensada
1 cuchardada de agua
1/8 cucharadita de sal
2 onzas de chocolate amargo
1/2 cucharadita de extracto de vainilla

Mezcle la leche con la sal y el agua y hierva a baño maría. Agregue el chocolate. Ponga sobre agua hirviendo y cueza a fuego alto, meneando constantemente, hasta que la salsa esté espesa y tersa, cerca de 20 minutos. Retire del fuego y mezcle en la vainilla.

SALSA DE CITRICOS

Rinde 3/4 taza aproximadamente

1/2 taza de azúcar
4 cucharadas de fécula de maíz
1 1/2 tazas de agua
3 cucharadas de mantequilla
2 cucharaditas de ralladura de limón o naranja
6 cucharadas de jugo de limón ó 6 cucharadas de jugo de naranja (dependiendo del sabor que desee que predomine)
1/8 cucharadita de sal

Combine todos los ingredientes y cueza a baño maría. Sobre agua hirviendo, meneando constantemente hasta que espese.

Está salsa es deliciosa para postres de pudines, gelatinas o nieve.

SALSA JUBILEE

Rinde 1 1/2 tazas aproximadamente

1 taza de cerezas en almíbar (si no están disponibles las cerezas puede usar otra fruta en almíbar)
1/4 taza de brandy
2 cucharadas de licor de cerezas (kirsch), o, si no está disponible puede subtituirlo con licor de naranja

Caliente la fruta, agregue el brandy que ha sido ligeramente calentado. Encienda y cuando la flama se haya apagado, agregue el kirsch u otro licor. Sirva sobre nieve mientras está todavía muy caliente.

Si desea, puede mezclar la fruta con el brandy y calentarlos juntos y no encenderlos antes de agregar el licor. El flamear el brandy es más para efecto que por necesidad y, por lo general, se hace en la mesa.

SALSA DE CARAMELO

Rinde 2 tazas

1 taza de azúcar
1 1/2 tazas de leche
1 cucharada de harina
3 yemas de huevo, batidas
1/2 cucharadita de extracto de vainilla

En una sartén pequeña, cueza el azúcar a fuego lento hasta que dore. Mezcle la harina y leche, poco a poco, hasta que estén bien incorporadas. Agregue el azúcar caramelizado. Hierva a fuego lento durante 3 ó 4 minutos, meneando constantemente. Ponga las yemas de huevo batidas a baño maría. Agregue la mezcla de caramelo y el extracto de vainilla y cueza sobre agua hirviendo, meneando con frecuencia hasta que espese.

SALSA BUTTERSCOTCH

Rinde 2 1/2 tazas aproximadamente

1 1/4 tazas de azúcar mascabado, bien presionada
2/3 taza de miel de maíz clara
4 cucharadas de mantequilla
2/3 taza de crema ligera

En una sartén o cacerola gruesa combine el azúcar, miel de maíz y mantequilla. Póngalas a hervir a fuego lento y cueza, meneando constantemente, hasta que una pequeña cantidad sumerjida en agua fría, forme bolitas suaves. Agregue gradualmente la crema. Retire del fuego y menee para mezclar.

CONSOME CONCENTRADO DE POLLO

Rinde 2 cuartos

Está es la misma receta para cocer pollo a fuego lento como para simplemente preparar consomé. Por lo tanto, cuando cueza pollo a fuego lento, siempre use agua suficiente para que sobre algo de caldo. Si reserva el líquido sobrante del pollo cocido, hace mucho más rico el consomé que cuando usa solo menudencias y huesos, como en está receta.

2 libras de mollejas de pollo
2 libras de pezcuezos y espinazos de pollo
1 cebolla grande, pelada y picada
1 poro, lavado y las puntas cortadas, pero con la mayoría de la parte verde (opcional)
4 dientes de ajos, pelados y toscamente picados
1 hoja grande de laurel ó 2 chicas
2–3 ramitas de perejil
1 cucharadita de tomillo seco, molido en el molcajete
½ cucharadita de romero, molido en el molcajete
6 granos de pimienta
3 litros de agua
Las puntas verdes de 3 tallos de apio
1 cucharada de sal

Ponga a hervir todos los ingredientes en una cacerola grande. Después de unos minutos, saque la espuma de la superficie y reduzca el fuego a que hierva a fuego lento. Tape y cueza a fuego lento durante 2–2½ horas. Cuele el caldo a través de un cedazo forrado con varias telas gruesas, a otro recipiente. Enfríe por completo en el refrigerador, y cuando el consomé esté frío, quite la grasa de la superficie. Si usó mollejas de pollo, reservelas para comerlas. Refrigere o congele el caldo hasta que lo necesite.

CONSOME CONCENTRADO DE PESCADO

Rinde 6 tazas

2 libras de esqueletos y cabezas de pescado, ó 2 libras de pescado espinoso (no use pescado aceitoso)
3 tazas de agua
3 tazas de vino blanco seco
1 ó 2 rebanadas de limón con cáscara
1 tallo grande de apio, ó 3 puntas
1 cebolla chica, rebanada
1 cucharadita de semillas de hinojo
1 hoja chica de laurel
1 zanahoria mediana, rebanada
1/2 cucharadita de perejil fresco
4 ramitas de perejil fresco
6 granos de pimienta, machacados
Sal

Lave bien el pescado y retire las agallas de las cabezas. Combine en una cacerola grande todos los demás ingredientes, excepto la sal. Ponga a que llegue a hervir, reduzca la flama y cueza a fuego lento 20–30 minutos. Cuele. Ponga sal al gusto.

CONSOME CONCENTRADO DE RES

Rinde 2 1/2 a 3 cuartos

2 a 3 libras de huesos (res o ternera)
Harina
5 libras de trozos de hueso de pierna con algo de carne
1 cebolla grande, pelada
1 zanahoria, lavada
1 poro, lavado y sin puntas
1 nabo blanco, pelado
4 dientes de ajo, pelados, enteros
1 hoja grande de laurel ó 2 chicas
2–3 ramitos de perejil fresco
1 cucharadita de tomillo seco
1 cucharada de sal

Espolvoree ligeramente en harina los huesos y el trozo de hueso de pierna con carne. Colóquelos en el asador y ase con la parrilla en el nivel más bajo (o coloque en el horno precalentado a 500°F. en la parrilla del centro) hasta que la carne y los huesos estén delicadamente dorados, volteando de vez en cuando. Después de dorados, coloque los huesos y la carne junto con todo los demas ingredientes en una cacerola grande con suficiente agua para cubrir. Ponga a que llegue a hervir sobre fuego alto durante 5–6 minutos, quite la espuma de la superficie. Reduzca el fuego hasta que el agua hierva a fuego lento. Tape y cueza durante 3 horas. Retire la cacerola del fuego, saque los huesos con la carne para usarlos como carne hervida, luego cuele el caldo a un tazón grande con el cernidor forrado con tela. Refrigere toda la noche, luego retire la grasa de la superficie. Regrese el caldo al fuego y hierva a fuego lento durante varias horas más, para reducir el consomé. Luego cuele el caldo una vez más y refrigere o congele hasta que esté listo para usarse.

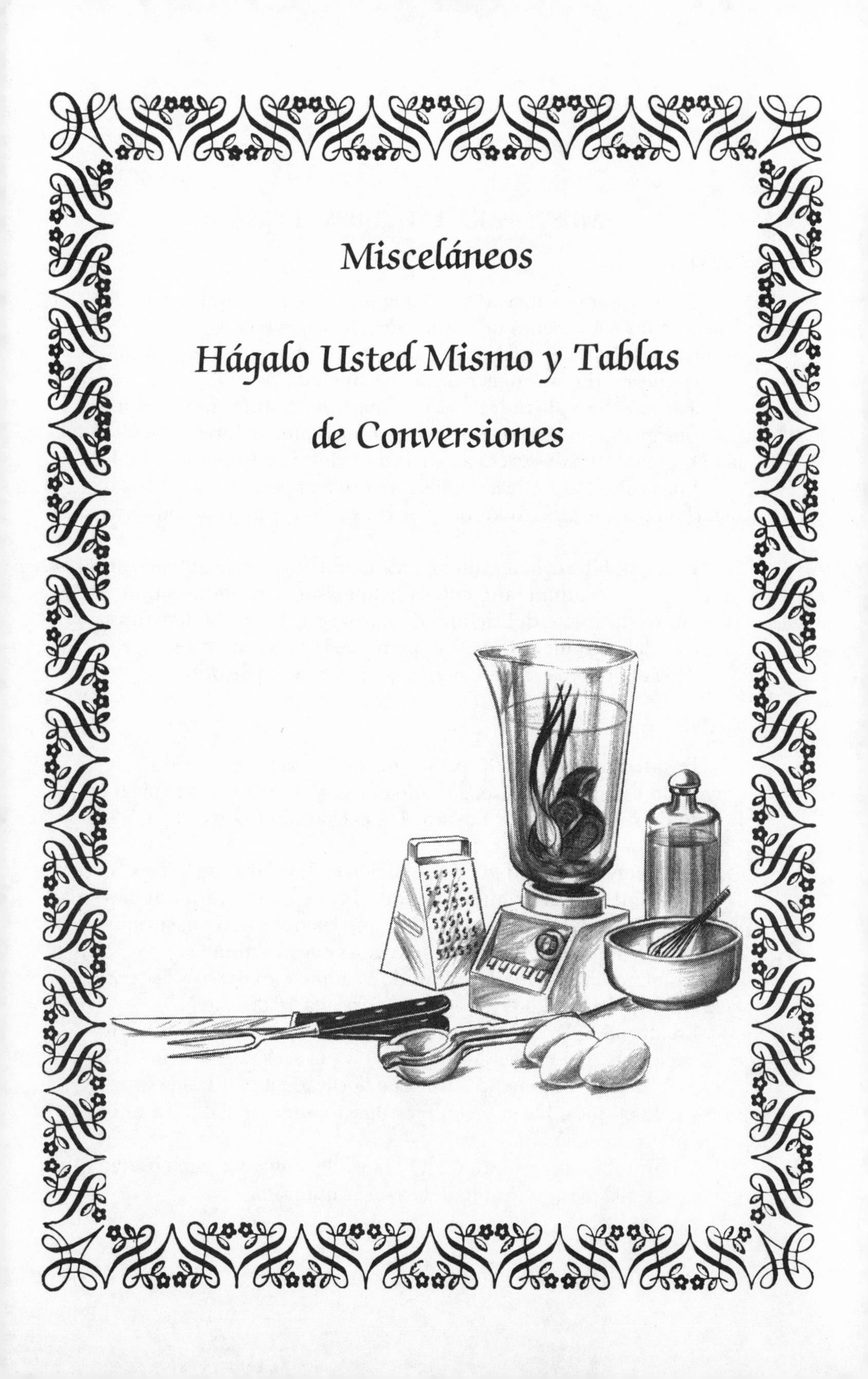

Misceláneos

Hágalo Usted Mismo y Tablas de Conversiones

AJUSTE PARA ALTITUDES ALTAS

PANES:

Para altitudes superiores a 3,500 pies, use un poquito más de líquido o un poco menos de harina, debido a que esta es más seca y absorbe más líquido en altitudes altas. Sin embargo, en un día lluvioso es necesario usar más harina que en un día seco.

También, en altitudes altas, la masa se levanta más rapido, por consiguente, para obtener un sabor más completo, permita que la masa se levante dos veces antes de darle forma y levantado final.

En recetas para panes rápidos, reduzca el polvo de hornear, o bicarbonato de sodio, o ambos, en 1/4 cucharadita o un poquito menos.

Para estabilizar la acción de levantamiento y para obtener un mejor pan de levadura, aumente la temperatura del horno durante 10 minutos al inicio del tiempo de horneado. La regla acostumbrada es de un aumento de 20°F. pero puede variar de receta a receta. Haga la prueba cuando hornee un pan nuevo por primera vez.

PASTELES:

En altitudes de 2,500 pies o más, reduzca la cantidad de agente de levantamiento; por ejemplo, el polvo de hornear, bicarbonato de sodio o cremor tártaro, 1/4 cucharadita por cada 1,500 pies.

Disminuya la cantidad de aire batido en las claras de huevo. Si la receta pide claras de huevo batidas duras, no permita que lleguen a estar muy duras y secas, sino que las debe batir hasta que las claras de huevo formen picos suaves y se vean satinadas.

Aumente la cantidad de líquido usado en 2 cucharadas por taza en altitudes de 2,500 pies o más, por cada 1,500. pies.

En altitudes de 3,500 pies o más, aumente la cantidad de harina 1 cucharada por cada 1,500 pies.

Aumente 10°F. la temperatura de horneado en altitudes superiores a 4,000 pies, hasta 6,500 pies, luego aumente 25°F. en altitudes arriba de 6,500 pies.

En altitudes superiores a 2,500 pies, disminuya 1 cucharada, por cada 1,500 pies, la cantidad de azúcar usada.

HERVIR Y FREIR GRASA, PROFUNDO:

Ya que el punto de ebullición de los líquidos es más bajo en altitudes altas, el proceso de cocimiento sobre la estufa, tarda un poco más.

También deberá aumentar de 5° a 15°F. la temperatura de la grasa para freído profundo, dependiendo de la altitud donde esté cocinando, y también dependiendo del tipo de alimentos que esté friendo. Pero jamás permita que el aceite u otra grasa humee antes de introducir la comida. Si es posible, utilize un termómetro y pruebe la comida particular a su altitud. Pruebe la temperatura introduciendo un cubito de pan de 1 pulgada. Si se dora en 50 segundos el aceite tiene la temperatura correcta.

SUGERENCIAS ACERCA DEL PESCADO

La técnica para saber cual pescado fresco debemos elegir y cual evitar, es muy fácil:

1. Los ojos deben estar brillantes, limpios, con pupilas identificables;
2. Las escamas deben estar brillantes y bien prendidas en el pescado;
3. Las agallas nunca deben ser de color gris.

Deshiele en leche el pescado congelado. Esto elimina los olores del pescado y cualquier posible olor del congelador.

Si congela el pescado fresco para uso posterior, lávelo muy bien en el chorro del agua fría y congelelo, ya sea en una bolsa de plástico o en un envase de cartón de la leche, o en otro recipiente que pueda cerrar bien y que haya llenado con agua.

O, congele un pescado grande entero, envolviéndolo con mucho cuidado, en papel aluminio grueso, bien sellado y luego colocado en una bolsa grande de plástico, sacando todo el aire y sellado con una cinta o elástico.

Antes de cocinar un pescado fresco, remójelo en agua fría con 1/4 de taza de vinagre blanco, aproximadamente, agregando vino blanco o jugo de limón. Esto da al pescado de agua salada un sabor dulce y da un sabor delicado a todos los pescados. Rápidamente enjuage el pescado en agua fría y séquelo antes de cocinar.

CAMARON:

El camarón fresco siempre está firme, jamás está blando, y no tiene un olor fuerte.

El camarón congelado debe ser deshielado en agua fría con un poco de vinagre, o puede cocerlo congelado. Si lo va a cocinar congelado, sumerjalo rápidamente en agua hirviendo y póngalo a que se cueza a fuego lento.

No permita que el camarón llegue a hervir porque se hará glutinoso. Empiece a cocinar el camarón en agua fría y, lentamente, a que casi hierva, baje la flama y cueza a fuego lento solo hasta que el camarón esté rosa. Se aplica la misma regla para cocinar camarón mientras está congelado (ver arriba).

Puede cocer el camarón en su cáscara, y puede pelarlo y desvenarlo después de cocido, o puede pelarlo y desvenarlo antes de cocerlo. Cuezalo en agua ligeramente salada y drenelo inmediatamente después de cocer, y enjuagelo en un baño frío, y vuelva a escurrir.

Nunca sobrecueza cualquier pescado, incluyendo todo tipo de mariscos. Cueza el pescado solo hasta que la carne no esté opaca en color, pero que haya tomado su color final, blanco, rosa o rojo. Pruebe con los dientes de un tenedor (introduciéndolo hasta el esqueleto si está cocinando un pescado entero). Esta misma regla se aplica al callo de acha y ostiones. Si está cociendo camarón o langosta, el marisco está listo cuando se torna rosa o naranja.

Recuerde, si sobrecueze el pescado, este pierde su sabor y se hace glutinoso.

OTRAS SUGERENCIAS Y COMO HACERLO

TRATANDO CON HUEVOS AL COCINAR:

1. Ponga los huevos, las claras que batirá, a la temperatura ambiente antes de separarlos.

2. Nunca debe batir las claras hasta que estén secas, sino hasta que se vean duras y satinadas.

3. Para obtener más volumen y un producto final más esponjoso, debe separar los huevos y batir las claras por separado y agregarlas a los pasteles de forma envolvente, al final del proceso de mezclado. (Sin embargo, no olvide las reglas para altitudes altas, y

pruebe está sugerencia antes de preparar un pastel para invitados, si vive usted en un lugar alto).

4. Nunca vierta huevos crudos o yemas de huevo, ya sean batidas o no, directamente a una mezcla caliente. En lugar de eso, agregue un poco de la mezcla caliente a los huevos hasta que estos estén tibios, luego vierta los huevos tibios a la mezcla caliente. Esto evita que se cuajen.

5. Después de agregar yemas de huevo a la salsa, nunca permita que hierva. Esto provoca que se separe y cuaje. Caliente de acuerdo a las instrucciones de la receta, pero no hierva. Tampoco prolongue el período de cocción. Calentar los huevo es suficiente para cocerlos.

6. Si se cuajara, vierta toda la mezcla cuajada en un tazón frío y bata vigorosamente con un batidor de mano y, si es necesario, agregue un poco de crema fría.

COMO GUARDAR PASTA COCIDA HASTA QUE LA VAYA A USAR:

1. Nunca cueza la pasta más allá del punto de al dente.

2. Tan pronto como logre este punto, enjuague la pasta en agua caliente, drenela y cubrala con agua fría. Si la va a guardar para el día siguente, tápela y refrigérela hasta que la vaya a usar.

3. Cuando esté lista para usarla, ponga otra cacerola con agua a hervir, drene la pasta refrigerada y cueza 1 minuto en el agua hirviendo, drene en agua caliente y sirva.

4. Justo antes de servir pruebe si tiene suficiente sal, y si es necesario agregue sal al agua caliente.

5. Para cocer pasta, ponga a hervir el agua (3 litros para cada 8 onzas de pasta) a que esté hirviendo mucho antes de agregar la pasta, con 3–4 cucharadas de sal o al gusto y 1/3 taza de vinagre (para prevenir que la pasta se pegue unas a otras). Ponga a hervir de nuevo, a fuego lento y hierva con cuidado, sin tapar, hasta que tenga el punto de al dente (8 a 10 minutos dependiendo de la altitud).

COMO HACER FRESCOS DE NUEVO UNA LECHUGA O APIO, LACIOS:

Corte una pequeña rebanada de la raíz, a manera que el agua pueda penetrar, luego remójelos en cerca de 1/4 de pulgada de agua fría, en un recipiente, tape con una bolsa de plástico sin apretar, y metalo al refrigerador toda la noche. Luego saque, envuelva en toallas de papel, coloque en una bolsa de plástico y ate con un lazo, torciendo dos veces y regrese al refrigerador hasta que estén listos para usarse. Lo crujiente se obtendrá al meterlas en agua y refrigeralas toda la noche, y se mantendrá todo el tiempo que guarde la lechuga o apio, de la forma en que se le indicó.

COMO HACER SALSAS DE MANTEQUILLA O GRAVIES FRESCOS:

Use 2 cucharadas de mantequilla o grasa de la carne o pollo para cada cucharada de harina, y derrita la grasa antes de agregar la harina. Mezcle en el líquido, ya sea leche o consomé y sazonadores, gradualmente, luego cueza hasta que espese.

COMO ELEGIR Y ALMACENAR CHAMPIÑONES FRESCOS:

1. Si va a escoger champiñones frescos del montón en el supermercado, elija solo aquellos que estén secos y cerrados, no los que están abiertos y mostrando el interior café.
2. Si compra champiñones que han sido empacados en el supermercado, de inmediato retírelos del recipiente porque si los mantiene guardados en el plástico se hecharán a perder y se humedecerán más rápido.
3. Acomode los champiñones en una sola capa, sin tocarse, en una charola o plato, o de preferencia en una charola de nieve seca, completamente forrada con toallas de papel. La toalla de papel ayuda a mantener los champiñones secos y al cubrirlos completamente, los ayudará a retener su humedad interior. Es importante no colocar los champiñones directamente en la charola, póngalos encima de una toalla de papel que cubra el fondo de la charola.

De esta forma guárdelos en el refrigerador, pero los champiñones no pueden mantenerse más de 3 semanas antes de usarlos. Si se empiezan a secar, debe tratarlos como champiñones secos que se componen al remojarlos en un poco de agua durante unos cuantos minutos. Sin embargo, si se cubren adecuadamente, tal como se indica, estarán firmes y frescos cuando los saque de la charola; se mantendrán por lo menos 2 y, por lo general, 3 semanas.

No limpie los champiñones antes de guardarlos, solo inmediatamente antes de usar.

TABLA DE CONVERSIONES

1 onza liquida	29.573 mililitros	
1 onza seco	.028 kgr.	
1 libra	.453 kgr.	
1 kgr.	2.205 lbs.	
1 pinta (pt.) seca	.551 litros	
1 pinta (pt.) liquida	.473 litros	
1 cuarto (qt.) líquido	.946 litros	
1 galon (gal.) líquido	3.785 litros	
1 pulgada	2.54 cms.	
1 pie	30.48 cms.	o 0.304 metros
100 pies	30.48 mts.	
500 pies	152.40 mts.	
1000 pies	304.80 mts.	
1500 pies	457.20 mts.	
2000 pies	609.60 mts.	
2500 pies	762.00 mts.	
3000 pies	914.40 mts.	
3500 pies	1,066.80 mts.	
4000 pies	1,219.20 mts.	
4500 pies	1,371.60 mts.	
5000 pies	1,524.00 mts.	
6000 pies	1,828.80 mts.	
7000 pies	2,133.60 mts.	

TABLA DE CONVERSIONES

Para convertir de grados farenheit a centigrados reste 32 grados. multiplique por 5, y divida entre 9.

GRADOS FARENHEIT	GRADOS CENTIGRADOS
100	37.77
150	65.55
200	93.33
225	107.22
250	121.11
275	135.00

280	137.77
290	143.33
300	148.88
325	162.77
350	176.66
375	190.55
380	193.33
390	198.88
400	204.44
425	218.33
450	232.22

Index

Index